What Peopl Saying About
Chicken Soup fo ..

T0085706

"If love makes the world go around, romance makes it spin! *Chicken Soup for the Romantic Soul* will put a beat back into hearts who have forgotten that romance really does exist."

Catherine Lanigan
author, *Romancing the Stone, The Jewel of the Nile* and
The Christmas Star

"This is a perfect book to read as a couple—each story will reveal a new understanding of romance, and will bring you even closer together."

Suzanne DeYoung
author, *A Love Story Foretold*
Dennis DeYoung
former singer and songwriter for the
multi-platinum group STYX

"If you love to read about romance, passion and magic, you will love reading *Chicken Soup for the Romantic Soul.*"

Tara Hitchcock
news anchor, *Good Morning Arizona*, KTVK-3TV

"The most powerful emotion is love—*Chicken Soup for the Romantic Soul* is a positive and uplifting look at love and romance! This book is full of hope, inspiration and truly profound lessons in love."

Alfredo J. Molina
chairman and CEO, Molina Fine Jewelers

"My favorite definition of romance is that it is 'love in action.' You'll find that these stories demonstrate the subtle yet incredible power of this concept. You'll also find inspiration for creating your *own* 1001 ways to be romantic."

Gregory J.P. Godek
author, *1001 Ways to Be Romantic*

"Our best comes out when we are unafraid to show love. *Chicken Soup for the Romantic Soul* is filled with many wonderful, heartfelt reminders."

Roseann Higgins
president and founder of SPIES
<u>S</u>ingle <u>P</u>rofessional <u>I</u>ntroductions for the <u>E</u>specially <u>S</u>elective

"*Chicken Soup for the Romantic Soul* has everything—passion, adventure, tears, laughter and love. You won't be able to put it down, and you'll want to read it over and over again."

Arielle Ford
coauthor, *Owner's Manual: The Essential Guide to the One You Love*

"These beautifully told stories capture the true magic of love and romance in a way that will touch your heart."

Jo and Tommy Lasorda, married 53 years,
baseball Hall of Famer

CHICKEN SOUP FOR THE ROMANTIC SOUL

Chicken Soup for the Romantic Soul
Inspirational Stories About Love and Romance
Jack Canfield, Mark Victor Hansen, Mark Donnelly, Chrissy Donnelly,
Barbara De Angelis

Published by Backlist, LLC,
a unit of Chicken Soup for the Soul Publishing, LLC. www.chickensoup.com

Front cover design by Andrea Perrine Brower
Originally published in 2002 by Health Communications, Inc.

Back cover and spine redesign by Pneuma Books, LLC

Distributed to the booktrade by Simon & Schuster. SAN: 200-2442

Publisher's Cataloging-in-Publication Data
(Prepared by The Donohue Group)

Chicken soup for the romantic soul : inspirational stories about love and
  romance / [compiled by] Jack Canfield ... [et al.].

  p. : ill. ; cm.

  Originally published: Deerfield Beach, FL : Health Communications, c2002.
  ISBN: 978-1-62361-006-7

  1. Love--Anecdotes. 2. Anecdotes. I. Canfield, Jack, 1944-

PS648.L6 C484 2012
152.4/1   2012944055

PRINTED IN THE UNITED STATES OF AMERICA
on acid free paper

CHICKEN SOUP
FOR THE
ROMANTIC SOUL

Inspirational Stories
About Love and Romance

Jack Canfield
Mark Victor Hansen
Mark & Chrissy Donnelly
Barbara De Angelis, Ph.D.

Backlist, LLC, a unit of
Chicken Soup for the Soul Publishing, LLC
Cos Cob, CT
www.chickensoup.com

Contents

3. ROMANTIC MOMENTS

4. ROMANCE AND MARRIAGE

5. MEMORIES OF LOVE

6. LESSONS IN LOVE

7. FOR BETTER OR FOR WORSE

8. THE FLAME STILL BURNS

CONTENTS

Introduction

What does it mean to be romantic? For many of us, the concept of romance conjures up visions of fancy gifts and flowers, extravagant evenings out on the town, or exotic vacations for two at fascinating destinations. However, the true meaning of romance transcends these traditional stereotypes and offers us something much more precious, much more profound: *The heart of romance is magic—the magic all of us have felt when we've been touched by love.*

This magic of love permeates *Chicken Soup for the Romantic Soul.* We are delighted and honored to offer you this inspiring collection of stories that capture the true meaning of romance. They are stories of passion, of devotion, of tenderness. They are stories of patience, faith and trust. They are stories of renewal, rediscovery and redemption. Through each tale, we are invited into the private world of love shared by two people and given a glimpse of the amazing ways love expresses itself. Our idea of what romance means was changed forever as we read the stories contained in this book, and we believe yours will be too!

In a world that is often filled with turbulence, confusion and even darkness, love is the light that guides us to joy and makes living worthwhile. What touched us as we worked on this book was reading about how each contributor shared his or her appreciation and gratitude for that light of love, and the unique way it had transformed his or her life. There are stories about extraordinarily romantic moments that mesmerized us and took our breath away; there are stories about ordinary romantic moments that brought tears to our eyes as we contemplated the power that love contains in its utter simplicity. Each story is remarkable, whether it was written by an eighty-year-old man about his "bride" of fifty years, or by a wife and mother of three small children about the surprising ways she and her husband keep the passion alive, or by a woman who thought she'd lost the love of her life, only to have fate find him for her again.

Romantic moments come in many varieties. Some are wildly amusing, and you will find yourself laughing out loud, as we did, at stories that remind us all of the comical adventures that often go hand-in-hand with love. Other stories will make you sigh with satisfaction, as if you're reading the most riveting romance novel. And some will fill you with the kind of warm, peaceful feeling that we all experience whenever we take time to focus on the abundance of goodness and love that exists around us and within us.

Reading this book, you will discover romance where you've never known it to exist before. You will learn about how love isn't always expressed in the most eloquent words, but in sweet acts of caring and consideration that feed the heart in the most significant ways. You will be reminded of memories of love from your own past that perhaps you'd forgotten, memories that will be a part of you forever. You will look at the challenging times love sometimes goes through and marvel at how indestructible it is even in the face of pain and loss. Most of all, you will gain a new understanding of how the essence of true romance permeates the days and nights of love in ways you'd never appreciated before.

We believe that, ultimately, *Chicken Soup for the Romantic Soul* is about magic: the magic of how just a few words from your beloved can make your heart soar; the magic that occurs when you've given up on ever finding love, and then somehow, when you least expect it, love finds you; the magic of knowing how to keep falling in love over and over again as the years pass; the magic of discovering what we become when we truly love another human being.

If you are in a relationship, we hope the stories in this book will invite you to look more deeply for the bonds of love and expressions of caring you may not have thought were romantic, but ultimately are and will inspire you to cherish your partner even more. If you are not now in a relationship, our wish for you is that reading these stories gives you hope—that love will come to you at just the right time; that even now, your soul mate is looking for you, and that destiny will bring you together.

May the magic of romance always find you and fill your heart with wonder at the amazing power love has to transform us all.

1

FINDING TRUE LOVE

*The most wonderful of all things in life, I
believe, is the discovery of another human
being with whom one's relationship has
a glowing depth, beauty and joy as the
years increase. This inner progressiveness of
love between two human beings is a most
marvelous thing; it cannot be found by
looking for it or by passionately wishing
for it.*

It is a sort of Divine accident.

Sir Hugh Walpole

The Right Approach

Anyone can be passionate, but it takes real lovers to be silly.

Rose Franken

Back in 1959 Bud and I, new army second lieutenants, received orders for the same unit at Fort Sill, Oklahoma. We graduated together from OCS but did not know each other well as we had been in different sections. Our new assignments brought us in daily contact and soon we became good friends. An outgoing Irishman, Bud enjoyed telling tales of growing up in the Bronx and recounting humorous situations involving parents and siblings. The family picture displayed in his room included an attractive younger sister. From the way he spoke about her she was obviously popular and not lacking "gentlemen callers." The attraction was there—this was someone I wanted to meet. But she was in New York and I was in Oklahoma—a long way to be dating.

Eventually I got up my nerve and asked Bud if he would mind if I wrote his sister a letter. He looked a bit quizzical, but gave me the address and wished me luck. I pondered what approach would have the best chance of hooking her interest and receiving a reply. The standard "Let's be pen pals" did not seem the way to go. After some thought I sent the following letter:

Dear Rita:

I'm a friend of your brother. I'll come right to the point. I owe him some money. He said he would cancel the debt if I would marry his sister. As he related, the family has been trying to marry you off for some time—with little success! As fate would have it, I am looking for a woman of childbearing age who is in good health, capable of hard work, reasonably intelligent and comes from good stock! As you appear to meet these criteria, I have accepted your brother's offer, and so for better or worse, we will be married. Thus, consider yourself engaged!

Enclosed you will find a temporary engagement ring (cigar band). Wear it with pride! If you have any questions about the details of the marriage, our future life together or other minor points just let me know. I will complete my active duty obligation in the near future. You may select an appropriate date for our wedding any time following my discharge.

Your husband-to-be,
Ed

I had no idea if she would reply, or if she would toss the letter out, thinking, "What nut did my brother meet and why did he give him my address?" On the other hand, if she did reply this could be fun. About a week later a perfume-laden letter arrived.

She had taken the bait! It read:

Dear Ed:

Your letter certainly came as a surprise! I am grate-ful that my brother has arranged for someone to take me "off the shelf." I planned to wear my "temporary engagement ring" until I found out that it comes from a very "cheap" cigar! I don't mind the marriage commit-ment, but I want to do it in style and comfort. This brings me to certain "conditions" of our intended betrothal. Naturally you plan to keep me in the manner to which I hope to become accustomed. To be specific, we will need a maid/cook as well as someone who takes care of the house and grounds. I hesitate to set a date for our entry into marital bliss until you can assure me that such will be the case.

Awaiting your reply with a fluttering heart!

Rita

Ah, the challenge! This was getting good. I replied:

My dear bride-to-be:

It was gratifying to hear that you have accepted my proposal. Now we can plan our life together. Further, I can understand your reluctance to wear that cigar band, as it was from an inexpensive brand. You are absolutely right! I should have known that you were a girl with "class." Thus, enclosed is a band from a Dutch Master, a much better brand. You can wear this one with pride!

I am happy to report that the conditions you specified (housekeeper/cook and groundskeeper) can be met. You see, we will be living with my parents and, as you will soon find out, Mom keeps a clean house and is a good cook while Dad keeps the lawn cut and the house in good repair. If you would want Mom to wear a special apron or something, I'm sure I can talk her into it. We can even get a bit of a uniform for Dad. I'm sure that this arrangement will satisfy your demands.

I did have one other question. You signed your letter "with a fluttering heart." Were you implying that you have a heart murmur or some other type of cardiac condition? Your brother assured me that you were "as healthy as a horse" when I agreed to marry you. I'm just checking, as one can't be too careful these days! Also, I have no picture of you. Please send one at your earliest convenience.

Your husband-to-be,
Ed

Her reply came in about two weeks.

Dearest Ed:

Your plan for us to live with your parents is certainly an interesting arrangement. I can't wait to hear about other plans you have for our life together, as you seem so sensitive, romantic and intuitive. How lucky can a girl get! By the way, how much money did you owe my brother?

In response to your inquiry about a possible "heart condition," the answer is "neigh." You see, I am as healthy as a horse. However, the thought occurs to me that if I continue to respond to your letters perhaps I should have my head examined.

Sorry, I have no picture of me alone to send you. I have some with boyfriends, but somehow it would seem "tacky" to send one of those. Thus, I've decided not to send a picture and I'm sure you'll understand. You'll have to admire me without the benefit of external props. Just think of me as perfection!

With bated breath I await your response!
Rita

Hum, how to respond? This one took some thought and a bit of research. The final product was as follows:

> *My dear Rita:*
>
> *In your last letter you wondered what our life would be like together. A great question! I see you as the perfect wife. The life of such a woman is described clearly in the Bible, specifically in the book of Proverbs, chapter 31. I quote some of the verses:*
>
> *"She does her work with eager hands.*
> *She gets up while it is still dark*
> *Giving her household their food.*
> *She puts her back into her work*
> *And shows how strong her arms can be.*
> *She weaves linen sheets and sells them,*
> *She supplies the merchant with sashes. Etc.*
> *Also: Her husband is respected at the city gates,*
> *And praises her good works to the elders."*
>
> *Obviously, the message needs to be updated to reflect our current culture, but the meaning is clear—you'll work your fingers to the bone and love it! Now be honest, isn't that the type of wife you always imagined yourself to be?*
>
> *This brings up another point, namely, the picture. Perhaps I wasn't clear regarding this. My words, or at least my intent, was not to give you an option regarding sending a picture. So let me be clear—send a picture. Again, it is important that we establish the proper line of authority for our life together. Remember St. Paul's statement, "Wives be subject to your husbands." The fact that we are not yet married is a minor technicality. So, I expect a picture!*
>
> *Regarding the money I owed your brother—it was*

$3. He said you were worth every penny.

One last point. You signed the last letter—"with bated breath." I just want to make sure that you weren't implying that you have a lung problem or persistent halitosis. I await your picture!

Your sensitive husband-to-be,

Ed

In a few weeks a small package arrived that obviously was a picture frame.

Enclosed was a picture of a girl of about seven or eight seated on a piano stool. She displayed a broad smile that reflected the absence of her two front teeth. A large bow in her hair complemented a fluffy dress. Score one for her! How do I respond? It took a while to develop the following:

My dear Rita:

Just a short note to let you know that your picture arrived safe and sound. I know our life together will be conflict free, given your willingness to follow the dictates of your husband-to-be. However, I would be less than candid if I did not confess that the picture took me by surprise. You see, in the picture you seem more mature than your letters have indicated to date! But, I guess some surprises are to be expected in any relationship.

One item we have failed to discuss—the dowry. Please let me know the assets you will bring into our marriage.

Your husband-to-be,

Ed

Several weeks went by without a reply. Had I pushed it too far? On the surface it was just good fun, yet I felt we were developing a relationship. I wanted to meet her and thought she had similar feelings. *Well,* I thought, *guess again.*

Shortly thereafter Bud advised me that he received a letter from Rita telling him that she was entering a convent, something she had always considered. She asked him to say good-bye to me and to let me know that she had enjoyed the letter writing and was sorry that we didn't have a chance to meet. I thought, *Were my letters the last straw, driving her into the convent?* I muttered to myself, *I guess it was the wrong approach!*

Soon my required active duty time was up and I returned home. Bud's commitment kept him in the army a bit longer. About six months later I received a letter from Bud inviting me for a weekend in the Bronx to celebrate his discharge. He noted, "As an added incentive I am featuring one ex-nun." How could I resist? I flew to New York and we met.

Our fortieth wedding anniversary is not too far away. It was the "right approach."

Edmund Phillips

Encounter on a Train

Journeys end in lovers' meeting, every wise man's son doth know.

William Shakespeare

When I first saw her in the station at St. Margrethen, she was boarding the railroad car in which I sat, shoving an enormous brown leather suitcase up the high step with her knee.

She was wearing earth colors: pants of brown corduroy, knitted vest patterned in orange and brown, Kelly green shirt with up-rolled sleeves. Dark eyes, dark hair, dark complexion, young, mysterious. After heaving her burden onto the overhead rack, she collapsed into a seat across the aisle from me, perspiring sedately. Then the silver, air-conditioned train quietly sealed itself to continue its five-hour run westward across Switzerland.

Alpine streams bubbled with icy meltwater, and the fields were ablaze with poppies, for the month was May. I attempted first to doze, then to strike up a conversation with the person next to me. No success there. I tried to doze a second time and couldn't, and then I noticed her again. She had produced a posy of wilted wildflowers from somewhere and was now holding it on her lap, her thoughts apparently upon whoever had given it to her. She had a strong but tranquil face. She was looking at the flowers and lightly smiling. I moved across the aisle and sat down facing her.

"Wie heissen die Blumen?" I asked. I knew that the salad bowl of German words at my disposal would not get me far. Perhaps speaking to her at all was a mistake. At any rate her only answer to my question about the flowers was a smile. *Ah,* I thought, *not German. Italian, of course. She's dark.*

I leaned forward to craft a more careful question about *i fiori,* knowing that if the conversational terrain should dip in that direction I'd have to beat an even quicker retreat. She still didn't answer me. The thought that she was mute crossed my mind, but I dismissed it. Since this was Switzerland, I had a final choice: French. The reply, however, was as before: a Mona Lisa smile. I began to wonder. I'd seen a stationful of Yugoslavs in Buchs that morning, back toward the Austrian border. Could she be one of them? The prospect of hearing her speak at last in Serbo-Croatian was discouraging. Better to go slowly now.

I leaned back, relaxed, and returned the smile as enigmatically as I could. I tried to look mysterious—a foredoomed task, considering my garb of crushable fisherman's hat, red long-john shirt, pin-striped mustard slacks, and leather running shoes. It didn't work. Just as I was about to pack it in, Mona Lisa spoke. *"Habla español?"* she asked. Why hadn't I thought of it? She's Spanish! A tourist, maybe, but more likely a *Gastarbeiter.* There were loads of Spaniards working in Switzerland.

With all circuits snapping to life, I strove to call up my meager store of Spanish while rummaging frantically through my bag for the right Grosset's phrase book. I commenced to address this person whose national origins were beginning to take form. She turned out indeed to be a Spaniard, on her way home to see her family. She was single, employed in a home for the aged in Altstätten, and incredibly, her suitcase was stuffed with Swiss chocolate.

Our conversation, unfortunately, was hampered by more than language difficulties, since I had been ill for twenty-four hours and was still required to take periodic and sudden absences. She proved to be understanding. She turned out, however, to be a poor judge of national costume or accents, taking me first for an Englishman and later for a German. I was apparently the first specimen she'd encountered from the Land of the Free and the Home of the Brave.

What we spoke of, exactly, I can't remember, but the day flew past, and I do recall we were in marvelous accord on a number of important issues. I dreaded our arrival in Geneva, where we would part, but by day's end we were there. We strolled for a while through the city's pretty streets, dallied over cappuccino in a sidewalk cafe, inspected shop windows in the day's failing light, laughed together, and filled conversational voids with banalities until my train came. Hers was due later, at midnight. I said good-bye with great reluctance. She appeared to share my feeling, but her people were beckoning from across the Pyre'nées, and my schedule called me to Italy before returning home. We exchanged addresses. I then boarded the train and left.

Today my life doesn't have the broad margin it had then. Like many other people, I raise children, commute, remodel and mow the lawn. But I sometimes think of those days when life could become so quickly and intensely bittersweet, when great possibilities could yawn in an instant.

In fact, one way I'm able to retain perspective on the here and now is by recalling the details of that particular spring day, with its chance meeting and sad good-bye. Occasionally I've recounted the event to others, too, but there I enjoy taking some liberties with the facts, making the girl somewhat more desperate and myself a bit more dashing or distant. In one of my versions the girl unabashedly pursues me. My wife especially enjoys hearing me carry on in this vein.

Even though she likes the story, my wife does find its variations astonishing. She insists that on the train she was not desperate, that I was not distant or dashing, and that she left Switzerland the following year to marry me despite the way I was dressed that day.

Kevin H. Siepel

"Falling" in Love

During World War II, I was employed at a research lab in Oklahoma. Men were pretty scarce at that time, of course. One day after the end of the war, a friend called me to come to her lab to meet the new fellow who had come to work for the summer while attending college on the G.I. Bill. So I went down for a short talk and to meet the guy.

As I left I heard a loud crash behind me. When I went back to see what had happened, he was sprawled flat on the floor. He had been sitting at a desk by the door in a swivel chair and had leaned back too far to watch me walk down the hall. All during our fifty-two years of happily married life, including eleven moves with three children, I have loved telling people this story of how my husband fell for me. He hastens to assure them that he actually was only leaning over to pick up a pencil.

Mary Mikkelsen

Glads on Monday

It's Monday and I'm leaving a meeting near my house and decide to take advantage of one of the perks of living in town: sneaking home for lunch.

I bank around the curve toward my house and suddenly remember I had procrastinated a little too much over the weekend and had neglected that dreaded of all chores: rounding up the week's groceries. After a quick turn into the grocery store, I discover no parking spaces in the first aisle of the lot. Quickly spotting an open slot in the next aisle two cars away from the sidewalk, I'm feeling rather smart as I smoothly idle in, slide the shift into first, pull up the brake, turn off the motor, jump out and head for the store.

Then I see the car.

In eight months of dating my recent girlfriend, I had never experienced the spontaneous, unexpected encounter. And now, ten days after she had called things off, I practically walk right into her car.

Every relationship has its rhythms. Ours, for some reason, had always peaked on Mondays. A couple of weeks after meeting, I had stopped by the store en route to dinner at her house and purchased a colorful bunch of gladiolas. Life was good back then. Not only were glads on special, but I discovered upon presentation that they just happened to be her favorite of all flowers.

Knowing a good thing when I found it, I would stop off every Monday, even those we didn't have a date. If she were at an aerobics class, I would sneak in her kitchen and arrange them on her dining room table near her back door for her arrival. She would always call and act surprised and appreciative. And I would always feel so coy.

As I step on the threshold of the electronic doors and grab a wobbly grocery cart, I suddenly recall a scene from the movie *Ghost* when the recently widowed heroine is confronted at odd times by the spirit of her late husband. I scan the checkout lines and don't see her, so I know I have a chance to pull off the plan: grab the glads, sneak up behind her in line and embarrass her in front of the check-out boys.

As I round the banana counter, I suddenly find myself two carts behind her. She evidently had arrived moments before. The best vector for cover is directly behind another shopper who is directly behind her—so I slowly trail past the blueberries and the orange juice. The glads are just ahead. *Surely, she won't grab a bunch for herself, will she?* My heart skips a beat as she lingers next to the display. If she reaches for a bunch, my plan will be foiled. I watch her eyes as she rolls past the long stalks banded in colorful array. I see a sadness roll over her face as if a mist had drifted in from the rows of moistened lettuce. Her mouth, so often bright with a soft smile, is taciturn. She turns and heads for the shelves of bread.

A moment of doubt falls over me. Maybe I'm being too cavalier with the raw wounds of the break up. *Or is it a break up, after all?* Life gets so messy when we entangle ourselves with others' expectations. Perhaps, I'm being pushed away just enough to be given a wide berth to display my need for the other. *But is that really her style or am I recalling the drama of an earlier entanglement?* Maybe I should abandon this farce and wander down to another grocery and pick up my basketful of items in solitude. But a chance for romance is not to be squandered, even in the sunset of a sweet good-bye.

So I abandon the cart by the ferns and grab a double bunch of glads. I hide behind the other shoppers until she makes the turn at the fish counter. But she isn't going left. She is doing a complete turnabout and heads back my way. I suddenly fall to my knees in front of the French loaves. She is two feet away, just on the other side of the rye. The woman beside me is beginning to grow nervous. The moment is falling apart. *What am I doing here,* I begin to ask? In *Ghost,* this other woman would not be able to see me at all. It would be so much smoother on celluloid. Perhaps romance has betrayed me again.

So I cash in the suspense and pop up in front of her over the breads and hold out the glads—water dripping on the cellophane wrap. "Here," I say, to the great relief of the other shoppers around me. "You forgot these."

The look of terror leaves her face and the eyelids fall again in pain. But she smiles and tilts her head and her shoulders drop. I place the bouquet in her cart and put my arms around her. She melts into me in that sweet way I have come to miss. She is at a loss for words. And I am relieved the moment has been pulled back from near-collapse.

There is not much more to say. We manage a little smile and inhale the sweet scent of the last glads of this all-too-short season.

Chris Schroder

A Love Story

She still remembers the moment she fell in love with him. It was near the end of their senior year of high school.

One Tuesday night, he called her up and asked her for a date. She heard the nervousness in his voice, so she reassuringly said, "I'd love to. What do you want to do?"

"Go to the movies," he said hopefully.

"What would you like to see?" she asked.

While considering the options, the real answer slipped out, "You."

Rob Gilbert
As cited in Bits & Pieces

Two Coins in a Fountain

Even as a kid my cousin Andrea always had big dreams! When we talked about being teachers or secretaries, Andrea talked of being a movie star. When we dreamed of going to the Mediterranean on holiday, Andrea dreamed of the Caribbean! (A long way from Scotland!)

As we grew up, she was not the prettiest of us, yet she had the most boyfriends. She was a little overweight and not that tall. But Andrea sparkled, both physically and mentally, and young men seemed to find that attractive.

Once on a double date, I marveled at her because she never had one moment's self-doubt or of feeling self-conscious. Because of this, she had the ability to say exactly what she was feeling; she made it seem like you were sharing something very personal with her.

It wasn't a surprise when she came in and announced, "Well, I am off to Rome to work as a nanny!" We all knew that Andrea had long ago decided she was in love with Rome and always said that is where she wanted to live.

She openly told us, "I am convinced I will meet this gorgeous Italian prince and we will fall madly in love!"

We laughed at that, but were all sad to see her go. She

kind of spread light around her and it was all much duller when she left.

Andrea arrived in Rome and settled in with the family for whom she was to be the nanny. They gave her a little apartment, and she already spoke Italian having always known she would need to use it!

Andrea took her young charge out a fair bit, to the Coliseum, the Spanish Steps, but mostly they went to the Trevi Fountain. "To anyone who has never seen it," she wrote to us, "you think of a little fountain in a square. It is huge, like a giant monument with water; it is breathtaking and beautiful."

She told us that you throw one coin in the fountain to return to Rome, two coins to find true love. "I have spent a fortune. I throw two coins in every time I pass, but it is an investment, I know it will work!" We laughed at that letter; same old Andrea, still the same big dreams!

One beautiful, sunny Roman morning, Andrea took Pierre Luigi out early, and they came to the Trevi Fountain. Andrea could not pass it by without throwing in her two coins, so they went down the steps and she threw in her coins.

She glanced up and two very handsome young men were watching her. The taller of the two asked her, "You weesh to return very much, eef you throw in two coins no?"

Andrea looked at this gorgeous young man, his hair a light gold brown, but his face somehow very Italian. "One is to return to Rome, two is for love!"

They both smiled and walked over to her, and the one who had spoken introduced himself. Marcello continued to study her smiling as he asked, "So you want to find true love, here on your vacation?"

"I live in Rome. I love Rome and I have always dreamed of falling in love with someone here. I am sure it will happen," she beamed at him. He kept smiling at her and asked where she came from, and the four of them ended up having coffee together in a little café.

Whatever she said at that first meeting, he seemed to be really taken with her and asked if she would go out with him.

Andrea met Marcello the next evening and asked him what he did for a living. It turned out that he played for Roma FC, the football team. Not only did he play for them, he was one of their star players. Andrea's Marcello was a very famous and much admired young man throughout Italy because he played for the national side as well.

When she wrote and told us about him and sent photographs, we agreed with how gorgeous he was. My younger sister Bertha said that she had read about him and that he was usually with some tall, long-legged blonde model or something. It would have made the rest of us wonder what he could see in someone ordinary like us. Andrea never gave that a second thought; she was already nuts about him and fully expected him to be nuts about her!

The thing was, amazingly, he *was* nuts about her. She wrote and told us that she saw him nearly every day, she had met his family. Then that he wanted her to give up her work and live with him in his beautiful villa high up in the hills that surround Rome. Finally we flew over to visit her, and lying at the side of his huge swimming pool, surrounded by hills and the distant tops of the buildings of Rome, she beamed at us. I asked her, "So is Marcello the Italian prince you always dreamed of?"

"Oh yes, Joyce, and more, he has asked me to marry him!"

When we met him, it took us all of five minutes to realize he was not just in love with Andrea, but he adored her.

He smiled every time his eyes rested on her. "There is no one like her," he told us. "She is so full of effervescence; she is like a bottle of champagne and I could not go back to drinking wine. She drifts off on flights of fancy, and I am running behind trying to find wings to fly with her. I love her very much."

They have been married for fifteen years and have three kids. She has seen a fair bit of the world, like she somehow always knew she would. Mainly though, she lives in her beautiful house with her gorgeous Italian.

I said to her one day about all her dreams coming true and she laughed. "You have to be determined to achieve your dreams, like throwing two coins in the fountain every time you pass, to make sure they come true!"

Joyce Stark

Six Red Roses

What the world really needs is more love and less paperwork.

Pearl Bailey

I still remember the day I first heard of my husband. It was Friday, June 14, 1985, but it would be a few days later before I actually saw what he looked like. Yet by September 6 that same year, we were engaged.

I'd been on my way out for lunch that fateful Friday when my supervisor called me. "Lori, there is a package for you at the front desk."

I turned to Janine, a friend and colleague. "Uh-oh. That doesn't sound good," I said.

We went down to the desk and saw my "package." It was a long narrow box, and since I'd never received flowers before, I didn't immediately recognize it as a florist's box. My brow scrunched in confusion, and I tore open the string. Inside were six exquisite red roses. The card was signed with an "X."

I looked to Janine. "Is this a joke?" I asked.

She shook her head. "Not that I know of."

Needless to say, we spent much of the remaining afternoon trying to figure out who had sent the flowers. Janine even called the florist for information. Although the lady was very helpful, she couldn't give us any names, since the transaction had been paid in cash. The only thing she could say was, "He seemed like a very nice young man." I rolled my eyes at that. It sounded like something my grandmother would say, and so far, her taste in men didn't exactly correspond with mine.

Later that afternoon, my supervisor joined our discussion. "You know," she said. "Someone was up here asking for your name the other day."

My eyes widened. "Me? What for?"

She smiled. "Well, now I'm wondering."

I continued to stare at her. I'm sure it was obvious this experience was totally new to me. "Well, who was he?" I asked.

"His name is Gerry. He works downstairs. I think his last name is Robidoux."

I had never heard of him. I looked at Janine. "Do you know who he is?"

She shook her head. "Rub-a-dub? No, I never heard of him."

"Great, I'm being stalked," I laughed.

Within minutes, several curious girls from our office went on a "tour." They returned with big smiles.

"So, how many horns does he have?" I asked.

They shook their heads. "He's cute!" they squealed, almost in unison.

I made a face. "Are you sure you were looking at the right guy?"

I still couldn't believe that someone even remotely male was sending flowers to me. The idea that he was cute, too, almost threw me into a tailspin. I was starting to think someone had made a huge mistake. Somehow, I must have walked in front of the girl he was asking my supervisor about at precisely the wrong moment, and she had given him my name by mistake.

When I brought the flowers home that night, my mother was there. "What on earth did you buy those for?" she asked as I arranged them in a vase. I shot her a look that said, "Thanks a lot, Mom." Clearly, this experience was new for all of us.

The following Friday, my supervisor approached my desk with a huge grin on her face. "Guess who has a package downstairs again?"

I raced downstairs and came back with another florist box. Inside were six more red roses, a bottle of Oscar de la Renta perfume and another card. It read, "Have a nice day." Again, the signature was a simple "X."

I looked up at the crowd assembled around my desk. I was stunned, and my reaction seemed mirrored in their eyes as well. "Well, this is kinda weird," I chuckled.

They laughed as I'd hoped they would, but I couldn't help wondering who was sending me these things. The other day, I'd walked right past the cute "Rub-a-dub" guy, and he looked right through me as if I weren't even there.

Right after that, I'd crossed him off my list of potentials. Now I could only wonder what kind of psychopath that left.

Later that night (yes, two dateless Fridays in a row if you're paying attention), I was telling the story to a girl-friend of mine. "It makes me feel a little creepy because I'm doubting that it could be this 'Rub-a-dub' guy. In the first place, he's too cute. In the second place, he had the perfect opportunity to talk to me the other day, and he totally ignored me. I just can't help picturing some stalker following me around now."

Well, as small worlds go, mine was no exception. My friend's boyfriend worked at the same place I did, and she

promised to ask him if he knew this "Rub-a-dub" character. It turns out he did. He knew him, and he asked him.

The following week, I received a phone call.

"Umm . . . hello, may I speak to Lori, please?" the voice
on the phone said.

I smiled. I knew right away. "This is Lori."

"Oh . . . well, um . . . you don't know me, but . . . well,
you know those flowers you've been getting? Well . . . um
. . . I sent them," he stuttered. I couldn't help grinning to
myself. It's usually me who's so tongue-tied.

"Who is this?" I asked.

"Oh . . . my name is Gerry Robidoux," he said.

The cute "Rub-a-dub" guy? I couldn't believe it. I
pointed to the phone, gesturing to my mom, who was
leaning over me, trying to catch every word.

"It's Mr. X," I mouthed.

After a few minutes of stilted conversation, we agreed
to meet at a local pizza parlor. I was still skeptical, but I
needn't have worried. It was as if the fates wouldn't allow
me to be disappointed now.

We met and talked for a few hours. The whole time I
couldn't help thinking that I could really fall for this guy.
He seemed so honest and sincere, and I could already tell
how thoughtful and genuine he seemed. Of course, his
big blue eyes weren't too hard to look at either.

Well, as I said, a couple of short months later, we were
engaged. I know to others that it seemed awfully fast, but
somehow we both knew it was right. We were anxious to
begin our lives together, and we were confident in our love.

That alone prepared us for the commitment that so
many couples seem terrified of.

As impulsive as it seemed at the time, it's a decision I've
never regretted, not for one moment, and it's made me
thankful I was blessed with such great instinct. I'm thankful every time he calls me just to say hello. I'm thankful

whenever he runs me a hot bath after I've had a stressful day at work. And I'm especially thankful every night when he wraps his arms around me as we fall asleep.

I remember something my grandma said right after I received those first roses. She sighed and said, "Oh, it's so romantic. And it'll be a great story to tell your grandchildren some day."

At the time, I just rolled my eyes and told her she was jumping to conclusions. But after fourteen years of marriage, two children and countless roses, I realize she was right.

Lori J. Robidoux

Real-Life Fairy Tale

Sometimes the heart sees what is invisible to the eye.

H. Jackson Brown Jr.

"My first girl! My first girl!"

It was our forty-fifth high school reunion. Bob Grove's arms were extended as he headed toward me. It was only a moment before he had me in the biggest bear hug I had ever experienced.

His twin sister, a close friend of mine, had called and told me he was coming, so I was watching for him. We hadn't actually talked to each other since 1938—forty-seven years before. What a thrill to have such an exuberant greeting!

He had been my "first fellow," too. He had been in my geometry class, and he wore glasses. I had just started wearing mine, and I was extremely self-conscious. Although I was worried about people making comments about my appearance I told myself, *At least he won't make fun of me. He'll be safe!*

As our friendship had grown, he had carried my books from class to class, had come over to my house to play cards and had taken me to parties. But we had never even held hands.

His sister told me he was now single and retired, and my husband had died over two years before, so we knew we were both unattached as we spent the rest of the evening together. He held my hand everywhere we went. By the end of the evening when it was time for me to go home (since I lived in town) he said, "Hey, wait up! I'll walk you to your car!"

He took my hand again and we headed for the parking lot. "Here's my car," I told him as I unlocked the door.

His hand had a tighter grip on mine as he pulled me back toward him, murmuring quietly, "When we were going together I was too shy to do this," and he kissed me gently on the lips.

I was taken by surprise, but enjoyed the feel of his warm lips on mine so much I returned the kiss before I hopped into my car.

Driving home I realized my heart was pounding, and it continued to do that all through the night—I could hardly sleep. *And it is only the first day of the reunion,* I kept thinking.

The next day we hung around together with old friends, then in the afternoon he asked, "Will you go with me to the dance tonight? I don't want to go alone. I want to sit with you!"

"Sounds good to me."

That night, while dressing for the big affair, I was looking forward to how great it would be to have his long arms around me. My two years as a widow had been devoid of any close, touching relationships, but I had adjusted well and hadn't been looking for a man. I couldn't believe how exciting it was to be with him. *It's just a fling. He'll be flying away before long,* I kept telling myself, hoping to calm down.

It wasn't long before he showed up dressed in his dark blue suit, his Stetson hat and cowboy boots. He was still a cowboy at heart even though he was a retired mechanical engineer.

Music from a small band filled the air at the party. It was more fun than I had imagined. Then a booming voice came over the loudspeaker, "Breakfast will be at 9:30! No need to get up early!"

"Too bad I won't be able to go to the breakfast," Bob said.

"What? You mean you aren't staying?"

"Nope, my plane leaves at 10:30, so I will be gone."

"But the breakfast is the most fun of all. I can't believe you didn't plan to stay for it!" I was upset, and I'm sure it showed.

He looked straight at me and made me an offer. "If you'll promise to spend the day with me, I'll change my reservations."

"Of course I'll spend the day with you. I'd love to."

That meant we would have all day Sunday together, just the two of us.

When he drove me home, I invited him in. We chatted a while, but it was getting late and soon he was leaving. This time when he kissed me goodnight, I returned his kiss with enough enthusiasm that he acted pleased and surprised.

Next morning I was so happy I went around the house singing "Oh what a beautiful morning, oh what a beautiful day!"

After the breakfast we took a drive out to our favorite desert vista, then returned to the hotel.

Sitting at a table in the bar was an old alum friend of ours. "Come on over and sit here," he said. "What's going on with you two anyway? You look so happy together."

Bob spoke up, "This is just the most fun I ever had!"

"Me, too," I chimed in, still excited over the way our day had gone.

"We decided to spend the day together," Bob explained. "I live in Corvallis, Oregon, fifteen hundred miles from here. No way can this last."

"What do you mean it can't last? Neither of you has any family to stand in your way. So what if you live fifteen hundred miles away? That's no excuse."

In those few minutes he convinced us to stop thinking of our fun times as a temporary situation. It hadn't taken much encouragement for us to feel closer from that moment on. It was a real "turning point" in our lives.

That night we had a late dinner and a romantic evening neither of us will ever forget.

Between phone calls and letter-writing, meeting each other in San Francisco three weeks later, and my going up to Corvallis to spend Thanksgiving with him (where we were snowbound for three days!), we made up for our lost years of togetherness.

We were married in March 1986, five months after we had re-met. Both of us were sixty-three years old.

At one time in my life, a long time before, I had wished that somewhere, sometime, I would find someone who would love me for the person I am, who would share my soul—a fantasy future. To think my wish came true!

It is still a thrill to be able to spend my "golden years" with someone so dear to me. We've been truly blessed to find each other again. There aren't many people our age (seventy-nine) who are so lucky!

Norma Grove

To Infinity

In 1974, when we were fourteen years old, Ralph and I became close friends. We used to sit in his front yard and eat cookies and talk for hours. Ralph had a girlfriend and I had a boyfriend, but I thought he was one of the nicest boys at our school.

A few years after graduation, I received an invitation to Ralph's wedding. I arrived alone and waiting outside was Ralph, receiving me with the kind and welcoming smile I had always known. We talked a while, and for some reason I turned and went back to my car and went home. We lost touch for several years. At our ten-year class reunion I looked up and, once again, there was that familiar smile. It was Ralph. "What happened to you?" I asked. "I've been getting divorced," he said with a twinkle in his eye. "Where have you been?"

"I've been getting married," I responded. We sat and reminisced all evening, promising to keep in touch. We contacted one another a couple of times a year and kept each other up on what was going on in our lives, but never saw each other until eight years later. My marriage ended and I found myself living alone in an apartment with my little daughter. Ralph called and asked, "Is there anything

I can do for you? Is your car running okay? Does your daughter need anything? Do you have enough money?"

I told him, "I need to see my old friend. It's been too many years." So we met for a beer and, once again, sat and went over old times. The hours flew by and next thing we knew we were asked to leave. The restaurant had closed.

We got together a couple of more times and found ourselves talking until the sun came up. As Ralph left, I found myself sad watching him go. One evening, I invited Ralph over to have pizza and watch a video. He came over and brought photo albums. As we went through the albums, I felt compelled to tell him that I felt I might be falling in love with him. Mortified with myself, I went in the bathroom and tried to figure out how I could escape from a second-story-apartment bathroom without being discovered! I was afraid I had just destroyed a precious friendship. I had stepped on hallowed ground.

When I returned, Ralph was sitting there with a Cheshire-cat smile on his face. "Lisa, I have loved you for twenty years. You have been the standard I have judged all women by. I don't want to let this opportunity slip past me." I told him that I was afraid that if it didn't work out, we would lose this priceless friendship that we had carried through the years. We agreed our friendship wouldn't be broken and that we had the potential here for something rare and priceless.

Sure enough, we were married nine months later. Engraved in our wedding rings are the words "to infinity." With my daughter, we became a family.

One day we came across his high school yearbook and decided to look up what I had written to him all those years ago. It was so many years back that I'd forgotten.

There was my handwriting. A full page long. And there I had written: "Ralph, You are the nicest boy I have ever met. I know we will be friends for the rest of our lives . . .

in fact, I love you so much that I think when we grow up we should just get MARRIED."

Who'da thought all those years ago as we sat in his front yard eating cookies that those two young kids really would be friends . . . and lovers forever . . . to infinity.

Lisa Ferris Terzich

Just Call Me Cupid

Laughter is the shortest distance between two people.

Victor Borge

It burns me up the way they've commercialized Valentine's Day. As I told Maggie, my wife, we've lost the spirit of it. "Originally a valentine was something personal, from the heart. A fellow would write some verses to his girl, something like that."

"It's certainly cheaper that way," she said.

"That has nothing to do with it," I said. "But a valentine should have a person's individual stamp. Nobody cares about the personal touch anymore. Take our boys . . ."

The boys had been after us to buy valentines to give their classmates. Sammy is in first grade and Roy's in third.

"Wouldn't it be more fun to make your own?" I asked them. They said no. Maggie said that made three of them. I was getting annoyed.

"Don't you want your children to learn to do things for themselves?" I asked her. "Instead of buying everything like a couple of robots?"

"Robots don't buy things," Roy said. "They make what they want."

Next day I decided to give the boys one more chance. I bought them a valentine kit big enough to make sixty-five valentines. After supper we spread it out on the dining-room table. I showed them how to punch out the parts and paste on the hearts and the lace. They got paste all over the table and started fighting over the scissors. I told them to cut it out. "You two are going to learn the joy of making something with your own hands," I told them, "if I have to rap your heads together." I went out to fix myself a drink.

When I got back the boys were gone. Maggie looked in to ask how it was going. I picked up a valentine to show her and the lace fell off. Cheap paste. It wouldn't stick to the paper. It stuck to everything else okay. My glass. My cigar.

The boys still weren't back. I mixed another drink. The first one had got spilled. At about 11:00 Maggie came in. She took a sip of my drink and picked up a valentine. "Interesting," she said. "The drink tastes like paste and the valentine smells like bourbon." I said I'd noticed. "You've done eight," she said. "Only fifty-seven to go."

I gave in and bought a couple of boxes of ready-made ones. They were pretty sleazy, and after the boys had put the names on, I slipped a chocolate heart in each envelope for a surprise. When I got home the next day, the boys wouldn't speak to me. It seems every kid in class had got a candy heart except Roy and Sammy. I hadn't thought of that.

"Okay," I told Maggie, "I'll go back and get them some."

Sammy wanted to go along to leave a valentine at a girl's house. When we finally located it, he wouldn't go up to the door—he said he couldn't reach the mailbox. So I delivered it. A couple of blocks later he said, "There it is. That's Sharon's house." We'd left the valentine at the wrong place.

We went back and I got the valentine out of the mail-box. As I started down the porch steps I met a man com-ing up. "You looking for me?" he said. I said no. He came up another step. "What do you want?" I said I wanted to deliver a valentine to a girl named Sharon.

"She doesn't live here," he said. I said I knew but I'd left the valentine by mistake and had to come back to get it. I showed it to him. The man sniffed. "You been drinking?" I said no, it was the valentine. I went down the steps. He followed me. "We've been bothered by prowlers here lately," he said, grabbing me by the sleeve. I pointed to my car: "If I was going prowling would I take a six-year-old boy along?"

"I never met a prowler before," he said. "How the hell do I know how your mind works?"

A woman called out from the house and wanted to know what was the matter. The man called back, "Fellow here says he's got a valentine for somebody named Karen." "Sharon," I said. "Sharon," the man said. The woman said nobody named "Sharon" lived there. "Oh, for cripe's sake," the man said, "don't you suppose I know that?" They were still arguing as I went back to the car.

Sammy said, "You sure took a long time."

"If you don't like the way I deliver your valentines," I said, "you can do it yourself."

When we got back from the candy store, Maggie said the boys had been invited to spend the night with their friend Buster. So I drove them over. I said they might as well give the rest of the chocolate hearts to Buster's mother—a little valentine present. Back home, I got the box with Maggie's present off the rear seat and took it in.

She acted surprised. "A valentine?" She opened the box and looked in. "Mmm—chocolates." I said what did she mean, chocolates? She held out the box.

"The boys were supposed to give those to Buster's

mother," I said. "My God, they must have given her *your* present. They were both on the back seat."

She said, "Maybe they didn't give her anything."

"Yes, they did," I said. "She came to the door and said thanks for the valentine. I told her to enjoy it and think of me. I thought it was the candy."

Maggie looked at me. "It wasn't candy?"

"No," I said, "it was a nightgown with hearts on it. A peek-a-boo nightgown." Maggie started to laugh.

"Damn it all," I said. "I was only trying to do something nice—and where did it get me?"

Maggie put her hands over her face and shook her head. She seemed to be crying. I patted her on the shoulder. "I'm sorry," I said. "I wanted to give you a nice surprise."

"You did." She wiped her eyes. "Just the thought . . ." and she started to laugh again.

"I realized that trying to be original was only a way of showing off," I said. "So this year I was going to buy you a valentine just like other husbands. I wanted—something sentimental and romantic. . . ."

"Come here." She held out her arms. I went over to her. "Do I have to wear a fancy nightie to be sentimental and a romantic?"

"Not for me," I said.

After a minute she said, "This is the nicest Valentine's Day I can remember." It was beginning to look better to me, too. The phone rang.

"Probably Buster's mother," Maggie said. I said probably. It kept on ringing. "It could be Buster's father," she said. "Could be," I said.

"Let it ring," Maggie said.

Will Stanton

2

LOVE AND ROMANCE

*The moment you have in your heart this
extraordinary thing called love and feel
the depth, the delight, the ecstasy of it, you
will discover that for you the world is
transformed.*

J. Krishnamurti

An Evening at the Waldorf

This is a true story about a young couple in love and the most glamorous hotel in the world. We are telling the story together because it is so indelibly a part of both of our lives that neither of us could tell it alone.

One rainy October evening, in 1948, I sat in my room at the Naval Academy in Annapolis, staring at a navigation lesson and thinking of Jean. I had met her the previous August in Chicago, just before my summer leave expired, and I had fallen in love with her. Three days later I was back in Annapolis, surrounded by rules and regulations, while she was a thousand miles away, surrounded by eligible bachelors. Things looked bleak indeed.

There was one bright spot on the horizon. Jean had promised to come east to Philadelphia for the Army-Navy football game in November. We had been invited to spend the weekend as houseguests of my uncle and aunt in New York. If there was going to be any hope at all for me, that weekend was going to have to be one that she would never forget. I shoved my books aside and wrote the following letter:

Room 5455, Bancroft Hall
U.S. Naval Academy
Annapolis, Maryland
15 October 1948

The Manager
The Waldorf-Astoria
New York City, New York

Dear Sir:

On Saturday afternoon, November 27th, I expect to pick my way across the prostrate bodies of the West Point football team to a seat in Memorial Stadium where a girl will be waiting— a very special girl who I hope will some day follow me from port to port on the "Far China Station." We will hie away by taxi to the railroad station where we will entrain for New York. Once there we will again take a taxi, this time to your hotel—and that, dear sir, is where you and The Waldorf-Astoria come in.

I am very much in love with this young lady, but she has not yet admitted to an equivalent love for me. Trapped as I am in this military monastery, the chances I have to press my suit are rare indeed. Therefore this evening must be the most marvelous of all possible evenings, for I intend to ask her to be my wife.

I would like a perfect table—neither too close to nor too far from the orchestra. There should be candlelight, gleaming silver and snowy linen. There should be wine and a dinner that will be the culmination of the chef's career. Then at precisely midnight, I would like the orchestra to play "Navy Blue and Gold" very softly, and I intend to propose.

I would appreciate it very much if you could confirm this plan and also tell me approximately what the bill will be. I am admittedly not getting rich on thirteen dollars a month, but I have put a little aside. So please give me your estimate of the cost—and I'll bet it will be plenty!

Very truly yours,
E. S. Ince
Midshipman, U.S.N.

I sealed the envelope and, before I could lose my nerve, stuffed it into the mailbox. The minute it was gone I regretted having sent it. It seemed to me that it was callow and smart-alecky and, above all, presumptuous. The manager of the most famous hotel in the world was certainly not going to be interested in the love life of an obscure midshipman. The letter would be thrown into the wastebasket where it belonged.

One week went by and then another. I forgot about the letter and tried frantically to think of some other way that I could convince Jean in thirty-six hours that she should spend the rest of her life with me. Then one morning I found on my desk an envelope upon which was engraved "The Waldorf-Astoria." I almost tore it to shreds in my eagerness to open it, and read:

Dear Midshipman Ince:

Your very nice letter has been receiving some attention from our staff here. Just for fun I am going to attach the reply from our maitre d', the famous René Black.

Frankly, unless you have private resources, I think it is entirely unnecessary to spend so much money. I would be happy to make a reservation for you in the Wedgwood Room and will see to it that you have a very nice table, the best of attention, flowers—and you and your girl order directly from the menu whatever intrigues you. You certainly can have a couple of cocktails and very nice dinners and a bottle of champagne for one third of what René Black suggests. However you are the only one who can make the decision so let me know how you would like to have us arrange your little party.

Best wishes.

Cordially yours,
Henry B. Williams
Manager

P.S. I think your delightful letter *inspired* our Mr. Black!

Needless to say, I hastily unfolded the piece of yellow paper on which René Black had typed his reply. Here is what it said:

When Lucullus dined with Lucullus, his gastro - nomic accoutrements were planned as you now do, every detail in presentation of the festivity. Times and manners have changed but little the unobtrusive elegance and distinctive "savoir faire" of amphytrionic distinction—to include hors d'oeuvre de luxe; the potage generally omitted by ladies (and not to be forced on her); the traditional fish course to be presented as an entr'acte of surprise; the resistance of the menu to show the bird being caught in the nest (which will help your philology in carrying the battle of the nuptials), or as we say in French, "la poulanie," and, like Talleyrand, will highly praise the artisan of the casserole as having been the Cagliostro of your machinations.

The price of this manoeuvre, including wines, gratuities, flowers, and everything named, will be in the vicinity of one hundred dollars, with which we hope your little cache is fortified for complete victory. Following is a description of your menu:

Black pearls of the Sturgeon from the Caspian Sea, stuffed into the claws of lobsters, and eulogising the God of the Oceans.

The Filet of Pompano known as the Demoiselle of the Atlantic, placed in a paper bag with the nomenclature "Greetings from the Poseidon."

The Breast of Chicken served in a little nest to represent the safety of the ketch, with its escort of vegetables and green salad.

An excellent dessert bearing the nomenclature "Ritorna vincitor" from Aida, and little galettes. A sweet liqueur to seal the anticipation.

Wines in small quantities but of choice bracket, of lip-smacking delectability. Pink champagne, flowers, candles, music, etc. All this will blossom with those hundred dollars that you were so provident to save.

I was thunderstruck with excitement and full of gratitude to the two busy men who had taken time to write, but I was also dismayed. I didn't have even close to one hundred dollars saved. With my November paycheck included, I would have a grand total of sixty-six dollars and twenty-five cents when I met Jean after the game, and there were train fares and other expenses to consider. Regretfully I wrote Mr. Williams that he had made a much closer estimate of my resources than had Mr. Black, and I would appreciate it if he would reserve a table for me.

I heard nothing further from The Waldorf. The days went by with no confirmation of my reservation—nothing. I was sure that my letter had never reached Mr. Williams, or that the whole thing had been taken as a joke. Finally it was the weekend of November twenty-seventh. The Brigade of Midshipmen went to Philadelphia and watched their inspired team hold highly favored Army to a 21–21 tie in one of the most thrilling football games ever played. After the game I rushed to meet Jean and she was just as pretty and wonderful as I had remembered her.

On the train to New York I blurted out the whole story and showed Jean the letters from Mr. Black and Mr. Williams. I told her that I wasn't sure that we had a reservation at all, and I questioned whether we should even go to The Waldorf. We decided that we should, and that, even if we didn't have a reservation, we would at least see the famous hotel. So we got into a taxi at Pennsylvania Station, and I said the enchanted words, "Waldorf-Astoria," trying to sound as though I said them every day. In minutes we were at the door.

We walked into the lobby. To the right at the top of a short flight of steps was the Wedgwood Room. There was a velvet rope at the bottom of the steps, and another at the top, with a majordomo posted at both places. A crowd of fashionably dressed couples was patiently waiting for admittance. They all looked fabulously rich. Jean and I were wide-eyed as we stared at the magnificence of the lobby. I looked at her, and she looked at me. Finally I gulped, "Here goes," and went fearfully up to the major-domo at the foot of the stairs. I felt like Oliver Twist when I said, "Sir, I am Midshipman Ince, and I wonder if you by any chance might happen to have a reservation for me."

Like magic he swept away the rope! "Indeed we do," he said, and suddenly we saw the headwaiter at the top of the steps smiling and saying, "Midshipman Ince?" "Yes, sir," I managed. "Right this way," he said, and snapped his fingers. A captain popped up out of nowhere like a genie from a lamp and led us across the room toward a beautiful table. Two waiters were leaning over it, lighting tall, white candles. . . .

Walking ahead of Bud, I looked in amazement at the table. Centered between the candles in a low white vase were flowers— white stephanotis and pink sweetheart roses. When the red-coated waiter seated me, I found a box at my place. Tucked under its ribbon was a card that read, "With the compliments of The Waldorf-Astoria." Catching my breath, I opened it and found a corsage of white baby orchids. A menu, unlike any I had ever seen, lay on the table in front of the centerpiece.

The menu was handpainted in watercolor. A gray navy ship steamed toward the upper right-hand corner, and highlighted on the left was a sketch of a girl's head with blue lovebirds in her hair. Printed with a flair in French, it read:

Menu

Le Fruit Ninon
La Volaille Bergerac
Legumes Testida
La Salade Pigier
La Friande Agrippina
Mayan en Tasse

Wedgwood Room   Nov. 27, 1948

At the very moment when our excitement over the flowers, the table and the menu had subsided to a point admitting of intrusion, our waiter said to Bud, "I have just one question to ask you."

(I was sure he was going to ask me if I could pay for all this!)

"Would you like a cocktail?"
We agreed that we would like a Manhattan, and that was indeed the only question we were asked all evening.
The dinner began. Silver sparkled and crystal glistened in the candlelight. Eddie Duchin and his orchestra played in the background. Service was constant, attentive and unobtrusive. We never felt a waiter near us. Everything simply happened as if by sorcery. Wines we had never tasted, "in small quantities but of choice bracket, of lip-smacking delectability," appeared with each course. The Fruit Ninon was splendid. La Volaille Bergerac was sealed in parchment, which the waiter slit to release its steaming aroma. The Legumes Testida never dreamed that under other circumstances one could think them beans. The salade was perfection. Everything was perfection. Each course was more lovely than the one that came before it, and every taste and flavor would have thrilled the most meticulous epicure.
About halfway through our dinner, a distinguished gentleman with silvery-gray hair and a large Gallic nose approached our table with a smile and said, "I am René Black. I just came over to make sure that you were not angry with me." Bud leaped to his feet, and I beamed as we poured out our thanks to the man who had planned this evening. He drew up a chair and sat down and talked, delighting us with anecdotes of his continuing love affair with his wife, the origin of omelets and a wonderful tale of a dinner party he gave his regiment in France during World War I. When we asked him if he had painted the menu, he smiled, turned it over, and quickly sketched the head of a chef with his pen. Under it he wrote, "Si l'amour ne demande que des baisers à quoi bon la gloire

*de cuisinier." (If love requires only kisses, what is the use of the
fame of the cook?)*

*After Mr. Black left our table, I looked at Bud. I had made plans
to come to see the Army-Navy game and to spend the weekend with
him, and the plans had been exciting. I had finished college and
was trying my wings as a "career girl," but as I fell asleep on the
Pullman on the way to Philadelphia, I wondered how I would feel
about the dashing midshipman I had met so briefly last summer.*

*Here we were in The Waldorf-Astoria Hotel in New York. I had
seen it from the street before and had listened to conversation about
Peacock Alley and the Starlight Roof, but now we were really there!
We had just talked with the famous René Black; we had been served
a dinner to delight royalty and were sipping wine together. How
wonderful. How wonderful. How wonderful!*

*A photographer came up to us and said, "Mr. Black has asked me
to take your photograph with the compliments of The Waldorf." The
flash caught us raising our glasses to each other, in perhaps the happiest instant ever recorded on film.*

A few moments later Eddie Duchin left his bandstand
and came to our table. The already legendary orchestra
leader was warm and friendly as he talked about the great
game Navy had played that afternoon. "I was cheering too,"
he said, and he went on to tell us about his own service in
the navy during World War II. When Jean's attention was
distracted for a moment, Mr. Duchin leaned over to me and
whispered, "'Navy Blue and Gold' at midnight. Good luck!"
He rose, grinning, and walked back to his piano.

He had hardly left when there was a stir and a buzz of
conversation on the other side of the room. Jean and I
looked for the source of the excitement, and then we saw
it! Our dessert, *La Friande Agrippina*, carried triumphantly
aloft across the dining room in a rainbow of colored spot-
lights. Great clouds of vapor billowed from silver cups
filled with dry ice at each corner of the silver serving dish.

In the center was a nest of ice cream within which rested two meringue lovebirds.

We had finished the delicious confection and were sipping a liqueur when the waiter told me that there was a telephone call for me in the lobby. I excused myself and followed him, wondering who in the world could be calling me, only to find the headwaiter waiting just outside the door. He handed me the bill and said, "We thought you might prefer not to have this brought to your table." I turned the slip of paper over fearfully and looked at the total. It was thirty-three dollars—exactly one third of Mr. Black's one hundred, and exactly what I had written Mr. Williams I could afford. It was clear to me that this amount couldn't even begin to cover the cost of the evening to The Waldorf, and equally clear that the reason the bill was presented with such exquisite finesse was to save me embarrassment had I not had thirty-three dollars. I looked at the headwaiter in amazement and gratitude, and he smiled and said, "Everyone on the staff hopes that all goes well for you."

Bud came back to the table gleaming and, in answer to my curiosity about the telephone call, said, "It was nothing important. Shall we dance?" I felt his hand on my arm, guiding me gently to the floor.

Other couples danced about us chatting and, it seemed to me, smiling on us as they glided past. I saw only Bud. We were living a fairy-tale evening, and it was all real. Bud was real, the midshipman who had charmed me during the two evenings we had spent together last August and who had existed since only through letters. I had spun dreams about him during those three months of paper and ink and now I looked into his face as we danced. "I'm in love!" I thought, "How wonderful. I'm in love."

At five minutes till midnight we were sitting at our table in a glow of happiness. Suddenly the wine steward appeared at my side with a small bottle of chilled champagne. He opened it with a subdued "pop" and filled two crystal goblets with the sparkling golden wine. I raised my glass to Jean, and at that moment the orchestra drummer ruffled his drums softly, as if in a command for silence. Eddie Duchin turned toward us, smiled, and bowed. He raised his hand and brought it down, and suddenly we heard the melody of that most beautiful and sentimental of all college alma maters. . . . "For sailormen in battle fair since fighting days of old have proved the sailor's right to wear the Navy Blue and Gold." It was the magic moment to which every other moment of the evening had led. I looked at Jean, my wonderful Jean, and with a lump in my throat said, "Will you marry me?"

Bud and I were married the following June. Now, over fifty years later, with our five children grown, our grandchildren growing, and the Midshipman a Rear Admiral, we sometimes turn the pages of the lovely wedding gift we received from Mr. Williams—a handsomely bound limited edition of the history of The Waldorf-Astoria. In it one can read of the princes and potentates, presidents and kings, who have been guests of that glamorous hotel. But there is one evening that is not included there—an evening in which kind, warm-hearted, gently romantic men opened a door of happiness for a young couple in love. That evening is ours, and its testimony is Mr. Black's wedding gift. Framed and displayed in a place of honor on our dining room wall, it is a watercolor sketch of a little chef tending his spit in an ancient kitchen. Printed in his familiar hand across the top he has repeated the words:

Si l'amour
ne demande que des baisers
à quoi bon
la gloire de cuisinier.

Bud and Jean Ince

To Begin Again

The way I see it, if you want the rainbow, you gotta put up with the rain.

Dolly Parton

The restaurant was crowded, and I waited at the bar until my wife's and my table was called. A fire roared nearby and a real tree stood simply in the corner, covered in small white lights and nothing else. I ordered my wife a glass of wine and sipped at my draft beer while she lingered in the bathroom.

No doubt she was drying her eyes and reapplying a third coat of mascara, I thought bitterly as I remembered the heated words and nasty barbs we had exchanged on the first leg of our trip from North Carolina to Florida.

We were going home to get a divorce. There was nothing pleasant about it. Neither of us were even trying anymore. . . .

We had pulled over at the first nice restaurant we saw. Of course, we had passed a hundred others that either hadn't lived up to her expectations or my price range. We blamed each other the more our hunger grew.

I grunted when the hostess told us that the wait was

over an hour. My wife sighed and disappeared into the ladies' room.

As I chewed on stale peanuts and ordered another beer, I watched the happy couples at the bar, basking in the firelight and looking forward to the new year they had no doubt roared in together romantically.

My wife and I had spent the first day of the new year storming around the house, dividing the CD collection and credit card bills. We had been married for four years, so there was a lot to go over.

I watched a young couple kiss. An older couple held hands. I recalled a happier time, not too long ago, when my wife and I would have been right there with them. Lingering over cocktails at the bar on purpose instead of just rushing in to get a table, eat and get it over with.

I thought of the past year and its few ups and many downs. It had started with a job transfer, and things had gone downhill from there. My wife said good-bye to her fourth-grade students, and we packed up the car and moved ten hours away. We had no friends, no family, and our first month's phone bill was enormous.

She found a job quickly and advanced easily, while I soon realized my new job was a big disappointment. She missed her family and her students, I missed my old job, and nothing worked out right. The move cost more than we expected, we rented an expensive apartment we really didn't need, and there was nothing to do in our new town but eat and watch TV. And fight . . .

Resentment grew with each passing month. But instead of talking to each other and sharing our problems as we had in the past, we turned to grumbling and grousing, fussing and fighting.

How could I tell her I felt unfulfilled and defeated at my new job? The job that had caused her to uproot her whole life and follow her husband to a small town in the mountains of North Carolina?

How could she tell me she hated going into work every morning and felt unfulfilled without being in a classroom?

In the end, neither of us told the other anything. When we spoke at all, it was to yell or accuse or snipe or bark.

My wife appeared at the bar, looking beautiful despite her puffy, cried-out eyes. I felt guilty at her tears, and each drop was like a knife in my heart. There was a time in our life when the thought of making her cry had brought tears to my own eyes. But now each drop was like some stupid point on an invisible scoreboard.

I watched her cross the room and felt a lurch inside my stomach as I thought of my life without her.

"How do I look?" she asked instinctively, and I had to laugh. It was a question she asked constantly, all through the day and night. An inside joke we'd shared for years, soon to be shared no more.

She thought I was laughing at her makeup, and she quickly downed her wine with a sour expression on her face that had nothing to do with the vintage.

Our last name was finally called, and we rushed through soup and rolls. Silver clinked on fancy plates and we chewed in silence. There was so much I wanted to say to her, but after all that we had decided, what was the point?

Telling her I still loved her would only make our decision that much more difficult. . . .

After ordering dinner I excused myself to go to the men's room, stopping on the way to place a reassuring hand on her shoulder. Not surprisingly, her body clenched at my touch.

While inside the men's room I heard the door burst open behind me and then the sound of water running, but my flushing couldn't cover the sound of sobbing as I emerged from the stall.

A middle-aged man in a collared shirt and Dockers stood blubbering in front of the sink. He snuffled and snorted when he saw me, and I reached for paper towels and handed them to him in an unceremonious lump. He used them all and still the tears flowed. His face looked ruddy and flushed, and his washed-out eyes beseeched me to understand as he explained himself through his sobs.

"I'm sorry," he choked. "It's just . . . the tree and the lights. I thought I was ready. I thought I could do all this. But then I heard the Christmas music and I just . . . it's the new year already. Why do they have to keep playing them? I just couldn't do it. I'm sorry. I tried."

"Tried to do what?" I asked gently, hoping I wasn't prying. His pain seemed so intense, it was all I could do not to join him myself.

"Be . . . normal," he explained, blowing his nose shortly after. "My wife. You see . . . she died six weeks ago and I—"

"Six weeks!" I shouted, fear clutching my young heart. "I couldn't get out of bed if my wife had passed away six weeks ago." Despite the current state of affairs of my marriage, I suddenly realized this statement was all too true.

He nodded, as if I had any idea what kind of pain he was experiencing.

"I know," he nodded again. "I know. But . . . I managed to make it through Thanksgiving by drinking my way through a tropical cruise. I even managed to eat and sleep my way through Christmas. And . . . I thought I should be well by now.

"But Christmas was always her favorite. I never stopped to listen to all of those silly Christmas songs until this very night. My appetizer came, my drinks, my salad. It all just sat there while I listened to the words. Over and over. Then I just started bawling. I'm sorry, you must think me a fool."

Just then the men's room door burst open again, nearly

knocking me to the ground. Two young men of college age rushed to surround the crying man. They wore expensive sweaters and grave expressions and called him "Dad."

They asked if he was all right and turned their backs to me as they cleaned their father up in private.

The small room grew crowded, and I left them to their task. I wanted to ask the man how long he and his wife had been married, but by the age of his grown sons I assumed it was well beyond twenty years.

I watched my wife's young face aglow in the candle-light, her fine hands curved around the stem of her wine glass. My legs felt leaden as I joined her at her seat, taking the chair beside her and pulling her into my arms just as the tears came.

"What's wrong?" she whispered into my hair as I clung to her chest. Her tone held no scorn, only bare and naked concern that her husband should feel pain.

After so many hateful words, so many petty barbs, I was still her husband.

"I'm sorry," I said, looking into her eyes.

Her tears spoke her truest fears, and in seconds we were tripping all over each other's apologies. Relief overflowed our hearts as we spoke.

"I'll find a job back home," I sputtered. "I'll work two jobs, whatever it takes. I miss our family, I—"

"We'll both find jobs," she joined. "You'll see. We'll be fine. We'll start all over. Last year was horrible. This year will be fresh and . . ."

When our apologies and plans were spent, she held me close and whispered two words in my ear: "What happened?"

But how could I explain that in one quick bathroom visit I had lost her, and then found her, all at the same time?

Rusty Fischer

"Let's face it, Paul. Our divorce isn't working out."

Reprinted by permission of George Abbott.

Love Notes

Where love is concerned, too much is not even enough.

Pierre de Beaumarchais, French dramatist

I could say that a winter breeze had sent snow flurries dancing against our windowpane as we cuddled in front of a glowing fire, sipping spiced cider, alternately nuzzling each other and cooing about the depth of our love.

I could say that—but it would be a lie.

The early November storms had melted, leaving an endless landscape of gray trees and mire green earth. It fit our moods. My husband and I vacillated between extreme joy over the life of our two-month-old son and extreme distress over our lack of sleep or time for each other. Our conversation, especially for the past two weeks, sounded less like the cooing of lovebirds and more like the barking of pit bulls.

I had returned to work after only six weeks' leave and on the tail of postpartum blahs. I felt fat and incompetent. My husband felt guilty and alienated. The few words in passing each morning and the brief hug and peck in the evening were, at best, meager tokens of the attention we desperately needed to give each other.

After one particularly exhausting day, I lay next to our precious infant, dreamily following the down of his cheeks and the satin of his neck and arm to his feathery fingers, when I . . . well, I fell asleep. I slept the dreamless sleep of the fatigued, while my dear husband waited, hopeful that I would rouse to finish the conversation we'd begun two days earlier. I felt his presence, vaguely, in the doorway of our room, but was drawn gently back into my drowsing stupor.

I awoke several hours later to the whimpering hunger of our baby and saw my husband sleeping soundly within arm's reach. After our son had settled back into blissful contentment, I rose for a drink of water. I stumbled into the hall and flipped the light switch. There, I found the first note, hanging from the frame of our family montage: "I love you . . . because we are a family."

My breath caught for a moment, then I ventured farther along the hallway, and . . . another note: "I love you because you are kind."

For the next half hour, I wandered through our home, collecting the precious bits of warmth and affection. On the bathroom mirror: "I love you because you are beautiful." On my satchel of essays: "I love you because you are a teacher." On the refrigerator: "I love you because you are yummy." On the TV, on the bookcase, in the cupboards, on the front door: "I love you because you are funny . . . you are smart . . . you are creative . . . you make me feel as if I can do anything . . . you are the mother of our son." Finally, on our bedroom door: "I love you because you said yes."

It was intoxicating, soothing—an embrace to carry me through the sleepless nights and draw me back into the joy of my every day. I slipped back into our bed and curled myself around my beautiful husband.

Gwen Romero

I Love You Anyway

It was Friday morning, and a young businessman finally decided to ask his boss for a raise. Before leaving for work, he told his wife what he was about to do. All day long he felt nervous and apprehensive. Finally, in the late afternoon, he summoned the courage to approach his employer, and to the businessman's delight, the boss agreed to the raise.

The elated husband arrived home to a beautiful table set with their best china and lighted candles. Smelling the aroma of a festive meal, he figured that someone from the office had called his wife and tipped her off! Finding her in the kitchen, he eagerly shared the details of his good news. They embraced and danced around the room before sitting down to the wonderful meal his wife had prepared. Next to his plate he found an artistically lettered note that read, "Congratulations, darling! I knew you'd get the raise! This dinner is to show you how much I love you."

Later on his way to the kitchen to help his wife serve dessert, he noticed that a second card had fallen from her pocket. Picking it up off the floor, he read, "Don't worry about not getting the raise! You deserve it anyway! This dinner is to show how much I love you."

Joe Harding

A Fragment in Time

The ultimate measure of a man is not where he stands in moments of comfort and convenience, but where he stands at times of challenge and controversy.

Martin Luther King Jr.

The day was a total disaster from the moment I awoke. The dog had decided the cat was a most interesting chew toy, much to the cat's indignant cries, and if that was not enough, the toilet overflowed onto newly installed carpet. The cat, once again in a pickle as she lifted each paw in disgust and shook the water from it, looking at me accusingly as if I had made her life miserable on purpose.

As I entered the kitchen to get a cup of coffee, I heard a scratching sound coming from my cabinet. I slowly opened the door as quietly as I could, and sitting in the back munching on a box of Cheerios was the fattest mouse I had ever seen!

I sighed and closed the door, hoping he was enjoying his breakfast. After all, the Cheerios were ruined anyway— he might as well have the rest! Before tonight, I would have to find some way of coaxing him out of the house and back in the field where he belonged!

I had twelve people coming for dinner and had not done the shopping. Time was slipping away, and my nerves were standing on end screaming, "Told you so!"

I locked the cat in the bedroom and scolded the dog, who looked at me with innocent eyes wondering what he did in the first place. Then I donned my coat and, totally frazzled, headed for the store.

There was a chill in the air as I pulled into the parking lot of the grocery store. The wind's icy fingers tugged at my coat as I hurried towards the door of the supermarket. I grabbed a buggy, and of course the wheels refused to go in the right direction, clattering through the aisles. *Fine!* I grumbled to myself. *A perfect ending to an already perfect day.* I decided that at least I would win the battle of the shopping cart. I shoved the cart next to the cashier's aisle and chose another that was more cooperative. Ahh, the sound of silence and smooth wheels; it didn't take much to bring a ray of sunlight into my life that day.

As I was standing in the produce section pinching the avocados, I heard that familiar annoying rattle of wheels, and I turned to the unfortunate person who'd obviously chosen my old buggy to say, "You have the shopping cart from hell!" What I saw changed the rest of my day into one I will never forget.

An elderly man with white hair and a face that was etched with wrinkles was pushing a hospital stretcher with one hand and pulling the basket from hell with another. He didn't notice the clatter or the wheels that went in different directions. He was busy guiding his wife, who laid upon the stretcher, closer to the produce so she could have a look.

She was a frail woman with gray at the temples and large blue eyes. Her hands and feet were twisted in odd directions and she could not raise her head but a tiny bit. He would pick up a piece of fruit and, with a sweet smile, hold it close to her, and she would nod her head and smile in return. They greeted everyone with a smile and a nod of their heads and didn't seem to mind that they were the subject of gawking and attention. Some people shook their heads in disgust that he would bring a stretcher into the grocery store; others whispered disapprovingly that they didn't belong.

I watched as he picked up a loaf of bread and touched her hand so softly. The connection between the two of them filled the space with so much love that it was palpable. I realized I was staring, as if to hold them in that moment of enchantment. Concerned that I was intruding, I forced my eyes to look away. I turned back to the avocado that was resting in my hand and noticed I had squeezed it a little too hard. I placed it back in the rack and moved to the dairy aisle, trying to catch another glimpse of this couple who seemed to be a magnet for my heart.

They had moved on to another part of the store, and I didn't see them again until I was finished with shopping and back in my car. I started the engine, and suddenly noticed that there, next to my car, was the elderly man and his wife. His vehicle had been parked next to mine, and as he put the groceries in the front of his van, his wife waited patiently on the stretcher.

He hurried to the back of the van, and a gust of cold wind blew the blanket off of her frail body. He lovingly tucked it back around her as you would tuck in a child before bed, reached down and placed a kiss on her forehead. With a twisted hand, she reached up and touched his face. Then, they both turned to look at me and smiled. I returned the smile with tears rolling down my cheeks.

What tugged at my heart and brought tears to my eyes was not the condition either of them was in. It was the love and laughter they shared in going to the store together and being as they always had been . . . in love and needing each other.

The man placed the stretcher in the back of the van and made sure it was secure, and then he came around to the driver's side and stepped in. As they were leaving, he looked at me once again and smiled with a wave, and as he pulled out of the lot, I saw a small hand wave from the back of the van, and the most beautiful, vibrant blue eyes returned my gaze.

Sometimes in life one is struck with an astounding realization—that within a moment of time, which seems to move in slow motion, one can grasp the total beauty of life and love in its purest form. It plays before your eyes like an old black-and-white movie with only the sound of silence and the movement of the actors who, without words, will touch your heart. In that fragment of time, sitting in the parking lot, I felt the pure radiance of the profound, unconditional love of two perfect strangers who crossed my path on what I had thought was going to be a disastrous day.

I started for home with my car full of groceries and my heart full of hope. This couple had taught me a priceless lesson—that the little things don't matter, and the big things are just small hurdles when there is enough love.

Victoria Robinson

Moving In with Frank

Although a bright and able man, my husband is almost completely helpless when faced with even the simplest domestic chore. One day, in exasperation, I pointed out to him that our friend, Beaa, had taught her husband, Frank, to cook, sew and do laundry, and that if anything ever happened to Beaa, Frank would be able to care for himself. Then I said, "What would *you* do if anything happened to me?"

After considering that possibility for a moment, my husband said happily, "I'd move in with Frank."

LaVonne Kincaid

The Gift of Life

Trouble is part of your life, and if you don't share it, you don't give the person who loves you a chance to love you enough.

Dinah Shore

I fell in love with my husband, Mike, after our first date. I had invited him to a Sadie Hawkins dance. He wasn't my first choice, but I am so glad fate had it that he was my second! A friend had encouraged me to invite him, saying, "Mike's the type of guy you could be with for the rest of your life." What wisdom from a sixteen-year-old!

He had every quality a girl could want. Handsome, kind, respectful, loving and caring . . . basically the very best friend a girl could have! He was a big high-school football player, and I felt like a princess when I was with him.

We dated into college, and with the Vietnam War facing us squarely in the face, we decided to get married. Yes, we were too young, but we would not back down on our decision, even without the support and blessings of our family. Love knows no obstacles.

On a short honeymoon trip to Corpus Christi, Texas,

Mike developed serious stomach pains. Terrified, I called the hotel desk to be referred to a local physician. The doctor said he was passing a kidney stone, and we should return home immediately. I remember the long, four-hour drive home. The wind was horrendous, and in those days cars did not have power steering! I could not hold the car on the road, so Mike, suffering incredibly, took the wheel of the car and took us safely home. He was my hero.

This incident began a long journey of living with chronic kidney disease. Mike never made the trip to Vietnam as he was immediately given a medical discharge from the service. He finished college and started a career as a manufacturer's rep in the furniture business. We had two wonderful sons. I made a career of being a full-time wife and mother.

Over a period of twenty years there were many hospital stays, kidney biopsies and some very scary moments. But with Mike's character and positive attitude, he would always bounce back and return to being a normal father and husband. On the outside looking in, we seemed to be an average, happy family, but on the inside, I lived each day wondering when the black cloud over us would finally burst.

In 1987, his time was running out, and the only alternative was to be put on a dialysis machine and go on the list for a transplant. Before starting the treatments, I surprised him with a trip to the beach, where he played one of the best rounds of golf he had ever played. He was so weak and so gray in color, and it was his fortieth birthday. For the first time in our married lives, he told me he felt defeated. He had fought going on the machine for as long as he possibly could. My heart was broken, even though I was grateful that this machine would keep him alive.

He approached the dialysis just like everything else he did in life. He made a game of it and would never allow it to bring him down. He would leave the treatments weak as a cat, eat a meal and go right back to work. People were just amazed at him.

Meanwhile, the list of people ahead of him was long, and relatives were ruled out for the transplant. To this day, I still cannot explain where this strange feeling came from, but I remember vividly sitting in the doctor's office with Mike's sister. He was explaining to her why she could not be a donor, when a voice in my head said, *You will do it.* It was so clear and so precise, and I have never before nor since heard a voice speak to me like that. I never doubted from that moment that I would be the donor, even though it sounded impossible at the time.

I kept thinking about it, and the answer came to me very easily. On the next visit with the doctor, I told him, "Look, Mike and I have the same blood type, is this correct? A cadaver kidney only has to match by blood type, correct? Okay, so if I got run over by a car today and killed, then my kidney would work for him, correct?" The doctor just looked at me as I pleaded my case. "So, let's let him have it while I'm alive to enjoy the rest of our lives together. . . . How about it?"

Sure sounded easy to me, but the answer was a flat no. A living, nonrelated donor could not donate a kidney. Saying no to me was like waving a red flag in front of a mad bull.

I spent hours researching and found that in the state of Wisconsin, husband-and-wife transplants had been done several times. So why not in Texas?

I gathered some support from a few physicians, and the case went before the hospital board. It took a while for them to reach a decision, and they even asked us to go through psychological testing. (I guess they wanted to make sure I wasn't crazy.) We both laughed driving home from the testing, because we could almost read each other's minds. He'd say, "I knew you would give that answer for that question," and I would reply, "Yeah, and I know which one you chose too!" Thank God we could laugh a little!

The Methodist Hospital board and staff in Dallas were finally convinced and ready to go. I never dreamed the delay might come from my own husband! The more he thought about it, the more he could not stand the idea of me going into surgery for him. After all this, he said he didn't think he could go through with it. In a quiet and very emotional moment, I just asked him the simple question, "I have watched you fight and be there for our family for the last nineteen years. We have been through all this *together*. Now what if it were me on that machine, and you knew you could do something to make me well? What would YOU do?" The surgery was scheduled.

Fourteen years ago, Mike and I made Texas history as the first husband/wife (living, nonrelated) transplant. I received phone calls from people all over the country wanting to do the same thing. Now it is not uncommon for nonrelated donors to be allowed to give "the gift of life."

Making history has never impressed me that much, but having a healthy husband for the last fourteen years, and looking at many more to come, is far more important.

Margo Molthan

The Heart and Cement of Texas

From the moment it is touched, the heart cannot dry up.

Louis Bourdaloue

Like so many of us, I grew up believing that a dozen red roses and a box of chocolates were a passable, if not ideal, Valentine's Day present.

I was wrong.

Mutual friends introduced me to Alfred around Christmastime. We hit it off right from the start, and less than two months later, we're only days away from celebrating our first Valentine's Day together. How could we make it special?

"Have you ever done anything romantic for a woman? Ever?" I asked him. There was a thoughtful silence while he gazed aimlessly around my living room. "Nope. Can't say that I have," he drawled. Alfred is from Texas.

Now, if my question seems abrupt, it's because my beloved Alfred is a superintendent in charge of building restaurants, and he has worked in construction most of his forty-something years of life. Based on stereotype, he loathes wearing business suits, spends a much-enjoyed portion of his day swapping dirty jokes with the guys, and can open a beer bottle with his toes since his hands are often too busy trying to unjam the door to the port-a-potty.

In short, male construction workers are not typically remembered for their romantic gestures toward women. At least, not the ones considered acceptable in polite society.

That same night, Alfred told me they would be pouring the sidewalks for his newest restaurant project the next day.

"You should carve our initials together in the wet cement," I suggested, half serious and half in jest.

"Awww. Now that would be romantic, wouldn't it?"

Two days later he invited me to the job site. "Besides havin' lunch with me, there's somethang I wanna show ya."

As we walked around the restaurant on the newly dried sidewalks, he showed me where he'd carved my initials not only once, but in THREE DIFFERENT PLACES!

"Does this mean there's something 'concrete' going on between us?" I joked. But the smile that just wouldn't leave my face showed how happy his thoughtfulness had made me.

And during our special Valentine's dinner that Saturday night, he presented me with a block of pinewood. Sounds pretty ordinary, I know. Except he'd jigsawed and sanded it into the shape of a heart.

"When did you do this?" I asked.

"This afternoon at work."

"Did the other guys see you make this? Didn't they tease you about it?"

"Heck, no. As a matter of fact, a couple of 'em wanted me to make them one for their sweethearts."

"And did you?"

"No, ma'am. I made this 'specially for you. 'Cause I reckon I love ya."

Then I realized that all the flowers, candy and God-only-knows what other kind of conventional presents could never compare to my custom-carved, heart-shaped, extraordinary piece of wood and my initials permanently etched in slabs of cement at a nearby restaurant.

In spite of all his subsequent denials, this crazy Texan had given me the most romantic Valentine's Day gifts of my entire life.

Have I mentioned how much I love Texans?

Barbara Zukowski

Three Times the Lover

On Valentine's Day, Tom asked me to have dinner with him. He insisted that my two daughters, ages nine and eleven, be at home when he picked me up.

When he arrived, he asked us to sit on the couch. From his pocket, he took three small boxes. One contained a diamond engagement ring. Each of the other two contained a heart-shaped ring with a tiny diamond in the center.

He proposed to all three of us and, needless to say, I didn't have a chance.

The four of us have been married now for almost thirty years.

Sherry Huxtable

Romance Isn't Always Roses— Sometimes It's Mulch

I'm easy prey for advertisers. As soon as the soft blur cuts across my television screen with the familiar diamond merchandising logo I glance balefully at my left hand. No sparkling solitaire there. Diamonds may be forever, but for me it's a plain band of gold.

Perfume commercials provoke dreams of swirling in chiffon, waltzing on terraces and gazing out across an azure sea. I drool over lingerie catalogues; the more Victorian lace and slinky silk I see, the more convinced I become that women in expensive negligees are more beloved than ladies in flannel. I'm definitely flannel clad most evenings and attired in painted, splattered sweatpants during the day.

I devour romance novels, and it's the romance that lures me. I sometimes even skip the sex scenes to get to the "good part"—the part where the hero tells the heroine how unique she is, how her humor, vulnerability, independence, sensitivity, strength or (fill in any other quality) draw him to her side. I especially love the authors who spark their love scenes with witty dialogue, clever Noel

Cowardish banter far removed from, "Do you need anything at the grocery store?" or "I've got to fix that toilet."

When my helpful computer pops up Internet ads for
flowers, I press my nose to the screen. When I surf into
spots advertising bed-and-breakfast inns with in-room
Jacuzzis, fresh flowers and chilled champagne, nasty
demons of resentment swirl through my head.

I forget that I don't even like champagne. I can convince
myself that I'm not loved, and that is so far from the truth.
Outside my window are hundreds of roses, their spring-
borne scent filling the evening air. My wealth of blossoms
thrive in raised flowerbeds that my husband built, their
roots protected by mulch he makes from autumn leaves.
Hollyhocks and hibiscus line the fence he put around the
yard to protect the tiny beagle I wanted for our son. We'd
negotiated with our kid—a dog in return for improved
grades. The report card wasn't up to par, but I thought
that every dog needs a boy. It wasn't my labor that put up
the fence. I didn't drive fifty miles out of town to find the
perfect puppy. Yet I was the one that wanted it to happen.
That's worth a bit more than a waltz on the deck of a
cruise ship with a few hundred strangers.

My husband doesn't waltz. He fixes the shower ceiling,
takes out the trash, checks the oil in my car and goes to
the grocery store.

We've never spent a night in a bed-and-breakfast tout-
ing fresh-baked cookies on your own private terrace.
We've backpacked through Europe staying in inexpensive
pensions with the bathroom down the hall. We'll never
have luxury, but we'll always have Paris—usually on frequent flyer miles.

About that diamond? I'm married to a man who would-
n't blink if I took "my money" and bought a diamond. So
while I succumb for an instant to the image of the romantic hero presenting the smiling heroine with a glittering

jewel, I value the space in my marriage.

I can spend hundreds of dollars on my hobbies. Buy fourteen pairs of black shoes or spring for weekly facials. He would never say a word. I'm married but completely free to do what I please and be who I am. It really is me that slides my feet into scruffy tennis shoes instead of high-heeled slippers. I laze around in flannel instead of dolling up in satin. Romantic dreams are a longing for appreciation.

Years ago a wise woman told me that, "He treats you like you're made of fine china. That wears well." Indeed it does.

Is romance roses? It can be, if you like pruning and mulching. Is it cruises under the stars? Well, we both get seasick. Romance is not in photo-op moments, it's in the day-to-day kindness that makes life comfortable. Is romance candlelit dinners with hovering waiters? My husband does a super stir-fry.

I need to turn off the television and put down the novel. I have all the romance I need.

Diane Goldberg

"Just the fact that your father hasn't taped
a football game over our wedding video
proves that it was a very special day to him."

True Love

If you have [love], you don't need to have any-thing else, and if you don't have it, it doesn't matter much what else you have.

Sir James M. Barrie, British playwright

I saw them walk in, he with his walker, proud and tall, she on his tail, uncertain of the fate awaiting her. With the peak upon us, the morning had been a whirlwind. This couple stood out like a sore thumb. At that time of year it was rare to have a married couple at my desk, let alone one in their sixties. It had been return after return filed by young ladies, girls almost, to claim the ever-popular earned income credit. These girls actually thought this was a good thing, these large refunds they received after an entire year of scraping and making do. They didn't want to earn more because they will lose that huge tax refund. How foolish these young girls were. They were mothers, yet still chil-dren. I wondered if they would ever have that same look on their face as the woman I saw walk in with her husband.

Ready for a change, I looked up as I finished with the client at my desk. My thoughts turned to wishing I would be the next in line when that older couple had their turn. Something about them captured my eye and my heart. In the midst of a divorce, romance was far from my mind. But I could sense romance as they walked through the door. The old-fashioned kind where the love had grown so big that it engulfed the two souls. I could see that on this couple's face. In the way they sat almost intertwined.

Picking up the clipboard I saw the woman look up anxiously. Apparently she knew I was going to call them next. "Clarence?" I said out loud. And the couple rose as I directed them to my desk. Relief washed through me as I wondered what their story was. She was shaky in that way that many older women are, not physically as much as emotionally and mentally. It was apparent he had protected and cared for her all their married life. She had that look of total trust and dependency. In turn though, I knew that things were changing for them. The presence of his walker was cruel evidence of a fork in the road for this couple.

I introduced myself, and she in turn introduced herself and her husband in a most genteel fashion. There was a question on her face. She had turned sixty-five during the tax year and the Social Security benefits she had received were a concern for her. He was trying to hush her. "Put that back, they don't deal with that here," he said as he refolded her papers and stuffed them back in her purse. I had given her enough answer to soothe her. She had worked during the tax year for perhaps the first time in decades. Many new experiences were coming her way.

The couple had never used a tax service before. Their daughter usually did their taxes, but things had gotten busy for her and they didn't want to bother her. With the advent of the rapid refund many people who would not normally use a tax service came in to have their returns done and get their refunds quick. This couple was no different. They needed the money and my heart broke at the reason. In the midst of conversation I heard him say, "I may not be able to work much longer, I have cancer." I felt my heart leap to my throat and it was all I could do to keep the tears on the inside.

I saw her breath catch as she heard the words. I knew there was terror hidden beneath those innocent eyes. Her beloved, her life and reason for being was being taken from her. She could not even drive herself around. There had never been a need for her to get a driver's license. He had chauffeured her wherever she needed to go for more than forty years. This was true romance, love at its finest. He was incapable of boiling water or turning on the washing machine. There had never been a need for him to do that. She did it.

I noticed his birthday was the next day and my heart skipped a beat. They applied for the rapid refund so I knew there was a chance I would see them again and on his birthday.

Another of their daughters came in the next day by their referral. I recognized the name on the coupon. I asked her what they were going to do for him and she told me all he wanted was that day, no gifts, no hoopla. He just wanted to spend it in gratitude for having another day. My heart ached to celebrate not only this man but also this couple, their strength and fortitude. They were not haggard from the ordeal of the cancer. They had just learned gratitude from it.

Musing on them as I had found myself doing time after time in the brief period since I met them, I realized that I had fallen hopelessly in love. This couple who walked into my life at a time when I was beginning to believe that true love did not exist changed me forever. I truly hoped there were no delays in processing and that I would see them again. I would not work the following day, and if the refund check was not ready then, I would miss seeing them again.

A couple of hours later as I handed out a refund check I noticed their name on the log. I wondered if I would have the privilege of wishing this man a happy birthday and seeing his bride again. I heard the door open and felt my heart leap as Clarence and Dorothy walked through the door. He with his walker, she close on his heels. Their faces radiated joy. He at having reached another birthday and she that her love was still by her side.

True to her nature Dorothy had obediently come in with her ID card ready. As Clarence reached for his wallet I shooed his effort away. They needed no identification, my heart knew immediately who these people were. "Happy birthday!" I said as I pulled out his check. I saw relief in her eyes though. They needed the money. Not only did he know it but he had not been able to shelter her from that knowledge. "Thank you," he said with a glint in his eye. After as much chitchat as I dared, I bid them good-bye. Watching them walk to the door I chanted, "See you next year," as we commonly do after handing out the refund checks. I heard him say, "I hope so."

I could only stand there, watching as if I had lost my true love. Tears welled up in my eyes at the ordeal these two had yet to come. But I knew without a doubt that their love would withstand even the cruelest journey.

Valerie Cann

Open Heart

Love's greatest gift is its ability to make everything it touches sacred.

Barbara De Angelis

My parents fell in love at first sight, and they've been in love for more than fifty-two years. They're not just comfortable with each other, or merely tolerant of each other's faults. They are still truly, deeply in love, with all the passion and heartache that wildly emotional state entails.

My father has always been more of a tease than a romantic, and he has regaled us with tales of his exploits all our lives. For example, the first time he and my mother ever spoke to each other was after World War II, after Daddy had just returned from Japan. He was driving his brother's brand-new car through town when he saw my mother go into a furniture store. Pulling over, he jumped out of the car and managed to slip into the store right behind her. My twenty-six-year-old mother, who was thinking about finding an apartment, asked the store owner to show her the twin bedroom set she had admired the week before. My father, a mere passing acquaintance, stepped up beside her and said, "Now Maude, we are not sleeping on twin beds."

They were married three months later, and they did sleep on one of the twin beds until they could afford a double bed. Fifty-three years later they still sleep in the same bed.

At age seventy-eight, my father had open-heart surgery. My seventy-six-year-old mother spent every night at the hospital, and every day beside his bed. The first thing Daddy said when they removed the tracheal tube from his throat was one of the most romantic things I've ever heard. He said, "Maude, you know what that doctor found when he cut me open? He found your name engraved on my heart."

Rickey Mallory

Message Received

I knew the answer before he even asked.

My boyfriend of two years dropped down on one knee, pulled out a velvet, heart-shaped box, and asked, "Will you marry me?"

Louis looked so adorable. Such a large, strong man suddenly turned so vulnerable. I couldn't have found a better mate, so gorgeous, caring and easygoing. He had become my best friend, and I knew in my heart that I loved him.

"Yes," I answered.

A wave of relief washed over his face, then a huge, boyish smile that preceded a passionate kiss. "Thank you for making me the happiest man in the world!"

That week, we set the date for August 8 of the following year, and I started to pick out cards for our engagement announcement—and the memories immediately flooded back.

This wasn't the first time I had planned a wedding. Five years ago, Jono, my first fiancé, had died unexpectedly only six months prior to our wedding date. Pain paralyzed my heart as unfinished grief and longing reared up. I realized that planning another wedding brought all my feelings to the surface. I wondered if I'd ever heal from that loss.

I thought I had gotten over losing him. Because I was so young—only twenty-three years old—when Jono died, family and friends expected I would move on and date others, which I had . . . but marriage? As the months passed, I began to ponder whether Jono, the angel, felt anger toward me for wanting to marry someone else. After all, I had once promised to be his one and only.

The next morning, I found myself praying. *Dear God, tell Jono that I know I said I would be his wife. But since you needed him, I've fallen in love with a beautiful man who treats me wonderfully. I'm very happy, yet afraid that Jono might be mad that I am going to have to break my word. Please have him forgive me. Tell him I'm sorry, and that I hope he will send me a sign so I know he approves.*

Just then, a knock on the door startled me. I jumped, almost expecting Jono to be there.

Louis came in. "Are you ready?"

"For?" I wondered.

"We've got premarital counseling today. Remember the pastor changed it to this morning."

"Oh, that's right!" Quickly I got ready, and we decided to take my car since it was faster than his.

"Are you okay?" Louis asked as he started the engine.

"Uh-huh," I nodded halfheartedly.

"You still want to marry me, don't you?"

I turned to him knowing I couldn't let this man out of my life. If only Louis knew how much I really did love him. In that moment, I knew without a doubt that I was willing and ready to break a solemn vow I'd once made to someone else, to move forward and marry Louis.

"Yes," I replied.

Louis stopped the car in the church's parking lot, stepped out and came around to my side to let me out. "Did you see my wallet anywhere?" He suddenly began patting his pockets.

"Maybe it's underneath the seat."

Louis went back to the driver's side as I walked around the car to help him search.

He found his wallet under the seat, but something else caught his eye. He reached farther back and pulled out a shiny gold object. "What's this?"

My hands flew to my face. I had lost that "Xs and Os" gold bracelet six years ago. It was my birthday present from Jono, given to me the last day he told me how much he loved me. I had searched my car many times looking for this special bracelet and had given up hope of ever finding it.

"Wow, this is beautiful," Louis said, impressed.

With some hesitation, I explained who had given me the bracelet so many years before.

For a moment, Louis just stared at the piece shimmering in the sun. Then he took my hand and tenderly fastened Jono's bracelet on my wrist.

"You don't mind my wearing it?" I asked.

"No," he replied. "Now you can think of it as a present from both of us."

Years ago, I had searched this car for days trying to find that bracelet with its message of "hugs and kisses" from my first love. As I watched it shine on my wrist, I knew my prayer to hear from Jono had been answered. I soaked in this divine moment and the symbolism attached to it now that the bracelet, Jono, Louis and I were all brought together at our church.

Louis took my hand and we began to walk into the church. Next to the brass door handle was a plaque that had the complete Bible scripture "Love bears all things" engraved. Louis opened the door for me, and I took one last look at the plaque. As we walked through the archway, my eyes focused on the next words, "Love is not jealous."

Michele Wallace Campanelli

3

ROMANTIC MOMENTS

What force is more potent than love?

Igor Stravinsky

Romance Is in the Eye of the Beholder

The supreme happiness of life is the conviction that we are loved.

Victor Hugo

Life is so very busy. I think at times we all get so lost in the hustle and bustle of everyday life that we forget what it was that made us fall in love with our spouse or our significant other. Thankfully, I remembered.

My husband works hard. Many times his hours are long and his employment usually takes him away from the homefront about one quarter of the year. I'm not complaining, mind you, because that was the same job that enabled me to be a stay-at-home mom and pursue my dream of writing. Yes, I'm a mother of three active boys and a published romance author. Naturally you'd think my life is full of romance. It is. My days consist of plotting and arranging the romantic lives of my characters so that the outcome is the proverbial "happily ever after." I love happily ever afters. This story is one of those.

I've never considered my husband of nineteen years to really be the romantic type. Sweet as he is, he isn't one to make dinner reservations at an exclusive restaurant, or buy me a mushy, lovey-dovey card "just because." I do get flowers for all the proper occasions and the cards do come then, but is that really romantic? I never considered it to be, especially when the vast majority of the female population was getting them, too. I had always wished for a little more. . . .

One day while I was working, several strange "incidences," for lack of a better word, crept into my mind. I was trying to concentrate on my current work-in-progress but "they" wouldn't leave me alone. "They" weren't any huge revelation or any spectacular plot points I could use for the rancher hero I was working on at the time, either. They didn't have to do with the elusive heroine I was still trying to get a grasp on. No. These were different. Very different. They were about my husband. For some strange reason I couldn't get out of my head the last business trip he went on. He brought me back a pound of Ghirardelli malt balls and the romance novel I'd been meaning to buy. Then there was that fax I received that simply said, "I love you." Could those two things fall under the romantic category? I decided they could. They most certainly should. Other special moments flooded my mind as if a little keeper in my head had opened some "dam of memories." I remembered, vividly, the time my husband got the kids to bed early. No small feat, let me tell you! I was in the basement scrubbing a baseball uniform, wondering what made me angrier, those coaches who encouraged kids to slide when it was raining and muddy, or the league who purchased the white pants. When I came up from finishing the chore, a scented bubble bath had been drawn, wine poured and candles lit. Has anyone ever been bathed by their spouse or significant other in an atmosphere like that? I can tell you firsthand that that was romantic! Those white baseball pants were soon forgotten and the coaches all forgiven. Then I fondly remembered another time, when the kids were at Grandma's. My so-called unromantic hubby packed us both sandwiches and we rode bikes to the covered bridge in our town. We sat there, holding hands, eating and watching the geese and ducks. Just the two of us, just "being."

It hit me, then, as I stared at my computer monitor, the words "Ray loves Tina" endlessly floating across the screen—the screen saver was something else my sneaky husband had changed once before going out of town—how unfair I'd always been in my thinking. Was my husband romantic? Heavens, yes! I realized I could go on and on with those special moments, all the way back to when we first got married. You may not think it's romantic for a man to travel on business with a container of deodorant that has his wife's picture taped to the front, or finding Hershey Hugs and Kisses that had been strategically hidden all over the house because he wants you to know he misses you and is thinking about you while he's gone, but I sure do.

I know it's been said that beauty is in the eye of the beholder, but I think the same goes for romance. We all need to look for those special moments—and cherish them! I'm just thankful this romance author finally reflected and realized, again, what a hero she's married to!

Tina Runge

Handmade Valentines from the Heart

Treasure the love you receive above all. It will survive long after your gold and good health have vanished.

Og Mandino

I was the tender age of sixteen and my husband was only seventeen when we were married in 1966 in Welch, West Virginia. There weren't many jobs available in our small town. We had been married only two months when my husband found out that Trailways Bus Lines was taking applications for various positions.

My husband drove one hundred miles to Roanoke, Virginia, to apply for a job with the bus company. They contacted him the next week to come back to take a test that was one of the requirements for being hired. So once again, he drove the one hundred miles to take the test. A few weeks later, he was notified that he had been accepted to a position as an apprentice mechanic. This offer was a great opportunity for us, but I was heartbroken when I found out that the job was in Roanoke and that we would have to move. We knew no one who lived there. It was

very hard for me to move so far from my family and
friends at such a young age. We found a small furnished
apartment, and I was lucky to find a job as a sales clerk at
Woolworth's during the day, but my husband was scheduled to work from midnight to 8 A.M. So as he came home
from work each morning, I was getting ready to leave to
go to work.

Naturally, we had very little money, so when
Valentine's Day came around that first year, I knew we
couldn't afford to buy anything for each other. I felt so
bad that I wouldn't be able to buy him a present—not
even a card.

After he left to go to work the night before Valentine's
Day, I couldn't sleep. So I decided to stay up and make a
Valentine's Day card for him. I didn't have any construction paper, so I had to use regular notebook paper. I
worked so hard to compose a poem for him. I knew what
I wanted to say, but I couldn't seem to put it on paper. It
took me most of the night, and by the time he came home
the next morning it was done!

I had made a valentine for my valentine. I felt foolish and
childish as I handed him my homemade valentine, hoping
that he wouldn't laugh at it. I held my breath and watched
as he opened it and started reading it. On the front of the
simple piece of paper, I had written the following:

We may not have a lot of money
To buy a card that's cute and funny.
But what we have can take the place
Of a paper heart with fancy lace.
We have each other, and that's the best,
Now open the card and read the rest.

On the inside, I had colored a large red heart and written "I Love You." I stood waiting and watching, afraid that
he would start laughing at any moment. When he had

finished reading it, he slowly raised his head and looked at me. Then the corners of his mouth started moving up! But all he did was smile tenderly.

While looking into my eyes, he reached down into his pocket. When he pulled his hand out, he was holding something. He told me that he had made it for me during his lunch hour, but he had been afraid to give it to me. He said that he thought I might think it was silly, and that I might laugh at it.

I took his hand in mine and turned it over. As I looked down, he slowly opened his fingers, and I saw a small heart made out of aluminum. While I had stayed up all night making him a valentine card, he had been cutting out a heart for me from a piece of aluminum. He said the guys he worked with had laughed at him for making the heart, and he'd been worried about giving it to me.

I still have the aluminum heart, and I keep it in my desk. Every once in a while when I open the drawer and see it lying there, all those memories come flooding back to me. Over the years, we've been able to buy each other very nice, expensive presents for Valentine's Day. But none has ever been as dear or meant as much as those handmade gifts made from our hearts the first year that we were married.

Evelyn Wander

Norma Shearer's Dress

We are shaped and fashioned by what we love.

Johann Wolfgang von Goethe

Before World War II, my husband and I lived in Ardmore, Pennsylvania, outside Philadelphia, in a fifty-dollar-a-month apartment. This was almost half my husband's monthly salary. Though we could not afford even a radio, we managed to pay for two babies. Occasionally, upon my husband's insistence, I went to a movie. Both of us couldn't go, and, anyway, who would mind the children?

We were wondrously happy in those struggling years. On sunny afternoons I piled the children into a canvas buggy and did the five-and-tens, just to look. The thing I yearned for most was a one-egg poacher, which cost fifteen cents. I would pick it up, examine it from all angles and return it to the counter. I didn't have fifteen cents to spend. Incredibly, this caused me no real unhappiness. In those days we simply accepted things as they were.

When we entertained, it was with conversation, games and bowls of bright red apples.

The one thing that did make my husband feel poor was

the dress I wore during my pregnancies. It had belonged to an older, larger sister. It was a depressing mustard-yellow print, large enough for me to "grow into." In the daytime I wore a wraparound Mother Hubbard, but in the evenings it was always the same mustard-colored print.

The night we first met, my husband had said I reminded him of Norma Shearer, a great movie idol of the time. I, too, had dark hair that fell over one side of my face in the fashion of the day. But there, I am certain, any resemblance ended.

One evening my husband told me of a dress he'd seen in a shop window. "I wish I could buy it for you," he said. "It looks like you; it looks like Norma Shearer."

"Where would I wear it?" I asked. "Be sensible."

But every day thereafter, when I walked the children, I stole a look at The Dress. It was made of *mousseline de soie,* in a design of pastel diamonds, the colors delicate yet deep and true. The dress hugged the mannequin from waist to knee, flaring out around her silver-slippered feet. Its black velvet belt was caught up under her bosom, with a flower whose petals were made of the same material as the dress. It was not only my kind of dress, but any woman's dream of the perfect dress—beautiful and timeless. The price was twenty dollars.

I told my husband to stop brooding about a luxury we couldn't afford. If I had twenty dollars, I'd buy new shoes for everybody, which is what we needed most.

One day, as I was looking for chalk, I found twenty dollars! The previous Christmas my husband's company had declared an unexpected bonus—a week's salary, twenty-seven whole dollars extra. Unaccustomed to such a bonanza, we had squandered seven dollars on shrimp, artichokes, anchovies and wine. The remaining twenty dollars we tucked into a box of chalk in the dresser drawer for safekeeping. Then we forgot it completely.

How could we possibly have forgotten so vast a sum? We had been operating on a strict budget so long that the extra money had been, for the moment, merely a beautiful piece of green paper, not to be translated immediately into shoes, groceries or entertainment.

When my husband came home, we laughed and laughed, fingering the crisp bill between us. And then we put it back.

It rained the next day, so I didn't go for my usual walk. That night my husband came in with a large box under his arm. We looked at each other wordlessly. He put the box in the bedroom. We had a quiet supper, put the children to bed and then my husband said, almost unbearable excitement in his voice: "Put it on, honey. Put the dress on."

I went into the bedroom, slipped the dress over my head and looked into the mirror. It was my dress. It was, indeed, perfect. And so was I. I was Norma Shearer.

The dress became the symbol of purest joy in our house, illuminating our lives as nothing would ever do again. Each Saturday night I put it on and had a special date with my husband. We danced to the silent music in our hearts and talked for hours, as we used to before we were married.

Hope stirred again within us. Bold new plans. Of course, the money in the chalk box was never mentioned; it had, after all, been an illusion. There wasn't enough money in the world to pay for what we had anyway.

Now the dress lies in the bottom drawer of the cedar chest. It has been there a long time, and although the flower has curled a little around the edges, the colors are as bright as ever. I have only to think of that dress to feel again the warmth and delight of that long-ago time. Sometimes as I lie wakeful in the night, I remember my husband turning to me and saying: "Why aren't you asleep? What are you thinking about?"

"The dress," I would tell him.

And again, I can feel its rustle. I remember dancing without music. I close my eyes and I am Norma Shearer again, just for tonight.

Marion Benasutti

Our Honeymoon Flight

We love because it's the only true adventure.

Nikki Giovanni

Dennis and I almost missed our honeymoon flight and were unable to get seats together. When we were airborne, I wrote my new spouse a flirtatious note: "To the man sitting in 16C. I find you very attractive. Would you care to join me for an unforgettable evening? The lady in 4C." A flight attendant delivered it.

A few minutes later she returned with a cocktail. The man in 16C was flattered, she told me, but said he must decline my offer since he was on his honeymoon. I was still laughing when we landed. "Thank you for the drink," I said to my groom.

"But I didn't send you one," he replied.

He had been sitting in 14C.

Cindy J. Braun

The Surprise

An archaeologist is the best husband a woman can have; the older she gets the more interested he is in her.

Agatha Christie

I separated the curtain of my hotel room window slightly and peeked outside. Both the door and the window of my ground-floor room faced the hotel's busy walkway. Not only could I see when someone was coming, but a passerby could see in, too. And he or she would certainly get an eyeful. I was dressed (if you could call it dressed) in a black lace bustier, black thigh-high nylons with elastic lace trim and a black garter belt. And, just as the article titled "How to Spice Up Your Marriage" suggested, I completed the scant outfit with what countless women's magazine surveys guarantee men can't resist—black high-heeled pumps. This attire was part of a planned seduction of my husband. The starring role in a live peep show I was not. I had already been embarrassed enough for one day. Checking into the hotel by myself, with virtually no luggage, in the middle of the afternoon raised quite a few curious and suspicious eyebrows. I didn't plan on attracting any more unneeded attention—not even for the sake of "spicing up" my marriage.

When I didn't see my husband approaching, I let the curtain fall back into place. I walked over to the suite's full-length mirror. As I studied the reflection, I couldn't help but think that the article that had suggested this romantic rendezvous had definitely lacked some vital information. For one thing, it neglected to mention how the lacey elastic band in the nylons squeeze your upper thighs so tightly that unless you have a figure like a Victoria's Secret model—which I most certainly do not— an extra roll of fat will bulge out above the stocking. Why didn't the marriage expert/author who wrote of sexy surprises and provocative garments include a warning? "Beware: If you are over the age of twenty-five, or if you have ever been pregnant, this outfit may be hazardous to your thighs." Why weren't the manufacturers of these unflattering stockings required to print a disclaimer on their packaging that read: "Thighs in these nylons may appear larger than they are."

I turned around to try to see how my backside looked in the new panties. The oh-so-skinny, oh-so-young lingerie saleslady insisted they would look fabulous with the other lacey garments I had chosen. She obviously underestimated the amount of cellulite I had hidden in my jeans. I decided right then I had to do one of two things: I had to change out of this ridiculous get-up or I had to start drinking. Considering all the time and effort I spent picking this lacey ensemble—not to mention the money—I opened a bottle of champagne.

I wasn't actually nervous about my husband's reaction to my body. After all, he'd seen me in a teddy or two, watched my belly expand with each of our three children, and been a firsthand witness to the changes in my body over the past sixteen years. I had just never presented myself to him in such an erotic manner. I looked like a stripper. What if he didn't appreciate seeing me looking so—sexual? And what if he didn't like the idea of spending all his money on a night of lovemaking—when we could have done almost the same thing at home, for free?

I refilled my glass with more champagne. I needed to relax. I told myself that I was just nervous because he was late. Of course he would love this surprise. Over our sixteen years of marriage, Ron had always been receptive to my somewhat unpredictable and romantic nature, even the time we treated ourselves to a second honeymoon for our tenth anniversary. We were waiting by the luggage belt when I said, "Ron, I have a great idea."

"Oh, God," he jokingly moaned. "What am I in for?"

"Well, wouldn't it be fun to pretend we're on our honeymoon?"

"Why?"

"Because people treat you differently. They give you that extra smile that says, 'Ahh, aren't those two kids in love just the cutest?' And then, before you know it, we feel like newlyweds." Before he could answer, I gave him my most persuasive smile and pleaded, "Please, it'll be so romantic."

"Okay, whatever you want," he said.

He never regretted playing my newlywed charade; we pretended to be honeymooners on that trip and every trip since then.

I'm not sure if it was the reminiscing or the champagne, but suddenly I was infused with excitement. I was about to pour myself another glassful when I heard a knock on the door. He wasn't supposed to knock. Why would he knock? I had done just as the article had directed. I waited until I knew he was out of the office and left the room key inside a small wrapped jewelry box. I attached a note, which I lightly sprayed with his favorite perfume, that read:

> *Dear Ron,*
>   *Meet me at Danford's Inn at 7:30, room 102. I can promise you this—you won't be sorry!*
> *Love,*
> *You-Know-Who*

A ridiculous thought occurred to me as I heard another more forceful knock at the door: *What if he didn't know who You-Know-Who was? Or worse, what if he thought he knew, but didn't really know, and he was now angry at You-Know-Who for plotting this outrageous scheme?* I had to take a deep breath. Panic and nerves, and most probably alcohol, were making You-Know-Who you-know-what—crazy.

"Are you there?" I heard him call. "Kath? Are you there?"

"Yes," I said as I released a sigh. "Just a second." He didn't sound angry in the least. And, luckily for both of us, he knew it was me who left him the note.

I slid the lock open. Being careful to stand behind the door so I was hidden from view of the walkway, I opened it.

"Oh Ron!" I exclaimed. "They're beautiful!"

"Anything for my beautiful wife," he said as he handed me a dozen roses.

"Thank you," I said almost shyly. I couldn't believe it, but I was actually blushing.

After closing and locking the door, he turned and took a good look at me. His eyes visibly widened as he absorbed the surprise of my risqué attire. I'm not sure whether his slow smile was a result of pleasure or shock, but he said, "Thank you. This is a nice surprise."

I smiled in return and whispered, "Anything for you."

It was as though I did this all the time.

Katherine Gallagher

Calling Long Distance

If we all discovered that we only had five minutes left to say all that we wanted to say, every telephone booth would be occupied by people calling other people to tell them that they loved them.

Christopher Morley

I read about a man who called his wife from an airport pay phone. When he had used up all his coins, the operator interrupted to say he had one minute left. The man hurriedly tried to finish his conversation with his wife, but before they could tell each other good-bye, the line went dead. With a sigh, the man hung up the phone and started to leave the little telephone cubicle. Just then the phone rang. Thinking it was the operator wanting more money, the man almost didn't answer. But something told him to pick up the phone. Sure enough, it was the operator. But she didn't want more money. Instead she had a message for him.

"After you hung up, your wife said she loved you," the operator said. "I thought you'd want to know."

Barbara Johnson

Keeping the Passion of Love Alive

Young love is a flame; very pretty, often very hot and fierce, but still only light and flickering. The love of the older and disciplined heart is as coals, deep burning, unquenchable.

Henry Ward Beecher, American clergyman

Imagine that you've decided to build a fire, perhaps while you're camping, or at home in your fireplace. You carefully choose the logs, the kindling, and after lighting a match to start the fire, you watch over it until you're sure the fire is burning strongly and steadily. Then you sit back and enjoy the comforting warmth, the delightful play of the flames, the magical light. You don't need to be as vigilant about keeping the fire blazing, since it has enough fuel for now. But at some point, when you notice it's getting a little colder, or the light is growing dim, you realize that the fire needs your attention again. And so you rouse yourself from whatever you've been doing and add more wood, or adjust the position of the logs so that, once more, the flames can rise high.

Even if you've neglected the fire for a while, even if it

appears to have died out, you see that the embers still radiate a deep, orange glow that can only be created by hours of extreme heat. The embers are deceptive, and they contain great power within their quiet light. Although by themselves they produce no flames, they can ignite a newly added piece of wood in seconds, suddenly rekindling the full force of the fire, transforming the dormant coals into a roaring blaze.

We can learn a lot about the passion between two lovers by thinking about what we intuitively know about building and maintaining a fire. When you first meet someone and fall in love, you carefully court and seduce him or her, adding the right amount of intimacy, the perfect amount of commitment until the fire of passion flares up between your hearts and your bodies. For awhile, this blaze burns brightly on its own and you grow accustomed to the joy it brings into your life. *How lucky we are,* you tell yourself, *to have such a passionate relationship!*

But one day, you realize there is less light, less heat between you and your mate, and that, in fact, it's been that way for some time. You don't feel the same intense degree of physical attraction, the same desire to unite, the same stimulation you once felt with each other. *The passion is gone,* you may conclude. *I guess I've fallen out of love. This relationship is over.*

How many people ask themselves, at this critical point in a love affair, if the fire of passion has died down simply because no one has been tending it, because no one has added the fuel necessary to keep it burning? How many people walk away from the smoking embers of their marriage, certain that the fire has died out, without noticing that the coals of love still contain enough heat to reignite into flames, if only they are given a chance?

Respect the fire of passion, the fire of love. Understand that to stay alive, it needs to be honored, to be cared for, to be tended as diligently as you would tend a fire you had built in the wilderness to help keep you warm and safe from harm. Feed the fire of your love with kindness, communication, appreciation and gratitude, and it will always blaze strong and brightly for you.

Barbara De Angelis, Ph.D.

Dating Again

When our children had all left home, I read an article that was meant to help couples deal with the empty nest. I explained some of the ideas to my husband. He nodded in agreement to all the things I said.

Then I told him the article suggested we spice up our marriage by going out on dates.

He answered, "With each other?"

Mary J. Davis

Ready to Be Entertained

It had been a crazy week at work for both of us. On our way home one Friday night, we knew it was time to break out the Blockbuster card, pick up a movie and order in some pizza.

On our way to the video store, my wife, Nikki, asked me what kind of movie I was in the mood to watch. After the long week before, I knew right away I wanted a comedy. So I told her, "I'm in the mood to be entertained. How about a comedy tonight?" She readily agreed.

Inside the store we started our search for the perfect movie that would leave us gasping for air from laughing so hard. Somehow we got separated as our eyes were focused not on each other, but on the myriad of choices on the shelves.

A few minutes later, Nikki came over and grabbed my arm as if she were terrified. "What's wrong?" I asked her. "Are you all right?"

In a trembling voice, she said that, no, she was not all right. It seemed that when we became separated, she ended up standing next to someone else ... who was wearing the same color slacks and shoes that I had on. Without looking up to make sure it was me, she had casually leaned over and, in a seductive voice, asked the stranger beside her, "So, you're in the mood to be entertained, huh?"

The shocked stranger had turned to Nikki with a perplexed look on his face, wondering if this woman he had never met was actually propositioning him in the middle of Blockbuster. Realizing her mistake, Nikki had stammered out an embarrassed apology and fled in my direction.

I don't remember the movie we got that night, but I know it wasn't as funny as what happened while selecting it. I still tease Nikki about trying to pick up strangers in the video store. But I haven't taken her up on her suggestion to write my name on the front of my shoes so that she can make sure she's talking to me when we are there.

Dennis Rach

CLOSE TO HOME

"I want an action-adventure film, she wants a romantic comedy. I just don't see how we can resolve this!"

The Camping Trip

It's not where you go or what you do, it's who you take along with you.

Anonymous

It was raining sideways and thundering so loud that the house shook. Anne sat in the middle of the hardwood floor surrounded by sleeping bags, camping stove, groceries and a tent. She wondered if the tent would be able to float in the ocean-sized puddles that were forming on the leaf-covered ground.

In a few minutes Sam was supposed to arrive for their anniversary camping trip. They had hardly seen each other the last few weeks. They were both bogged down with graduate thesis and research projects. In addition to their schoolwork, Anne taught two classes a week and Sam worked full-time for his mentor. They knew the only way they could spend some time together was to go out of town, away from phones, computers and professors asking for last-minute favors. This trip was going to be their reunion as well as their one-year anniversary celebration.

"Just my luck," Anne said out loud. "We finally have plans and it has to rain on our camping trip. We're cursed!"

The front door opened and there was Sam, clad in soggy hiking boots and clothes so wet they looked like they were melting.

"Who's cursed?" he asked, plopping down on the splayed sleeping bags. "Certainly not us. Two wildly in-love newlyweds about to go on the world's most fabulous camping trip?"

Anne shook her head. "You don't really want to go camping in this weather?"

"You bet I do!"

Before Anne could answer, Sam stood up and walked around the room. First, he unplugged the phone, then the computer. He pulled down the shades and covered the television with the orange afghan they kept on the couch. Then he began setting up the tent in the middle of the living room floor. He brought the George Foreman grill in from the kitchen and set it up next to the tent and lit a fire in the rarely used fireplace.

"Now," he said smiling, "have you ever seen a more beautiful campsite?" He opened his arms wide and Anne rose and stood in his embrace, laughing as she surveyed their campsite.

"Never."

That night after they roasted hot dogs on the George Foreman grill and toasted marshmallows in the fireplace, they were tucked inside their sleeping bags. Sam circled his arms around Anne's waist.

"Sam," Anne said, "when we planned this night, I imagined that by now we would be watching the sunset behind House Mountain and sipping on some champagne, but, somehow, this makes it all the more special. We don't need a romantic sunset, or a fancy bottle of champagne or beautiful scenery—we just need each other, forever. Together we can make any situation work out right."

Anne and Sam just celebrated their ten-year wedding anniversary. To celebrate they did the usual; they went on a romantic camping trip—right in their own living room.

Meghan Mazour

CLOSE TO HOME

"Do you want to be the one to go outside
when it's minus-15 to get some firewood?
All right then, quit complaining!"

Hello, Young Lovers

The miracle is this—the more we share, the more we have.

Leonard Nimoy

He appeared almost Lilliputian, dwarfed by the big hickory rocking chair he occupied on the porch of the old Riverside Hotel in Gatlinburg, Tennessee. But we could hardly help noticing him on that warm mid-April day: While others lounged about in casual attire, he wore a dark-blue pinstripe suit, a Harvard-crimson necktie and a straw boater. The gold watch chain draped across his tightly buttoned vest glinted in the sunlight as he rocked ever so deliberately.

He watched bemusedly as I stepped from the Jaguar XK-150, my pride and joy, and walked to the opposite side to open the door for Diane, my bride. His eyes followed as we trailed self-consciously behind the luggage-laden bellboy, and he smiled a knowing smile when we neared his rocker.

"Hello, young lovers," he said. Our honeymooner status was unmistakable.

The man we came to know as Mr. B was in the dining room, sitting alone with a cup of tea, when we entered late the next morning. His eyes came to life when he saw us. He rose with some effort and beckoned us toward him.

"You'd make an old man very happy if you joined me," he said with an octogenarian's formality. I wonder even now why we did. Perhaps it was the angelic expression his face assumed. More likely, it was our honeymooner self-consciousness—we'd been found out by an elder and felt compelled to comply with his wishes.

He was a Canadian, an attorney, he said, still practicing in Winnipeg. But he'd been spending Aprils in Gatlinburg for almost fifty years. He and his wife would come with their son and daughter and explore the mountains on horseback, getting to know every scenic vantage point of Mount Le Conte, every turn in the tumbling Little Pigeon River.

After the son had died and the daughter was grown, Mr. B and his wife had kept up their visits. And he still made the annual trek even though his wife had died three years earlier. The mountains and the valley were touchstones for him, sites of pleasant memories that were revived with each visit.

"I've had a love of my own," he said, his eyes misting. He asked detailed questions about our wedding and told us in detail of his own, some sixty years earlier. During brief periods when a conversational lapse threatened, he softly hummed "Hello, Young Lovers," the song from *The King and I*.

That night he sat alone during dinner, careful, he later told us, not to "get in love's way." But he glanced often in our direction, and we knew he was not alone; he was deep in reverie, dining with his own true love. Returning to our room following an after-dinner walk, we found a ribbon-bedecked bottle of champagne. An accompanying card read: "See Mr. B in the A.M. for instructions as to its use."

He was waiting for us in his rocking chair after breakfast, the look of a leprechaun on his face. He handed me a piece of paper on which he had sketched the river, a place where we could leave our car, a footpath and points at which large boulders made it possible to cross the cold mountain stream on foot. His shaky-handed path led eventually to a river pool indicated with an X.

"The champagne is to be chilled in the pool," he said. "You are to spread your picnic lunch on the grassy knoll to the right of it. It's very secluded. A very romantic spot." We could only gape at him, certain he was spoofing.

"Your picnic basket will be delivered to you here on the veranda at precisely noon." He was on his feet then, moving away. He turned and added: "It was our favorite spot, our secret place."

We never saw Mr. B again during our honeymoon. We wondered whether he'd fallen ill. But inquiries to the hotel staff were answered with, "Oh, he's around," or "He often likes to be alone."

Our firstborn was almost three when we next visited Gatlinburg, and Diane was six months pregnant with our second son. We approached the aging hotel not in the Jaguar, but in a practical sedan. Our arrival went unnoticed.

But when we walked into the hotel lobby the next morning, our son toddling ahead, the old man was sitting in an overstuffed lounge chair. Seeing the child, he stretched out his arms, and our son, as if drawn by a magnet, ran into them.

"Mr. B!" we exclaimed in unison.

He smiled that beatific smile.

"Hello, young lovers," he said.

Philip Harsham

Who's Lucky?

It was Lucky's sixtieth birthday. Lucky's husband of forty-one years threw a big celebration in her honor. Their whole family was there.

Just before they brought out the cake and sang "Happy Birthday," one of their granddaughters asked her grandpa why everyone always called Grandma "Lucky."

"Oh, it's a nickname I gave Grandma right after we got married."

"Well, do you call her Lucky because she really is lucky?" the inquisitive child asked.

"Oh, I think Grandma definitely has a lucky streak, but that's not why I called her that."

"Do you call her Lucky because she brings you good luck?"

"I think Grandma has always brought me good luck, but that's not why I called her that."

"Okay, I give up," the young girl said, "What's the reason?"

Her grandfather spoke as if he were thinking out loud. "I have always called Grandma 'Lucky' to remind myself how lucky I am to be married to her."

Bits & Pieces

Head to Toe

Now that I'm four kids past twenty-five, my body shows some signs of wear and tear. So when we vacationed at a Washington coastal resort I was—I'll admit it—*jealous* of the flat-stomached, stretch-mark-free bachelorettes frolicking in the pool.

When the kids pulled out their swimsuits, I looked pleadingly at my husband, Andy. "Please take them in," I said. "I just can't go out in a swimsuit in front of all those twenty-somethings." He gave me a puzzled look, but took the children swimming while I watched the baby nearby.

That night Andy came in with a mysterious bag, from which he withdrew a bottle of fuchsia nail polish!

"I'm going to paint your toenails," he announced.

"You're going to what?"

"Paint your toenails," he said, taking off my socks.

This is silly, I thought. *I don't even paint my toenails.*

But my husband was insistent.

"Why are you doing this?" I asked.

"Because," he answered, brushing on the first coat, "I want you to know you're beautiful from head to toe."

I looked at the guy who's been with me through fifteen years of bills and babies. He had not only protected me from embarrassment, but adorned me. I thought of those twenty-somethings with the flat stomachs and I didn't feel jealous anymore. Instead I felt grateful.

Katherine G. Bond

4

ROMANCE AND MARRIAGE

For one human being to love another; that is perhaps the most difficult of all our tasks, the ultimate, the last test and proof, the work for which all other work is but preparation.

Rainer Maria Rilke

Hubby's Special Gift

True love comes quietly, without banners or flashing lights. If you hear bells, get your ears checked.

Erich Segal

I stood just beyond the doorway. And I watched. And I listened. And I smiled. He didn't know I was there. And he spackled. And he sang. And he cursed the wrong size screws. And he sang. And he measured. And he knocked over a box of nails. And he cursed. And I giggled. Quietly. Lovingly.

Hubby was building a room. A room just for me. A "proper" room for me to write in. And I swear, although I could be wrong, he said to himself, *She's gonna love this room!* And I swear, although I could be wrong, I whispered to myself, *Yes, she's gonna love this room—because you built it, just for me.* And then I smiled, I guess too loudly. He looked up and saw me.

Puzzled, he pushed back his baseball cap and asked, "What are you looking at?" I giggled, "You." He smiled, "Do you like it—do you like your new room?" I smiled, "I love it—I love my new room." And he smiled. Loudly.

And then he proclaimed, "No more of you sitting on a hard stool with no back, writing on a stupid workbench in a dingy workshop with no windows, poor light . . ."

"And," I interrupted, "no more with you sitting in your stupid Barcalounger bugging me while I write." I winked. He winked back. And then with all seriousness he said, "Now you have a proper room with proper accoutrements and proper lighting and I'm even gonna install a proper pencil sharpener so you can keep your pencils properly sharpened so that you can write properly." I didn't have the heart to tell him that I write with a pen. He built this room just for me—pencil sharpener and all. I loved that.

Soon I was in my proper new room ready to write. Properly, of course. I had my proper chair, proper desk, proper lighting and even my proper pencil sharpener. I was set. But something wasn't "proper." I couldn't write. I didn't get it. The room was perfect and proper—a dream. And then I got it. I grabbed my pad of paper and pen and went into the dingy workshop with poor lighting and sat on the hard stool with no back. Puzzled, Hubby looked up at me from his Barcalounger. "What's wrong?"

"I couldn't write," I said. Seriously, he asked, "Is there something wrong with your new room?"

"Seriously," I replied, "Yes . . . you're not in it." He smiled. Loudly. And then I wrote. Properly.

Lisa Bade Goodwin

"No, I'm not happy you bought me flowers for absolutely no reason. It's our anniversary."

Road to Romantic Ruin
Is Paved with Practical Gifts

No man should marry until he has studied anatomy and dissected at least one woman.

Honoré de Balzac, French novelist

The other day my son and I were talking, and the subject of women came up, and I realized that it was time he and I had a Serious Talk. It's a talk every father should have with his son; and yet, far too often, we fathers avoid the subject, because it's so awkward.

The subject I am referring to is: buying gifts for women.

This is an area where many men do not have a clue. Exhibit A was my father, who was a very thoughtful man, but who once gave my mother, on their anniversary, the following token of his love, his commitment, and—yes—his passion for her: an electric blanket. He honestly could not understand why, when she opened the box, she gave him that look (you veteran men know the look I mean). After all, this was the deluxe model electric blanket! With an automatic thermostat! What more could any woman WANT?

Another example: I once worked with a guy named George who, for Christmas, gave his wife, for her big gift—and I am not making this gift up—a chain saw. (As he later explained: "Hey, we NEEDED a chain saw.") Fortunately, the saw was not operational when his wife unwrapped it.

The mistake that George and my dad made, and that many guys make, was thinking that when you choose a gift for a woman, it should do something useful. Wrong! The first rule of buying gifts for women is: THE GIFT SHOULD NOT DO ANYTHING, OR, IF IT DOES, IT SHOULD DO IT BADLY.

For example, let's consider two possible gifts, both of which, theoretically, perform the same function:

GIFT ONE: A state-of-the-art gasoline-powered lantern, with electronic ignition and dual mantles capable of generating twelve hundred lumens of light for ten hours on a single tank of fuel.

GIFT TWO: A scented beeswax candle, containing visible particles of bee poop and providing roughly the same illumination as a lukewarm corn dog.

Now to a guy, Gift One is clearly superior, because you could use it to see in the dark. Whereas to a woman, Gift Two is MUCH better, because women love to sit around in the gloom with reeking, sputtering candles, and don't ask ME why. I also don't know why a woman would be ticked off if you gave her a fifty-six-piece socket-wrench set with a seventy-two-tooth reversible ratchet, but thrilled if you give her a tiny, very expensive vial of liquid with a name like "L'essence de Nooquie Eau de Parfum de Cologne de Toilette de Bidet," which, to the naked male nostril, does not smell any better than a stick of Juicy Fruit. All I'm saying is that this is the kind of thing women want. (That's why the ultimate gift is jewelry; it's totally useless.)

The second rule of buying gifts for women is: YOU ARE NEVER FINISHED. This is the scary part, the part that my son and his friends are just discovering. If you have a girlfriend, she will give you, at MINIMUM, a birthday gift, an anniversary gift, a Christmas/Chanukah/Kwanzaa gift, and a Valentine's Day gift, and every one of these gifts will be nicely wrapped AND accompanied by a thoughtful card. When she gives you this gift, YOU HAVE TO GIVE HER ONE BACK. You can't just open your wallet and say, "Here's, let's see . . . seventeen dollars!"

And, as I told my son, it only gets worse. Looming ahead are bridal showers, weddings, baby showers, Mother's Day and other Mandatory Gift Occasions that would not even EXIST if men, as is alleged, really ran the world. Women observe ALL of these occasions, and MORE. My wife will buy gifts for NO REASON. She'll go into one of those gift stores at the mall that men never enter, and she'll find something, maybe a tiny cute box that could not hold anything larger than a molecule, and is therefore useless, and she'll buy it, PLUS a thoughtful card, and SHE DOESN'T EVEN KNOW WHO THE RECIPIENT IS YET. Millions of other women are out doing the same thing, getting farther and farther ahead, while we guys are home watching instant replays. We have no chance of winning this war.

That's what I told my son. It wasn't pleasant, but it was time he knew the truth. Some day, when he is older and stronger, we'll tackle an even more difficult issue, namely, what to do when a woman asks: "Do these pants make me look fat?" (Answer: Flee the country.)

Dave Barry

"Well, for goodness sake, Helene—you were right!"

©Mort Gerberg, 2002.

Saturday Nights

Perfect love is rare indeed—for to be a lover will require that you continually have the subtlety of the very wise, the flexibility of the child, the sensitivity of the artist, the understanding of the philosopher, the acceptance of the saint, the tolerance of the scholar and the fortitude of the certain.

Leo Buscaglia

I think I need a Saturday night.

Oh, sure, I get my share of Saturday nights. There's one at the end of every week—that one night where I can stay up to watch TV because (a) I haven't worked all day, so I'm not totally exhausted, and (b) I don't have to go to work the next morning, so I can sleep in if I decide to catch the eighty-seventh showing of *An Affair to Remember* on PBS's late movie.

But, of course, there's nothing on TV, unless you count the Nick-at-Night *Beverly Hillbillies* marathon. And—even though I didn't have to go to the office that morning—I still had to buy the groceries, clean the house, plan meals for the week and carpool various children to soccer games, birthday parties and skating rinks. It's Saturday night, but I'm still asleep before midnight.

Besides, that's not the kind of Saturday night I'm talking about anyway. I'm pretty comfortable with these "Saturday night as the end of another fun-filled, action-packed week" gigs. What I need is a Saturday night the way it used to be, when each weekend held its own promise, its own potential, even its own magic. When the air was heavy with possibilities, and the night—dancing with nervous laughter and furtive gazes—was full of maybes.

Not the least of which, of course, is this—"Maybe tonight is a beginning."

You remember what beginnings look like, don't you? They're usually lit by soft flicks of candlelight and set to the tune of a deliberate piano. You glance across the table and look into your companion's eyes, holding his gaze for as long as possible before dropping your eyes. Your conversation is whispered and intense, filled with enough references to world events to prove that you're informed and intelligent, and enough wry comments about pop culture to establish that you're aware but not overly impressed. And then comes that moment when you make contact—when fingers accidentally brush while passing the bread basket, or your high heel collides with his loafer under the table as you shift ever so subtly in your seat—and suddenly you feel that spark, that heat, and your head is full of nothing more than that single unrelenting thought—*maybe this one could be THE ONE.*

Of course, most of those Saturday night companions didn't turn out to be THE ONE, but that's not what mattered anyway. What mattered was that feeling—the excitement, the potential, the nervous butterflies pirouetting in my stomach. It seems I've traded that feeling in—and I made a good deal, giving up that potential and excitement for a trusted companion, a faithful lover, something real and reliable and consistent. Still, every once in a while, I miss the possibilities and questions, the hopefulness and uncertainty. Every once in a while, I miss feeling something new, instead of "same old, same old."

Every once in a while, I miss Saturday night.

And I miss more than just the actual date part, the shadowed restaurants and expensive meals and adult conversation part (although that in itself is something to long for as you watch your children inhale Happy Meals under the unforgiving glare of neon). I miss the preparation, the anticipation, the fuss and the fawning that led up to that moment when the doorbell rang and your palms started sweating just knowing he stood on the other side.

Hours before that moment arrived, I would begin my preparation. First would come the steamy shower, the thorough soaping down, the frothing shampoo and the extra-extra-rich conditioning. I wanted to be more than squeaky clean—I wanted to eliminate all the humdrum scents of the week so I could liberally apply my "scent of the season" (usually something heady, romantic and memorable—just the way I wanted the night to be).

Slipping into my terry cloth robe, I would plug in all the necessities—the hair dryer, the hot rollers, the electric brush. I'd curl each strand of hair around a roller as I practiced looking interested and mildly flirtatious, raising an eyebrow and tilting my chin at my reflection in the mirror. "Oh really? That's fascinating," I'd comment as I plucked my eyebrows. "Tell me all about it," I'd say as I rubbed moisturizer into my elbows and hooked my laciest bra around my back.

I'd find just the right outfit—not too fancy (I didn't want him to think I thought this was a "major occasion") but not too casual (because nothing romantic ever started while wearing gray sweatpants). Something attractive, alluring and that would float around me as I swirled in his arms on the dance floor—just in case we ended up cheek to cheek.

I'd unroll my hair and flip my head to give my curls the right bounce, the proper fullness. Then I'd sprinkle baby powder in my shoes, spray my hair with cologne and apply a sweep of blush across my cheeks. I checked the mirror one last time as the doorbell rang. The butterfly wings started flapping, but I was ready.

"Ready for bed?"

A voice brings me into the present. Okay, so the voice is familiar, the butterflies are stilled. It's been a long day, a Saturday, the kind we live now. The kind that is full of kids and carpools, Power Ranger videos and long, competitive games of "Aggravation." The kind that finds me in sneakers (easier to chase a five-year-old!) and T-shirts (liberally stained with grape jelly).

The kind I wouldn't trade for all the Saturday nights in the world.

Still, I was feeling a bit nostalgic, a bit wistful and more than a little bit old. I woke early the next day (why not? I was asleep by eleven) and touched Scott's shoulder.

"I want a Saturday night," I said, so close to his ear. "I want to be young and in love, to be open to new things, to be swept off my feet. I want a night that lasts into the early hours and leaves me breathless with the possibilities."

He turned and smoothed my hair, disheveled from a hard sleep. "Um, will you settle for a Sunday morning?" he whispered. I held his glance a bit longer than I should have, and we began our dance in sweatpants as the sun came up on another week.

Mary Lebeau

A Fool in Love

When you live with a man for thirteen years, you become a well-rehearsed advocate of the unwed state. While people rarely question the decision to marry, the decision not to marry must be continually defended. As dependably as your dental hygienist sends the checkup reminder, you are asked to explain your rationale. By your mother, your friends, the UPS guy, your mother.

No one is pestering me of late. They're sending flowery cards that say, "On Your Engagement."

I'm not marrying the man I lived with for thirteen years. That ended. (See? Good thing we didn't marry.) What began a year later has turned me, like a shipyard winch, 180 degrees around.

July 3 was our first date. By August he was on my speed dial. Mid-October, the *M* word made its debut. Here was a man who loved things about me I never knew existed (the way I whistle my *s*'s, for God's sake). He wooed me with construction-paper hearts ("I found this on my sleeve. I'm sure it belongs to you") and picnics on the living room floor. He brought me to his cardiology appointment and showed me his heart on the sonogram. "It's yours," he said, gluey wire things hanging off his chest, the doctor peering over his half-glasses. He left a high school picture on my desk (bad tie, long hair brushed like Lassie's) signed, "Where are you, Mary? When will I meet you? "All this when I didn't need to be wooed. I was in love with everything, the big picture and the everyday details. His children, his neck, the way he folds laundry.

I digress. This is not about love. No one questions love. Be in love, sing it high and low, throw a party, eat cake. But why change tax brackets over it? This is the odd thing: Here I am, altar bound, yet I still see no rational reason to submit love to the confines of a legal document. Marriage grew out of an early business deal: I'll keep the home fires burning and you'll bring things to put on them. My world doesn't work this way. I bring home my own mastodon steaks; that's how I like it.

Equally anachronistic is the notion that marriage is binding. Only a fool (and my mother) would argue it holds a couple together in times of trouble. Divorce is not global circumnavigation. It's simple and commonplace. If someone wants badly enough to leave, he or she will leave.

Yet, yet, yet, yet. If my man presented the preceding arguments to me in an effort to lobby for cohabitation over marriage, I'd be deeply disappointed. Flattened. Emotional road kill. God help me, I want to be this man's wife. I want to go where he goes and know who he knows. I want to wear a gold ring though all my earrings are silver. I want to be half of a whole—united, consumed, glommed, linked as tight as it gets for as long as we live.

In part, I suppose, the change comes of maturity. When I was twenty-five, I wanted the future to be unimaginable. I was on my way, in motion. If you haven't reached your potential, how can you know who's right for you? What if you become rich and important? Will you, could you, still be happy with the guy who runs slide shows at the planetarium? Life changes quickly in your twenties.

You're in a fast car. Marriage is some old coot riding the brakes.

But eventually the clouds clear and you can see the future. It isn't quite what you pictured—who, in their youth, pictures incorporation, perimenopause, condo conversion?—but it's solid and real, and there's a comfort in knowing, more or less, what's coming. And one of the things you realize is that if you could find someone just right, someone you loved like the best pal you ever had and the worst crush you ever had, it would be awfully nice to have that person in the seat beside you along the way.

Now that I'm thirty-eight, marriage no longer feels like a sacrifice. It feels like the winning lottery ticket. Nothing more perfect than this, I am certain, is ever going to appear on the misfolded, coffee-stained road map of my life. I know what Johnny Cash was talking about with that line: I find it very, very easy to be true.

I used to balk at the idea of lifelong fidelity. I wanted the falling part of falling in love. But lifetimes have been wasted chasing that. What did I gain for decade and a half of relative freedom, my dalliances, my so-called open relationship? A few heady affairs, chance encounters far away. The heart leaping off a cliff and flying through the air. And, shortly thereafter, hitting the ground. Heart pulp. Guilt and regret. The knowledge that by refusing to commit myself fully to a relationship I destroyed it.

I had romance all wrong. As a man I'll call Bob said, upon hearing me extol the splendors of off-the-cuff, on-the-road romance, "That's not romance. Romance is turning down the fling with the local smooth chest, going back to your hotel, and calling the person you love." (Bob was, at the time, cheating on his girlfriend with me. But bless him, he was torn.)

Something else I failed to grasp is that all marriages are

group marriages. I am marrying a man; his delightful, beautiful, children; his warm, welcoming parents; his sister; his cousins; their families. A whole clan of hearts and minds that wants me to sign on. What could be more wonderful? My own family was small and cut-off, a lone asteroid out of its orbit. Growing up, I had no grandparents and never got to know my aunts and uncles. I pictured my family tree as one of those bald, spiky pines on a burned-out hillside. No wonder I was such an independent lass. Independence is sweet, but not as sweet as belonging. Marriage is a second chance to belong.

Would I belong if we simply lived together? Past experience says no, not really. In my world, to share a house with someone but not marry sends a message to him, to our families, to everyone who matters to me. It's a message I don't wish to send anymore. It says, I love this man, but I'm not sure he's it.

Of course, no marriage comes with guarantees. But you have to go into it believing, knowing, heart laid bare and eyes amist, that this is it, for better and worse, richer and poorer, liver spots and arthritis. If you do this and believe this, the what-ifs of divorce are moot.

I sometimes wonder if I've given in to the pressures of society, if I'm tired of being the odd one out, of not getting spousal health benefits, of not knowing which box to check under "Marital Status." Yet it wasn't society at large that got to me but my own circle: the unwavering and unignorable fact that, without exception, the people I love most are married, or would like to be. None of them makes decisions by following convention. There must be something to this.

At times I used to think that the people who wanted me to be married simply wanted me to be yoked. Stop traveling the globe, they were saying, stop having adventures. Be bored and predictable like us. I no longer believe this.

I think they wanted to see me married because they wished me well. They wanted me to have a reason to stay home.

Mary Roach

The One-Sweet-Potato Thanksgiving

One can endure sorrow alone, but it takes two to be glad.

Elbert Hubbard

The first call came at the end of October. Our middle son had decided he wouldn't try to come home for Thanksgiving from college—too many papers due and California was too far away. However, he'd already been asked to join a friend's family for dinner, so we shouldn't worry; he wouldn't be lonely.

In early November our oldest son called; his wife's brother, whom she hadn't seen since their August wedding, was going to be in New York for Thanksgiving. So would it be all right if they spent the holiday with him instead of coming to Texas to spend it with us? Of course, we said, knowing how homesick she had been for her French family.

Later that month when our youngest son decided it wasn't worth two days of travel from his Vermont college to spend two days with us for Thanksgiving, we weren't too disappointed. After all, we still expected my parents and sister for the holiday. And then my mother called: "Honey, I'm sorry, but the doctor just told your dad absolutely no travel for the next few months. Could you come to Oklahoma?" After briefly considering the twenty-hour round-trip for a four-day holiday, I reluctantly said we couldn't.

So, in the chilly afternoon light that Thanksgiving Eve, my husband and I loaded up our car and our old dog and left Houston for New Braunfels and our first Thanksgiving alone as a couple—ever. What would that feel like for us? When his parents were alive, Thanksgiving had always been their holiday with us, usually at our condo in New Braunfels. After their deaths, we had continued the ritual of spending Thanksgiving there, but always with some of our family around. Accustomed to the traditional feast and family visiting, would we be desolate?

With none of the usual holiday preparation to do the night before, we went to bed early and cuddled. I slept ten hours. Thanksgiving dawned bright and cold; we spent the morning side by side on a loveseat. A fire blazed, and we took pleasure in self-indulgence; I read months of accumulated magazines while my husband watched the Oilers.

Early in the afternoon, just an hour or so before we intended to eat, I went into the kitchen to start dinner. I remembered other years when I had arisen at dawn to make stuffing, prepare the turkey for roasting, roll out pie dough and set the table, sitting down for the first time in many hours when dinner was ready and then finding myself too tired to really taste the food. So I wasn't really sorry to be making dinner for two instead of eight—or eighteen.

Feeling hungry, my husband wandered into the kitchen and saw a single yam sitting on the counter. With a look of mingled surprise and regret, he asked wistfully,

"Only one sweet potato?" I knew he was recalling other Thanksgivings—hot, steamy kitchens fragrant with cloves and butter and roasting turkey, every horizontal surface covered with delicious dishes. As I put my arms around him for consolation, I too remembered the ritual of Thanksgiving in my childhood.

At my grandparents' Kansas farm there were always enough aunts, uncles and cousins in attendance to set at least two tables, starched embroidered cloths centered with autumn leaves and pinecone-and-paper-bag turkeys. Grandmother Mary would serve an enormous turkey oozing juice from its golden, cracking skin; pans of giblet dressing baked crispy on the top, moist and steamy inside; candied sweet potatoes topped with melting marshmallows; pork roast and a platter of chicken for those who didn't like turkey; yeast rolls; cinnamon-flecked applesauce; pickled peaches studded with cloves; creamed corn; green beans cooked with bacon; white potatoes whipped into peaks gilded with butter; and a cut-crystal bowl of ambrosia. Later there would be pie— mince and pumpkin, of course, but also cherry and peach—a coconut-topped layer cake, plates of black-walnut cookies and a box of my grandfather's favorite chocolate-covered cherries. And lots of storytelling and reminiscing as we sat pushed back from the table, somnolent and stuffed.

Now I leaned back and looked at my husband still in my embrace and said, "It's a Texas-sized potato—and besides, neither one of us really likes sweet potatoes that much." He agreed, we kissed, and then returned to the fire for a glass of champagne and paté with crackers. I set the table with a folk-art pilgrim couple, a small bouquet of flowers and some turkey paper napkins. We sat down, blessed our food and our absent families, and talked about how grateful we were for what we had accomplished as parents. We congratulated ourselves that this new ritual of spending a holiday alone was proof that we had given our children permission to lead their own independent lives.

We ate the simple meal—a small honey-glazed turkey breast, wild rice, broccoli, green beans and that solitary baked sweet potato—and shared a nice bottle of chardonnay. Dessert was a pumpkin cheesecake from our favorite bakery. Cleaning up the kitchen took ten minutes, and then we both had a long nap. No, I didn't miss the hours the women spent restoring order in Grandmother's kitchen after the holiday meal.

We spent the rest of the weekend doing as we pleased. We talked about retirement and the children and our jobs. We shopped, we saw a movie, my husband played golf, I read and wrote. One sunny afternoon we walked through Landa Park, numbing our fingers in Comal Springs. At the end of three days we returned to Houston, refreshed, restored and mellowed by intimacy unencumbered with the usual holiday chores and responsibilities.

We've had two more one-sweet-potato Thanksgivings since that first one; the menu changes from year to year, but one sweet potato remains a staple, the symbol for a holiday alone as a couple. Perhaps one day we will again have a houseful of people for Thanksgiving, and I will happily polish silver, iron linens, plan menus and cook for days. Or perhaps not. Spending holidays as a family of two, we've learned not to mourn what cannot be but instead to relish what we have—solitude and time together.

SuzAnne C. Cole

A Penny More
Precious Than a Diamond

Elizabeth Taylor, the actress, received an equally famed diamond from her then husband, famous actor Richard Burton. It was covered in all the media: the carat ring was so huge, and so rare and so priceless.

I too received something quite priceless. Let me explain. You who are sentimental, stay with me. Back in the early 1960s, my husband of ten years or so and I took a long, leisurely, romantic walk in the countryside following some railroad tracks. It was a beautiful, early fall day, the sunshine warm on our backs, a chance to talk without children interrupting, or even to be quiet as we held hands walking along. We would stop and laugh occasionally, thoroughly enjoying each other's company and the outdoors. We had walked quite a while when the wail of a locomotive could be heard in the far distance. My handsome husband instantly dropped my hand and ran quickly some distance up a slope to the railroad tracks. I couldn't see what the mad dash was about, and when he returned he wouldn't say.

When we arrived home several hours later, he asked me for my charm bracelet, with no explanation as to why he wanted it. I obliged and started to prepare for supper while he went to the garage. A few minutes later he handed the charm bracelet back to me, and I saw what it was all about. Since the bracelet was gold in color, and not silver, he had taken a penny from his change pocket, flattened that Lincoln penny on the track, all the print forever erased, drilled a tiny hole, and attached my newest, most valued charm, saying, "This is so you'll always remember our walks together."

My wonderful husband died some years ago, but all I have to do is hold my penny in my arthritic hands and I have him and that day from the sixties all over again. It's as valuable to me as Elizabeth's "rock" was to her, only more so.

Mrs. B. Bartlett

Happy Valentine's Day, Dear.
Here's Your Mesh Body Stocking.

*A hundred men may make an encampment,
but it takes a woman to make a home.*

Chinese Proverb

Christmas is officially over. Today I dragged the tree with its fifteen remaining needles out to the curb, tied the Christmas lights into one great big ball like I found them, and dumped the odd remains of two ham-a-ramas and a jalapeño cheese log into the cat's dish, which caused him to immediately jump up onto the telephone stand and look up the address for the Humane Society's self-admittance wing.

But it's done. Kaput. *Finé.* The yuletide has ebbed. And not a moment too soon, because now it's time for . . . Valentine's Day.

Not to worry though, because this year I'm ready. Last February I was fooled by the pact my wife and I made that we weren't going to bother with Valentine's Day. What I thought she meant was that she didn't expect a gift. What she really meant was that only a chump would think it was okay not to get his wife—who was put on this earth for no greater reason than to serve her husband's every need, although said husband could count on serving certain needs himself until further notice—a gift.

And even though it was quite a bonding experience camping out in my backyard in February with my brother-in-law, who had wondered why everyone was buying flowers on Washington's birthday, I think I'd rather spend the rainy season inside this year.

So I grabbed the garbage bag full of Christmas cards and wrapping paper to drop off at the local landfill and headed off to the Hallmark store—that magical place full of those beautiful poetic musings that women love. I settled on a card with a romantic, soft-focus photograph of a young couple laughing and hugging in a wooded glen, taken no doubt just seconds before they realized they were standing waist deep in poison oak.

Then I headed across the mall to the lingerie store. The place was mobbed with guys all holding intimate apparel, trying to picture their wives in them. One guy was holding his selection upside down wondering, I suspect, why the thing had snaps at the neck. I was about to explain when a saleslady approached wearing a button that said "All Our Bras Are Half Off." She looked frazzled. Her hair was mussed. Her makeup was smeared, and she had bags under her eyes.

"Let me guess," she said. "Gift for the wife?"

Before I could compliment her on such a quick assessment of the situation, she moved me to one side and yelled over my shoulder. "Please don't mix the satin panties up with the silk ones."

Two guys, who were each holding a dozen pair of panties, smiled sheepishly, like they just got caught during a midnight raid at the female dorms.

"I hate Valentine's Day," she muttered. Then with a

forced smile she asked, "So, what did you have in mind?"

"I dunno. Something sexy, I guess."

"Novel idea. What's her favorite color?"

"Uhh . . . brown?"

"Brown? Brown's her favorite color?"

"Green?"

"You don't know, do you?"

"Well, our cat is gray and white and she likes him a lot." I thought briefly about the cat and wondered if he'd still be there when I got home. Meanwhile, the saleslady moved me to one side again.

"Sir. Siiirrrr."

A large, bald man in a three-piece suit glanced up.

"It's Velcro," she said. "As you have no doubt observed, it will make that same sound over and over."

She shook her head, turned her attention back to me and was about to speak when a tall, thin guy approached us wearing a teddy over his T-shirt and boxer shorts.

"Whaddya think?" he asked.

I thought the red was a little too bright for his complexion and was about to say so when the saleslady jumped up onto a clearance counter and addressed the entire store.

"Okay. Here's what we are going to do. I want every one of you to take out the amount of money you want to spend and step up to the counter. I will hand you an item that costs that amount of money. Do not worry about the color or size. Your wives will be in here to exchange your gifts tomorrow. Now, who's first?"

We all hesitated. She held up her watch.

"The mall closes in fifteen minutes, gentlemen, and they are predicting a particularly cold February this year."

I thought I caught a whiff of damp tent. Then I quickly took out my wallet and got in line.

Ernie Witham

CLOSE TO HOME JOHN McPHERSON

"They're *perfect*, Charles! I'll think of you
every time I wear them."

The Forever Card

On a shelf in my bedroom closet is a dusty, wooden box where I keep special treasures. It is a tiny museum, of sorts; my past is preserved there. Childhood photos, post-cards, graduation tassels, holy cards and newspaper clippings carefully lie together. Stored away are bits of fur from beloved pets and even wrapping paper from the box that held my engagement ring. But of all these precious mementos, one is most revered—the *forever* card.

Twenty-five years ago, after spending Christmas Eve with our three rambunctious children, my husband and I finally rested. Like other parents the world over, we were exhausted. This quiet, alone time was magical as we sat near the glow of the Christmas tree. I reached over to the end table and handed my husband a card that I had carefully chosen for him.

On the front of the card was a scene, reminiscent of drawings from the much-loved children's book, *Goodnight Moon*. A man and woman slept sweetly alongside each other; a patchwork quilt covered them. A small, gray cat (much like our own cat, Jessie) was curled up at the foot of the bed, warming their toes, and a fireplace burned softly in the corner. A little Christmas tree sat atop an end table and through the parted window curtains, snow fell softly in the night sky. A feeling of serenity emanated from the picture. The card opened to a simple, beautiful expression, "Merry Christmas, I love loving you." My husband and I both cherished that card; it captured the affection we held for each other. I saved that card and added it to my box of treasures.

The following Christmas, I shopped for a new card for my husband, but I couldn't find one as meaningful as the card from the previous year. On Christmas Eve, as once again we sat alone together under the warmth of the tree lights, I offered my husband the same card. When he opened it he whispered, "I remember this card," and he smiled as he gently kissed me. A feeling of comfort surrounded us as we sat in silence. For more than twenty-five years, we have repeated that custom and we are always left very moved.

Over the years, much has changed and life has thrown us a few punches. Still, on Christmas Eve, after the house is quiet, we sit alone by the glow of our tree and I tenderly place in my husband's hands our card. I believe that we look forward to that one special moment more than anything else during the holidays. Like our skin and hair color, our card has wrinkled and faded with the passage of time. But one thing remains the same—the love we have for each other will last *forever*.

Susan J. Siersma

The Frosty Moment
Called for Ice Cream

Every time I receive a wedding invitation, I envision the unique personalities of the two people about to wed. I think of what they love, what they share, what makes them laugh. Then I go to the store and buy them all the same thing: an old-fashioned ice-cream maker.

Every couple's response is the same. First, they look puzzled, then they recover to utter a quick pair of "thank yous." Then they set the thing aside like a book opened at Christmas amid a mountain of toys.

The newlyweds will head off on their honeymoon, then return to settle into the day-to-day business of being husband and wife. They'll unpack the ice-cream maker and set it on a closet shelf or in the garage and forget about it. Time will pass, and soon the wedding silver will need polishing, the toaster will fill with crumbs, and somehow life will seem all too ordinary. Then one of them will think of ice cream!

My husband and I were just such a couple. We opened an ice-cream machine at our wedding reception. The giver was a purist, selecting a model with a genuine oaken bucket, a large-capacity tin and a hand crank. She grinned knowingly as we labored to disguise our surprise and managed a pair of hesitant smiles. We never took the machine out of its box to appreciate the bucket's polished-oak staves or the perfect fit of the wide paddle in the tin. Instead, it was quickly crated with the other gifts and shipped to our new home.

After a carefree honeymoon, we settled into the predictable lifestyle of two newly married, working professionals. We negotiated day-to-day duties, deciding who did the laundry, bought the groceries, cooked the dinner, cut the grass. Within months, the structure and routine of married life were in place. We purchased two rooms of furniture, six potted plants, a lawn mower and a dog. Life was good.

Then it happened. We had our first fight. In the long-established form of my youth, I slammed the bedroom door, threw myself on the bed and cried. My husband went out to play basketball. Hours slipped by, and without the attention that I'd expected to elicit from my rookie spouse, I quickly grew tired of crying and being alone. Finally, he returned, carrying a paper bag.

I hoped it held flowers. Instead, he pulled out a bulky, rectangular sack, which he laid with a disappointing thud on the counter.

"What's that?" I asked, keeping an angry edge to my voice.

"Salt," he answered. "Don't we have an ice-cream maker someplace?"

"In the garage," I said, stingy with my words. He brought the box into the living room and sat it on the floor, obviously as an invitation for me to come and help. But I didn't. I shifted plates and pots, pretending to cook dinner. All the while, I was watching to see if this city boy I'd married could figure out how to assemble a machine he'd never used in his life.

He made it as far as screwing the wooden handle onto the iron rod. After that he sat back and scratched his head, a scene that forced a smile across my face.

"You ever use one of these things?" he yelled toward the kitchen.

"Yeah," was all I said.

It turned out that ours was a model almost identical to the one I grew up with, so it took only minutes for me to assemble the pieces and punctuate the task with a satisfying glare of superiority.

"Do we have all the stuff we need to make some?" he wondered.

"Yeah. Take this outside. Hammer some ice. I'll make the cream," I said, loving the chance to direct this technically awkward though handsome man, whom I was mad at for something.

With everything assembled, I began to turn the crank, relieved by the rattle and slush of churning ice and salt. "I'll take it from here," my husband said, kneeling beside me and placing his hand on the crank next to mine. I let him take over. He smiled as his arm flew. The look on his face reminded me of my childhood days.

Often, amid the chaotic summers that vibrated with the energy of five school-free children, my mother would say, "Let's make ice cream!" Taking turns at the crank united us as a team with a mission. The process of turning a few basic ingredients into ice cream was a magic that never lost its power to delight.

An hour later his smile was a sweat-glazed grimace, and the hasty strokes had turned laborious and slow.

"It's getting hard—it must be done," he gasped.

And I suspect it was. However, something made me pretend to give it a test turn then say, "Another ten minutes."

The ice cream was the best I'd ever eaten. Our anger, cooled by time, task and a frosty dessert, retreated. Along with it went the energy needed to sustain the dispute. Suddenly, our diverse opinions seemed nothing more than a natural variation in personal tastes, as unworthy of battle as different flavors of ice cream.

Unfortunately, we didn't always make ice cream when we had a disagreement.

Like many couples, getting angry, arguing our positions and reaching a series of small settlements became something of a routine. There's a lot of waste in such a way of life. But until we experienced a major emotional jolt, we didn't see that.

Months after our first fight, my husband was in a plane crash. Although all the people on board survived, the day marked a turning point. We didn't disagree for a long time after that. Instead, we moved into a new level of maturity in our marriage. We decided that life needed fewer routines and less strife, and some unspoken logic dictated that it wouldn't hurt to have a little more ice cream.

In the spirit of our new philosophy, we threw a party, announcing to our guests that they had to make the dessert—homemade ice cream. Some of our friends were novices, believing that the whole thing started with a carton.

Others couldn't wait to start cranking. Everyone agreed that it was a delicious way to have fun.

The making of ice cream bonded us as a group, and soon everyone who came that night, even the bachelors, bought ice-cream makers. Every get-together became a new theme in ice cream. We tried peach, peppermint, chocolate, blueberry and even an experimental cinnamon-honey.

After a decade of making ice cream, our machine broke. But with a young child and a new baby, our hands were too busy to crank out desserts. I felt like a deserter when I bought an electric model. But our family had doubled, and it didn't seem unreasonable to make use of a modern appliance and a power source.

It's been twenty-two years and three machines since we opened that oddest of wedding gifts. I'm heading out to buy another one—for a wedding present, of course. I know the couple will be surprised and puzzled, but I'm used to that reaction. Eventually, they will discover, as we did, that few things in day-to-day life can't be improved with ice cream.

Susan Sarver

Hooray for the Ho-Hum Marriage

It is an extra dividend when you like the girl you've fallen in love with.

Clark Gable

Then the prince swept the lovely young maiden into his arms and carried her home to his castle. And they lived. . . .

What I want to see is a federal study of all these princes and princesses seven years after their happily-ever-after marriages. The truth is that life isn't made up of the continual highs found in the initial stages of courtship. Yes, the flirting is fun and the chase exciting. But after a while your system needs a rest.

It's called the second stage. All of a sudden the man who wanted you morning, noon and night prefers watching the football game, falls asleep while you're revealing your innermost secrets, and forgets the four-year anniversary of the first time ever he saw your face.

Actually, settling in is the best thing about a marriage. No longer do each of you have to do a little tap dance to win approval. You've won each other's acceptance, and that is not to be undervalued.

Yet as time progresses, you look at the glorious union that you were sure would be filled with Kodak moments. You see a house that has to be cleaned, car pools that have to be organized and a husband who looks as weary as you feel. You ask, "This is *it?*"

Now comes the third stage when you come to terms with your marriage and why it's worth the ups and downs. What saves the relationship is that your plus column is fuller than your minus column. Maybe he doesn't tell you how incredible you look when you've spent three hours putting yourself together (minus), but he unloads the dishwasher without being asked (plus). Although he doesn't surprise you with tickets for a weekend in Miami (small minus), he treats both you and your parents with respect (big plus).

Maybe you don't have his newspaper and slippers waiting for him (little minus), but you ask him about his day, and are even interested in his response (super plus).

Then there are the things your husband does that say: this man cares about me. He makes me feel loved. It's a security I wouldn't trade.

Who else but someone who loved me would agree to take our teenage daughter shopping because her taste in clothes makes me want to gag?

Who else but someone who loved him would travel twenty miles out of the way because he was too stubborn to ask directions, and not say, "I told you so."

Who else but someone who loved me would kiss my sleepy head before he leaves in the morning and not tell me I look like Medusa on a bad day?

Who else but someone who loved him would pick up his trail of underwear and socks that never quite made it to the hamper and not question his upbringing?

Who else but someone who loved me would insist I meet him every Thursday night for dinner? By the time we sit in the restaurant and have a chance to do what we do at home (exchange the stories of the day), we usually don't—because we're alone and forced to share more of our feelings, to laugh a lot. The net result, after eighteen years of marriage, is romantic (super plus).

Although no marriage is continually blissful, it can be pretty good most of the time. The reason we lasted through arguments, money worries, kids' traumas and midlife crises is not that our relationship is always like the Fourth of July. It's because the fundamental reason for our marriage has outlasted the craziness of day-to-day living: We love each other. That's my idea of "happily ever after."

Trish Vradenburg

The Anniversary

It has been wisely said that we cannot really love anybody at whom we never laugh.

Agnes Repplier

My wife and I celebrated our seventeenth anniversary the other day. Not in commemoration of our wedding, but in recognition of our first date (we were high school sweethearts). And, as we were reminiscing, I admitted that our relationship almost never got off the ground.

"What do you mean?!" my wife demanded.

I smiled. "I was afraid of your dad."

The man was, and still is, huge. He was the proverbial father teenagers would look at and say, "I'M GOING TO DIE!"

"But you were brave, for me," my wife said sweetly. "What did you do when you knocked on my door? Did my dad answer?"

"All dads answer the door on first dates," I replied. "If I remember it right, my tongue swelled up in fear and I almost suffocated to death."

"Did my dad say anything to you?"

"No, he just stood there staring at me. I think he thought I was raising money door-to-door for the mute."

"Why do you think that?"

"He gave me a dollar."

"Well, apparently, you were okay—he let us go out, didn't he?"

"True," I replied. "But before we left, he looked at me, then he looked at you, and then he looked at my car."

"Why?"

"It was like he was telling me a little story through telepathy."

"What was the story about?"

"A horny high school student who now walks with a limp."

Her eyes flashed with a sudden realization. "Is that why you never held my hand in front of my dad?"

I nodded. "I was afraid he was going to say something."

"Like what?"

"Like, 'Hey, Romeo, do you want to keep that arm?'"

Of course, our first date was nothing like a week later when I went over to my future wife's house. It was the day before I was set to leave for spring vacation with my family. Her parents were gone, so, like high school kids do, we necked on the sofa.

Next thing I know, her parents are rolling into the driveway an hour earlier than planned. With my hair tousled about, I start going nuts, shouting "Our Father, who art in heaven," while my future wife was behind me spitting into her hand and smoothing down my cowlick.

Positioning myself on the couch to look as if I had been reading an interesting *National Geographic* article on apple maggots, her dad walks in and proceeds straight to the living room like a bounty hunter.

"Hi," I said, greeting him like a hoarse soprano. I would have also waved, but I got a paper cut from clutching the magazine like a life preserver, and I was trying to stop the bleeding with a linen doily.

Finally, as beads of sweat were rolling down my neck, the giant spoke in his deep, dark voice: "So, when are you leaving, Ken?"

"Right now," I answered, jumping up to go.

He looked at me for a moment, and then started laughing. "I meant on vacation."

"My dad still loves to talk about that," my wife remarked.

I can only hope to be half as scary when my daughter starts dating.

Ken Swarner

"That's how my dad looked
when I told him I was going to marry you."

Reprinted by permission of Martha Campbell.

The Little Things . . .

Love is a great beautifier.

Louisa May Alcott

It's the little things he does every day with love and affection. I often try to take the time to reflect on how lucky I am to have someone who cares so completely for me. The most powerful examples of his love for me, his wife, are the ways in which he makes sure that I am taken care of, not in macho, overprotective ways, but in caring expressions of tenderness and devotion. One such day that I will always treasure occurred in May 1993.

Jeff and I had been married for just over a year and a half. We were expecting our first child, who was due in August. Fortunately, my pregnancy was proceeding uneventfully, other than what almost all other expectant mothers go through adjusting to our body's changes. I suffered with morning sickness throughout the entire pregnancy. Of course, it was not just restricted to morning hours. My husband was right there with me, rubbing my back, as well as cleaning up after me when necessary.

My sleep patterns were so messed up that I thought I

would never again see a good night's sleep. Every little thing bothered me. Any noise, movement, light, heat, cold, you name it. But the worst disruption of my sleep was not being in a dark enough room. I wanted complete darkness. As my hormones began to dictate my behavior, I became angry at the street light outside, the neighbors' security floodlight and even the moon for shedding such light into my bedroom.

On this day in May 1993, Jeff had put in a full day at work, which for him began at 4:30 A.M. He found time to go to Home Depot and purchase a window shade. He purchased a shade in the heaviest material he could find so that the most light would be eliminated from the window. The window shade had to be custom cut to fit our odd-sized window. He installed the shade before I arrived home from work.

When I arrived home, he escorted me into our bedroom and then into our adjoining bathroom where a bubble bath was waiting. I enjoyed quiet time in the bubble bath. When I was through, he brought me into the bedroom. He suggested that after my long day at the office I get off my feet and get right into bed. I agreed because nothing could have sounded better to me at that moment. But, of course, Jeff had another surprise waiting for me.

Jeff walked over to the window. I asked him what he was doing, and he told me to be patient. He gently pulled down the newly installed shade. The bedroom slowly turned from filtered sunlight to pitch black. He gave me a big hug, a soft kiss and told me to "Rest, sweet Sue." What a wonderful nap!

The wonderful sleep didn't come because of the darkness. It came because of the peace and love, which was all around me as evidenced in the tangible and priceless window shade, which is on my bedroom window to this day.

Susan M. Miller

Who, Me?

The entire sum of existence is the magic of being needed by just one person.

Vi Putnam

One of our family jokes was that any time we accused my husband of a good deed, prank or mistake, his reply would always be, "Who, me?" We told him we were going to have that engraved on his tombstone. In reality it would be fitting because it would remind us—"Yes, you . . ."

You who painted my toenails when I was eight months pregnant. You who held our baby in your arms after his surgery because you didn't want him to wake up in a strange bed. You who gave me seedless grapes and Cheez-Its for Valentine's Day because you knew that was what I liked. You who cried in front of me for the first time when my father died. You who always saw that your family had what they needed and most of what they wanted. You who never bought anything for yourself. You who required so little of me as a wife and denied me even less. You who knelt down to talk eye-to-eye with me as I sat in the chair in the living room the day my mother died. You who planned for our future from the beginning of our marriage.

You who I still love as inscribed inside your wedding band, "More than yesterday, less than tomorrow." You who fixed everything that broke, fell off or clogged up in our house. You who wouldn't spend three dollars for the right tool but would give one hundred dollars to a friend in need. You who went back to your parents in their illness to be the son they knew they could depend on. You who never ate the last cookie, biscuit or piece of pie. You who told me when I complained about the boys' spending: "Well, we're not paying bail money." You who would refer to an employee as someone who worked with you, not for you. You who gave me the good car to drive. You who found four-leaf clovers and told me the reason I couldn't was because I was only looking at the three-leaf ones.

You who took care of the dog no one wanted. You who bought me a new printer but never bought yourself a new reel. You who never let the boys leave to go back to school without your checking their oil and wiping off their headlights. You who never left my gas tank on empty. You who showed restraint and love by leaving me at least one word on the Jumble, even when you knew all the answers. You who taught me the fine art of the atlas. You who showed the boys how things worked, making repairs on them easier. You who always saw the beauty in a newborn white-faced calf.

You who found no job beneath you at the plant. You who sat through every play our children performed. You who lived "around" my knick-knacks, but did hide a few that were intolerable. You who no matter what I gave you to eat complimented it and my efforts. You who fought for the boys' rights to the sanctity and privacy of their own rooms. You who scraped my car windshield. You who told me to send the boys a check for a major need they had.

You who cleaned the frogs out of the pool skimmer because I was afraid of them. You who never came to bed on time, but made waking up a joy finding you there next to me. You who shared with my widowed mother the only bonus you ever got at work. You who would start or unload the dishwasher and let me read after dinner.

You who always thought things through and helped tame my impetuous nature. You who was known by your coworkers as a dependable peer and a fair boss. You who wore both sons' Eagle Scout Award pins on your suit lapel. You who raked the yard after mowing because you knew that was what I wanted. You who never stuck your finger through the bottom of the candy pieces in the Russell Stover box to see what kind each was. You whose hands could soothe all our hurts.

"Who, me?" you ask.

Yes, you—who made my two greatest dreams come true, making me your wife and a mother. Thirty blessed years later, yes, you.

Andy Skidmore

5

MEMORIES
OF LOVE

*Love is a force more formidable than
any other.
    It is invisible—it cannot be seen or
measured, yet it is powerful enough to
transform you in a moment, and offer
you more joy than any material possession
could.*

Barbara De Angelis, Ph.D.

The Hat I Stole for Love

A coward is incapable of exhibiting love; it is the prerogative of the brave.

Mahatma Gandhi

Kissing was out of the question when I was in Grade 5 in a Catholic school. Written expressions of love were also frowned upon—except for Valentine's Day, when a card was more a vote for the most popular kid than a message of real affection.

There was really only one chance in those days if a parochial schoolboy wanted to show his interest in a girl: He would steal her hat and hope she cared enough to chase him for it.

I have no idea how many times I stole Diane Tasca's hat. I do know my love for her was real, and one of the things I liked most about her was her pep.

Her pep lent energy to her response to my hat thefts. Invariably, hands would go to hips, and she would say, loudly, "Edward, give me back my hat this instant," followed by a few attempts to get it back. None was ever peppy enough to be successful. That would have ruined the game.

This was no common game of keep away. I never passed her hat to another boy, for instance, as this would have been a breach of trust. In taunting, such a move would have been inappropriate. But this was love.

One day a girl who was frequently the object of teasing was watching classmates jump rope when her hat was snatched. She wheeled around and lunged for it, but she was no match for the school-yard bully. Other Grade 6 boys joined in.

The hat was flying from boy to boy when, betraying my sex to stop what I saw as unfair play, I jumped in and brought it down. I returned the hat to its teary-eyed owner. Out of the corner of my eye, I saw Diane watching. I was surrounded by the taunters, threatening retaliation. Then the recess bell rang. Even the bully froze in his tracks.

"Get you tomorrow," he hissed.

I ran to catch up with my class, but I was a minute late. Sister Regina Christi caught me sneaking in. "Edward, do you have a good excuse for your tardiness?"

"No, Sister." To report how I had rescued the girl would have cheapened the event, of course. Instead, I shot a look at Diane. Her face was full of understanding, I thought.

"Edward, you'll stay after school."

Later that afternoon, as I was passing the convent on my way home, out stepped Diane, fresh from her piano lesson. I stopped at the end of the path and waited. "Walk you home?" I asked, surprising myself. As we meandered down Springfield Road, she said, "I saw what you did today."

"I did it for myself," I said. "When I see someone help-less being picked on, I feel sick to my stomach." There was some truth to this, naturally, though I hadn't thought it through until then.

"Do you like her?"

There! She was jealous. "Sure I like her."

"Do you like me?"

"Oh, yes, I *really* like you."

"Then why do you steal my hat?"

I was flabbergasted. Did Diane think I was as mean as the school-yard bully?

"Be-be-because I *like* you so much."

"Then that bully likes her, I guess."

I was getting in deeper. "No, he hates her."

"So you steal my hat because you hate me."

"No, it's the opposite."

"What's the difference?" Her pep was turning to pout.

I was floundering now. "Wait, look . . . if I didn't like you, I'd steal your hat and throw it to the other boys. But I don't. I keep it."

"Then you are selfish and don't want to share."

"Share your hat? No!"

"You want to keep it all to yourself?"

"I give it back to you, don't I?"

"Yes, but it's still ungentlemanly."

"Do you want me to stop?"

"Well, yes . . . and no," she replied, looking as though she were solving a math problem.

I felt helpless. It was the first time I had come up against a deeper wisdom.

"No, I don't want you to stop because I like the attention."

I was almost getting it, but not quite. "And yes?"

"Yes, I want you to stop because it interferes with my vocation—and yours as well, I think."

Today the word "vocation" can refer to any of the answers to the question, "What do you want to be when you grow up?" But in our tradition, it meant only one thing—being called to devote your life to God as a priest, a brother or a nun. Marriage would be precluded.

"Do you really think I have a vocation?" I asked.

"Well, I have thought about it a lot. How about you?"

"My mother wants me to be a priest, but my father has

warned me against taking a job where I have to wear a dress to work."

Diane looked up, her cheeks reddening from the shock of my answer. But when I couldn't keep a straight face, we both started laughing.

"Edward Patrick Stivender," she said, "you're twisted." Then she snatched my baseball cap and ran down the street. By the time I recovered from the surprise and caught up, she was at her door, my cap twirling on her finger. Diane giggled as she threw it back. Then she disappeared into the house, leaving me to figure out the meaning of the moment.

A few weeks later, Sister Regina Christi told the class that Diane had an announcement. As Diane faced the class, she avoided looking at me. "My father has been promoted, and we're moving away this weekend," she said, then sat down.

Moving? She's moving? I stared at her. She put her head on the desk. "We will have a good-bye party on Friday, right after our weekly tic-tac-toe game," Sister Christi said.

On Friday, as fate would have it, Diane and I were paired as contestants in our version of a popular TV game show, "Tic Tac Dough." Four lines were drawn on the board, producing nine squares, each representing a different subject. I won the coin toss to go first, but I said, "I defer to Diane."

She smiled at me. "Top, right square, please."

"The category is geography," Sister Christi said. "The question is, 'What is the major export of Texas?'"

"Crude oil," Diane answered.

"Correct. Edward?"

"Middle square, please, Sister."

"Arithmetic. How much is eleven squared?"

"One hundred twenty-one."

"Correct. Diane?"

"Lower right-hand corner."

"Spell the word 'encyclopedia.'"

Diane almost chanted as she spelled the word.

"Correct. Edward?"

"Middle, left square please."

One boy shot me a look of consternation. Middle left would leave Diane a space to win. I couldn't explain to him in sign language that I was just trying to show my affection. Sister was smiling at me though. At least she got it.

"The category is civics. How many seats in the United States Senate?"

"Ninety-six."

"Correct. Diane?"

"Middle, right square please."

"This is for the win. Quiet please. Name the seven sacraments." The boys groaned. This was too easy. Grade 2 stuff.

"Baptism, Confirmation, Penance, Holy Eucharist, Holy Orders, Extreme Unction . . ." Then Diane paused. We held our breath. She had skipped Matrimony. Could it be that she forgot? Diane looked at me, then in a voice beyond pep, said, ". . . Taking the vows of a nun: poverty, chastity and obedience." A groan from the girls, a cheer from the boys.

"Wrong. Edward?" All the boys had their fingers crossed.

"Baptism, Confirmation, Penance, Holy Eucharist, Holy Orders, Extreme Unction and Matrimony." The boys were cheering. The girls looked crestfallen. But Diane was grinning from ear to ear as she shook my hand in congratulations.

Later, after we sang "For She's a Jolly Good Classmate" and lined up for a piece of cake, Diane began cleaning her desk out. I asked if I could carry her books.

"No books to carry," she laughed. "But you can carry

my hat." She held out the easiest one to steal, a tam with a yarn clump at the top—a perfect handle. I put it on my book bag.

The next morning my mind raced as I walked to Diane's house to return her hat and say good-bye. I was still confused about winning the quiz. Did she really forget Matrimony? Would I really never see her again?

Diane was standing in front of her house, next to a large moving van. There was a question on the tip of my tongue, but I was having trouble getting it out. Just then her mother saw us and called Diane to come in immediately. "We're almost ready," she said.

"I have to go, Edward," Diane said. Then she kissed me—full on the lips. Shocked, I stepped backward as she ran into the house.

"I love you," I called after her. I began walking down the street still trying to figure out why she had given the answer she had to the quiz question. Perhaps she really did have a vocation, and this was her way of telling me our love could never be.

Then it hit me. She had let me win. She did love me—or something like it. Elated, I threw my book bag into the air. In midflight, her hat slipped out and fell at my feet. I picked it up and ran back to her house. But the van was gone, and her family's station wagon was no longer in the driveway.

I ran to the door and knocked loudly. The sound echoed. They were gone. I'd never see her again. I held the hat to my nose and breathed in the warm scent of her hair. Then I hung it on the doorknob and walked down Springfield Road towards home.

Ed Stivender

"Getting love notes isn't half as
much fun as returning them."

Reprinted by permission of Peggy Andy Wyatt.

Will He Kiss Me?

Kissing is a means of getting two people so close together that they can't see anything wrong with each other.

René Yasenek

I met Chris on a double date, only I was with his best friend. Chris of course was with his old girlfriend, Paula. As we sat at the restaurant, our eyes kept meeting. He had the most electrifying blue eyes I had ever seen. When he talked I got lost in the sea of blue. He had the kind of eyes that could make all the girls swoon. I knew I should not stare at this boy across from me—he was not my date. His eyes were like magnets drawing me back. Every time I looked at him I found him staring at me as well. I tried refocusing on my date but to no avail. I went home that night dreaming of those blue eyes and wondering if I ever would see them again.

A week later, Chris called. Oh, how my heart started racing. I got so excited I had to sit down. When he asked me out, the only thing I could think to ask was "What about Paula?" He responded, "What about her?" He then went on to tell me that the two of them were over. Non-chalantly I agreed to go out. In reality, I was so ecstatic I could hardly contain myself.

Saturday he arrived right on time. He came in, sat for awhile and chatted with my mom. I couldn't take my eyes off him the entire time. I thought it was so sweet how he talked and listened to my mom, smiling and laughing with her. I was dancing on cloud nine.

Chris was a gentleman all evening. He opened my car door, offered his arm for me as we walked and always ushered me through the door first. When he brought me home he walked me to the house and greeted my mom. I fully expected a kiss at this time, but instead he said, "Thank you for going out with me tonight. I had a good time." Wondering what was wrong, I responded, "I had a very good time too." I thought maybe he wanted to make sure I had a good time before we kissed. But he said goodnight and left. I was bewildered. What had gone wrong? Half of me thought he didn't like me and that would be the end of it. The other half giggled at the thought of such a gentleman and was excited about the prospect of where this could go.

Monday I was standing at my locker when Chris came up behind me and gently touched me on the arm. I was very surprised to see him since we had never seen each other at school before. The school is huge with three floors and four different wings. There are so many students, it is impossible to know or have seen even half of them. But here he was, he had sought me out. I was very excited, and my heart raced as he asked me to go to a basketball game on Saturday. After he left I was so flustered I couldn't remember what I was supposed to take from my locker. I closed it and floated down the hall. I'm sure I had a faraway look on my face, along with a silly grin. I didn't have the right book for class, but I didn't care. All I could think about was Chris.

Saturday arrived and I was a bundle of nerves. I wanted our date to be perfect. I drove my mom crazy that day, with questions about my clothes, my hair, makeup and what I should say and how to act.

Chris was right on time to pick me up. He came in and again exchanged pleasantries with my mom. He was so polite and nice, and he genuinely had an interest in my mom and the conversation.

We arrived at the basketball game, and walking across the parking lot, Chris took my hand and held it until we reached the building. All the while my heart was racing. His hand, firm and strong, engulfed mine. I could sense his strength, but he held my hand with such caring and gentleness. He made me feel safe and protected.

When he took me home that night I was sure he would give me a kiss. But again he just thanked me, and we departed. I couldn't believe it—again no kiss! What was wrong with me? Was I imagining something between us that wasn't there? I was very confused and frustrated. I talked to my mom, and she said, "I think he is a gentleman." I responded, "Okay, but does that mean he likes me?" She shrugged her shoulders and winked at me with a smile on her face. I was so bewildered. I had never met anyone like Chris before, and I really liked him. But I was not certain how he felt about me.

The next week I didn't see Chris until Wednesday afternoon. He found me on my way to lunch. He asked if I knew how to bowl. Sarcastically I thought, *Bowling—this guy doesn't like me in a romantic way at all.* I responded unenthusiastically, "Yes, I've been on bowling leagues before." Suddenly his face lit up. "Really!" he said with excitement. "We need another person for our team. Someone dropped out. Can you come tonight?" I shrugged one shoulder and said, "Sure," feeling disappointed that we were never going to be more than "just" friends.

We went bowling that night. Our team won, and I really enjoyed being with Chris. Several times that night our eyes met, and I searched for some kind of a sign that he might still like me.

When he brought me home, he walked me up to the front door. I thanked him for inviting me to join the bowling league. As I turned to go inside, he gently touched my arm. I stood there looking into his dreamy blue eyes. He cupped my face in his large gentle hands. We searched each other's eyes for what seemed like a lifetime. Then as if we could read each other's minds we embraced in a long, passionate kiss. I was intoxicated with the aroma from his leather coat. I breathed deeply to savor the moment. Oh, at last, the kiss I had dreamed about. It was better than I had imagined. I was swept away. It was worth the wait. I knew in that instance there was a bond between Chris and me that would last a lifetime.

To this day I still savor that first kiss with Chris. That was nearly twenty years ago, although it seems like yesterday. I can still smell the leather of his coat. Sometimes I even take his coat out of our closet and breathe deep into it, relishing the memory of that first kiss. As for Chris, he can't figure out why I want to keep that coat around. It hasn't fit him for years.

Margaret E. Reed

CLOSE TO HOME   JOHN McPHERSON

8-23   closetohome@ucomics.com

Not long into the date, Brad hit the
Smooch-Matic button on the couch.

About Men/"A Love Affair"

No love, no friendship can cross the path of our destiny without leaving some mark on it forever.
François Mauriac

I remember the way the light touched her hair. She turned her head, and I saw her face. She turned still more, and our eyes met and held. We saw each other, a momentary awareness in that raucous fifth-grade schoolroom to which I'd just been assigned. I felt as though I'd been struck a blow under the heart. Thus began my first love affair, a surge of adrenaline, a rush of blood, a thing of innocence and pain that has lasted all my life.

Her name was Rachel. I suppose our story, noted in a romance now out of favor, is one of absurdity today, and—who knows?—the innocence may really have been ignorance, in view of all that has happened since. Whatever it was, I mooned my way through grade and high school, stricken at the mere sight of her, tongue-tied in her presence. Does anyone, anymore, linger in the shadows of evening, drawn by the pale light of a window—her window—like some hapless summer insect?

That delirious swooning sickness, asexual but urgent and obsessive, that made me awkward and my voice crack, is like some impossible dream now. I know I was so afflicted, but I cannot actually believe what memory insists I did. Which was to suffer. Exquisitely.

I would catch sight of her, walking down an aisle of trees to or from school, and I'd become paralyzed. She always seemed so poised, self-possessed, slightly amused. At home, in bed, I'd relive each encounter, writhing at the thought of my inadequacies, feeling less than worthless. Even so, as time passed and we entered our teens, I sensed her affectionate tolerance for me.

"Going steady" implied a maturity we still lacked. Her orthodox Jewish upbringing and my own Catholic scruples imposed a kind of idealism, a celibate grave that made even kissing a distant prospect, however fervently desired. As for the rest of it, we were babes in arms. I managed to hold her at a dance, and at a party—chaperoned, of course—we experienced a furtive embrace that made her giggle, a sound so childish and trusting that I hated myself for what I'd been thinking.

At any rate, my love for Rachel remained unrequited. We graduated from high school, she went on to college, and I joined the army. World War II was about to engulf us, and when it did I left for overseas in the first task force after Pearl Harbor. For a time we corresponded, and to receive one of her letters at mail call was the highlight of those grinding, endless months that became years.

Once she sent me a snapshot of herself, a guileless pose in a bathing suit, which drove me to the wildest of fantasies. I mentioned the possibility of marriage in my next letter to her, and almost immediately her replies became less frequent and personal.

I returned to the States for reassignment during the final throes of the war. The first thing I did on reaching home was to call on Rachel, whose recent mail had failed to keep up with me on my travels. Her mother answered the door. Rachel no longer lived there. She had married a medical student she'd met in college. "I thought she wrote you," her mother said.

Her "Dear John" letter finally caught up with me while I was awaiting discharge. She gently, compassionately explained the impossibility of a marriage between us, even had she not found someone else. Looking back on it, I think I must have recovered rather quickly, although for the first few months of having learned of her marriage, I think I didn't want to live very much. Like Rachel, I found someone else, whom I learned to love with a deep and permanent commitment that has lasted to this day.

Then, fairly recently, I heard from Rachel again—after an interval of more than forty years. Her husband had died. She would be passing through the city on her way to live with a daughter in California, and she had learned of my whereabouts through a mutual friend. We made a date to meet during her brief layover.

I felt both curious and excited at the prospect. In recent years, I hadn't thought about her, and her sudden call, one morning, had taken me aback. The actual sight of her can only be described as a shock. Was this white-haired matron the Rachel of my dreams and desires, the supple mermaid of that snapshot I'd subsequently lost?

Yet time had given us a common reference and respect. We met and talked as old friends and quickly discovered we were both grandparents.

"Do you remember this?" she said. We were sitting in a restaurant, and she reached into her purse and took out an envelope from which she extracted a slip of worn paper. It was a poem I'd written her while still in school. I examined the crude meter and pallid rhymes: "Will" and "thrill," and "strove" and "love." Watching my face, she snatched the poem from me and returned it to her purse, as though fearful I was going to destroy it.

I told her about the fate of the snapshot, how I'd carried it all through the war.

"It wouldn't have worked out, you know," she said.

"How can you be sure?" I countered. "Ah, Colleen, it might have been grand indeed—my Irish conscience and your Jewish guilt!"

Our laughter startled people at a nearby table. During the time left to us, our glances were furtive, oblique. I think that what we saw in each other repudiated what we'd once been to ourselves, we immortals.

Before I put her into a taxi, she turned to me and, with a resolute expression, said, "I just wanted to see you once more. To tell you something." Her eyes pleaded with me. "I wanted to thank you for having loved me as you did." We kissed, and she got into the taxi and drove off.

My reflection stared back at me from a store window on Fifth Avenue—an aging man with gray hair stirred by an evening breeze. I decided to walk home and entered Central Park. Her withered kiss still burned on my lips, something strange was happening. I was feeling lighter with each step. All round me the grass and trees were shining in the surreal glow of sunset. Then I felt faint and sat on a bench. Something was being lifted out of me. I was becoming someone else. Something had been completed, was ended, and the scene before me was so beautiful that I wanted to shout and dance and sing for joy—like Blake, like Whitman.

But that soon passed, as everything must, and presently I was able to stand and start for home.

John Walters

A Friend's Secret

The greatest weakness of most humans is their hesitancy to tell others how much they love them while they're still alive.

Orlando A. Battista

There's a moment in the Disney classic *Cinderella* when the ragamuffin heroine lays claim to her wayward glass slipper and Prince Charming adoringly sweeps her into his arms and waltzes her away. It's a scene that draws longing sighs from every woman who watches it. Why? Romance! That's what it's all about.

I've often wondered how that intangible sense of true love and romantic devotion makes the leap from celluloid to reality. I know it can happen. I've been around couples married for decades who still glow while sitting side by side, hands lovingly intertwined. Yet, as the child of divorced parents, and a divorcée myself, I also know that the course of true love never runs smooth. In fact, "Rocky Road" might better entitle the majority of marriages I've encountered.

However recently, a friend of mine told me a little

secret—a tale of love that brought tears to my eyes and, I must admit, a little envy to my heart.

Her story wasn't about the latest piece of jewelry that her husband gave her, or flowers he sent as my friend's husband passed away two years ago, just short of their fiftieth wedding anniversary. Now, at the age of seventy, she is alone, but thanks to her loving spouse, not always lonely.

For tucked away in drawers and cabinets throughout my friend's home are love notes scripted by her husband. Terms of endearment that he planted as romantic surprises during the course of their marriage. Over the years, she saved his sweet inscriptions, often leaving them in their original hiding places, his loving sentiments tenderly playing anew with each rediscovery.

Now that he is gone, my friend's life is a daily challenge of loving memories and sad yearning for this romantic man with whom she shared almost half a century of life. Yet in her indomitable way, she is continuing on with determination and enthusiasm. She is healthy and strong and lives each day with an interest in the world around her. She is surrounded by family and friends who support her and a community where she is acknowledged and respected.

Most of all, however, my friend endures with the inner sense that she is loved, truly and totally. Any time she thinks otherwise, all she has to do is open a kitchen drawer, or look in her bedroom nightstand, to find a reminder.

Although somehow I have a feeling that even without looking . . . she already knows.

Christina M. Abt

Beautiful Life—Beautiful Death

"Linda" means beautiful. How did her parents know she would have such a beautiful essence?

Today I started the morning by saying, "Don't worry about me, love," then immediately laughed out loud—with her. How ludicrous to imagine that Linda would not worry about me, the children she left behind, grandchildren she won't know or even unborn millions. For the first time I understood the nature of her worrying. To worry was Linda's way of expressing unconditional love, a love that reaches you and every living creature for now and in the future. If you knew Linda, you have felt it. She could not imagine that people might hurt others, or even lie or steal—it just was not in her being.

We meet many people in life, but few leave footprints on our heart. Linda wore spiritual clodhoppers with a velvet tread. She trampled our hearts in so subtle a way we may not notice the impact for years.

Eighteen months ago, melanoma excised from a small spot on her lower back six years earlier returned to a lymph node. We leveraged every resource at our disposal to get the finest care available, but to no avail. Despite feelings of denial, we began to prepare practically and emotionally for her likely death in the near future. In January 2002, we knew her likely life span was months. Not wasting time on regret, we seized the precious remaining time to savor our love and say good-bye. A week before she died, our children came to say good-bye—one lasting image is my young adult children curled up as if in their "jammies" on either side of Linda, cuddling with her quietly to soak up a lifetime of physical contact.

In the final days she began to slip away at home under hospice guidance. Although not in pain, she could talk only with great effort, and drifted in and out of awareness. Her sister and I sat quietly with her, reminding her of the love she had shared and the fullness of her life contribution. We found her stash of my love poems and letters over thirty years, and I read them all to her. We sat quietly for hours just holding her hand. In the evening we shared the magic of our last fire in the living room fireplace.

Her last day she slept into the afternoon, then moved into a coma of diminished awareness, eyes unfocused and cloudy, but peaceful countenance. Next came the death rattle of gurgled breathing. Alarmed, we called hospice and were told to look at her forehead and face—did she appear to be grimacing, struggling? No, not at all. We continued to calmly soothe her, hold her hands, play peaceful music, read poems, generally give her permission to leave us, as her life work was well done.

In the evening, by force of her ample will, she somehow escaped her death coma momentarily. She turned her head slightly, focused her eyes on me, moved her lips perhaps to say "Good-bye, my love." I kissed her. She returned the kiss. She turned to her sister and shared the same poignant good-bye, then fell back to the coma. The awesome, touching moment will be in my feeling memory forever. A few hours later, assured by a visiting hospice nurse that we had done all we could, we prepared for sleep. I kissed her goodnight and assured her I would be again by her side should she need me. I fell asleep.

Suddenly only minutes later, I awakened fully, glanced at Linda and felt she had gone—her breath had stopped, her lips were pale. I called her sister and we said our final good-byes to honor her remaining aura in the vessel that had carried her awesome life. Peacefully I sat by her side. She is peaceful, held by so many hearts on a quilted cushion of love.

Linda taught me to fully live within the mosaic of all the moments of life—moments that transcend, time, space, here, there; now, then, alive, dead—significant moments richly lived whose many facets define who you are.

Strange concept, beautiful death, but I feel its meaning. I was incredibly lucky to have thirty years as Linda's husband and to be at her side as she died. I am still learning from her. Though her physical presence has passed, my beautiful Linda will guide me for my lifetime.

Bruce Hanna

Prince Charming

At the touch of love everyone becomes a poet.

Plato

When I was a little girl, I used to read about love in all my favorite fairy tales. However, it wasn't until I experienced love myself that I really understood what it meant and how truly remarkable it could make me feel. . . .

We had been friends for a while, and he knew almost everything about me. If I was upset or angry, excited or scared he could always tell and knew exactly what to say to make the moment that much better. Whenever I had a bad day and just needed to cry, he always had a joke to cheer me up and make me smile. When something exciting happened, he'd be there to share in my happy tears and laughter. He knew me for who I was and I loved him just for being my friend.

As I entered my last year of high school, I had yet to find Mr. Perfect. My friends kept telling me that I was looking too hard, and that when I least expected it, Prince Charming would sweep me off my feet. It seemed to me as though everyone around me was finding his or her high school sweetheart, and then there I was, left behind with nobody. Prom was approaching, and everyone's biggest fear was going to his or her high school prom dateless. I knew that I was no exception and realized that I had to start looking again. I went out on dates with countless guys, but none of them seemed right. None of them were what I was looking for.

One night as I lay trying to fall asleep something hit me, which scared me more than anything had before. I loved him. My best friend . . . I loved him. I didn't know what to do, I didn't know what to think or feel or say. My heart was racing as I looked through pictures of us laughing and having fun together. The one person who I had never expected to feel this way about, yet here I was, so sure that I loved him. I cannot even explain the feeling I felt that night. It was if my heart had found its other half. Should I tell him? Should I leave it be? Not knowing if I'd have the courage to give it to him, I grabbed a piece of paper and wrote him a letter that will forever remain in my mind and heart:

Dear Jo,

As the time comes for us to almost graduate, it seems as though the past year has flown by. I knew from the moment we met that we would be forever friends. You have been there for me through the good times and the bad, and you have never let me down. Yet here I am writing to tell you something that I never thought I would. Telling you something that I never thought I could. You know how sometimes we talk about love, and I always tell you that I've never been in love before. That the only love I know is that of which my mother read me when I was a little girl. I was wrong. As I lay in my bed tonight I realize something that until now has been so unclear. You've been my best friend for so long that I was too scared to let myself love you . . . but I do. I do love you. I know it, because you are all I ever think about. Your happiness at times means more to me than my own. My binder is filled with doodles, all of which say your name. I circle your name, because we both know that hearts can break but circles go on forever. I know that I love you, because when I'm upset, the mere thought of you makes me feel a little better. I know that I love you, because when you are with any other girl . . . I'm jealous. I don't know what else to say, but I know that my heart never lies, and it is telling me that each ounce of my being . . . loves you.

Love always and forever
Your best friend,
Casey

The next day at school I slipped my letter into his locker, fearing what would happen. Would I lose the love of my best friend? Or would I gain the love of the person who I had loved for so long? The day seemed never ending. It dragged on for so long that the minutes turned into hours, and the hours into what felt like weeks. As the final bell rang, my heart began to pound. As I approached my locker, I noticed that there was a little piece of paper sticking out through the vent. I ran over, and grabbed the piece of paper. The few words written filled my heart with a love greater than I thought possible:

Dear Casey,

I never thought someone could put into words what I was feeling.

How did you know how much I loved you?

Love always,
Jo

I shoved the note in my pocket, and with a tear in my eye I took a nice long walk home. For the first time in my seventeen years I was overcome with a love that was greater than those found in the fairy tales. It was a love that filled my heart with this indescribable amount of happiness, and for the first time in my life . . . I had my very own Prince Charming.

Michele Davis

The Two-Dollar Bill

I sat there with trembling hands, holding the little tin box and wishing desperately I didn't have to tell my mother its contents. It was winter of 1977, and I had just flown back to Tulsa, Oklahoma, from Tucson, Arizona, where I had buried my dad. At the funeral, a heavyset woman with kind eyes handed me the little box and said, "Your dad wanted your mom to have this." She patted my hand and disappeared in the funeral crowd. As I opened the box, I saw half of a two-dollar bill, worn and crumbled. The stories I had been told as a child came flooding back with tears.

It was May 1939 when my mother and dad eloped. They were very much in love. Dad took his last dollar to buy gas for the borrowed car to drive to the nearby town to get married. He had saved a two-dollar bill for emergencies. He tore it in half, and they each promised to keep their half until "death do us part."

Mother graduated in August from nursing school, and Dad got a job driving a truck. In April 1940, I was born, and then eighteen months later my brother was born. They managed to save enough to rent a house in a poor neighborhood. We were a very happy family.

Then the world was at war. Dad was stationed overseas in the army. Mother went to work as a nurse while we lived with my grandparents. Dad came home in 1946 with a wounded arm, having been away for two years.

Over the years, their marriage began to fall apart. Dad was an alcoholic, and they had difficulties making ends meet. Mother continued her nursing career, supporting the family while Dad went from job to job. The verbal fights became intolerable for my brother and me through our teenage years. There were some good times, but too often I remember the bad ones.

I graduated from college in 1962, and my brother came home from the army. Dad moved from the home to an apartment, but the conflicts about his drinking continued. Then in 1965, he moved to Arizona where his stepmother was living.

I heard from Dad occasionally and knew that he was having lots of medical and emotional problems. Mother always said she didn't care what happened to him, although there was always a look in her eyes that made me believe she really did care. Never in all of those years was anything said by either of them about their half of the two-dollar bill.

But here I stood with a little tin box full of reminders of what was left of my father's life. Among these objects lay a fragile, half piece of faded green money.

As I handed her the box, I searched her face for some emotion. There was none. She opened the box, stared at its contents, then reached in gently and took out the worn bill. Nothing was said about it. As she left the room, she shoved the box back into my hands and simply said, "You can keep the rest of this." The next time I saw the bill was twenty-one years later.

After Mother died, I inherited the treasured cedar chest.

I often found myself rummaging through the quilts and objects left me by my mother and grandmother. One of those treasures was a big, bulky family Bible. One day, as I fumbled through its many pages, there it was—the worn green piece of money. It was placed between the pages and now pressed and uncrumbled.

Several times over the next few years, I would look at the bill and think about all the places it had traveled. Examining it closer, I noticed a few names scrawled and faded. I knew these must have been old army buddies. I wondered what happened to them after the war. I wondered, too, what ever happened to the other half of the bill.

On one occasion as I caressed it lovingly, I saw the names were gone! Suddenly the realization hit me. This wasn't Dad's half of the bill. Was it Mother's? I searched frantically in the Bible for the other bill. There it was!

My fingers shook as I slowly placed the two halves together. All of my senses reeled. I felt as though lightning singed my fingers. While I had assumed I only had the half that Dad had sent to Mother on his deathbed, I had the half that she had kept all of those years too.

Did she place them in different parts of the Bible for a reason? Had she placed them both there for me to find? I stood there trying to understand. Looking at the two-dollar bill, the story I had heard as a child came flooding over me. Words began drifting toward me from somewhere far away.

Now I understood. When they were married, they made a vow to each other. The two-dollar bill was a symbol of their love for each other. Through bad times and good times, that symbol was always with them. For better or worse, richer or poorer, in sickness or in health, and even "until death us do part."

April Felts

My First Kiss

I was nauseous and tingly all over. . . . I was either in love or I had smallpox.

Woody Allen

When I was in the first grade, girls were not only an alien species but (as every little boy knew) were also covered with cooties. So naturally, the boys stayed as far away from them as possible. Imagine, then, our dismay, when on the first day of school our teacher not only lined us up next to the girls but made us hold their hands as we marched to class.

Michael, a loud know-it-all kind of a kid, with big ears and straw-colored hair, declared to everyone in the back of the line that he would probably die as a result of holding his partner's hand. (She didn't much appreciate his prediction.) So I looked at my partner and wondered if I would die. She was a pretty little girl with short blonde hair and big blue eyes. Her name was Frances. And I thought to myself: *This ain't so bad.*

That's when I heard Michael declare: "It's bad enough holding a girl's hand but can you imagine kissing a girl!"

"Ohhh!" one kid moaned.

"Yuck!" another declared.

And a third little boy just stuck his finger in his mouth and mimed gagging.

But then there was Frances, with her rose-colored cheeks and freckled nose, and I said without thinking: "I don't know. Doesn't seem so bad to me." The icy stares that greeted me were the kind that we normally reserved for only the most heinous of transgressions: cheating, ratting on your classmates, or not sharing candy with your best friend.

"You're lying!" Michael declared in disbelief.

"No, I'm not," I replied, proud that I could defy him.

Not knowing what else to say, Michael remained silent. It wasn't until we were in the shadows of the coatroom that Michael and several other little boys challenged me on my claim. "So do it," he said.

"Do what?" I countered, pretending I didn't know what he was talking about.

"Kiss a girl," he pressed.

I hadn't really considered it but I wasn't about to back down now. "What's in it for me?" I asked, knowing that you never did anything for free.

Michael was stumped. What could he offer that was worth kissing a girl? Then a gleam came into his eye and he reached into his back pocket. Drawing out his deck of baseball cards, he held them under my nose. "I'll give you one baseball card for every kiss you give a girl." There were oohs and aahs of appreciation from the spectators. He was talking serious money.

I could feel my resolve starting to crumble. I just might have to kiss a girl. "Who would I have to kiss?" I said, playing for time, knowing that the teacher was bound to come and get us.

Michael looked around the coatroom for a suitable

candidate. Then he saw Frances. "You can kiss Frances," he said with a smile. "You liked holding her hand."

Frances had been standing there with a group of her friends. Like many of our classmates, she had stopped to watch our battle of wills. She turned a deep crimson red at having been selected. But Michael had made a mistake. I had liked holding her hand, and when I considered it, I had no problem with the idea of kissing her. So, like the gallant gentleman my mother always wanted me to be, I stepped up to her, took her hand and asked, "Do you mind?"

Frances shook her head mutely. And I, without so much as a second thought, leaned forward and brushed her lips gently with mine. The girls squealed with delight. The boys howled with dismay. Michael's jaw fell to the floor. And Frances remained speechless.

I held out my hand and Michael paid up with one of his prized baseball cards. Then, to everyone's surprise, I kissed Frances again—and again, and again, and again. By the time the teacher had come looking for us, I had earned fifteen baseball cards and the awe of my classmates.

Frances and I would hold hands in line, for the rest of that school year. I didn't get any more baseball cards from Michael, but it didn't matter. The memory of those first kisses was enough.

Arthur Sánchez

Be Mine

Don't cry because it's over. Smile because it happened.

Author Unknown

Although I have seen the day roll around at least thirty times now, for me there has been only one Valentine's Day worthy of the name. Like most, I have had the usual array of chocolate candies, cute cards and exotic surprises in see-through red thrown my way over the years—and have offered up more than my share of such treasures as well—but for the sheer romantic renown of the day, there has been but one. Fourth grade, Lori Lee. Quite possibly the most charming grade-schooler ever to carry a Josie and the Pussycats lunchbox.

Lori Lee introduced me to Valentine's Day with such grandiloquence that no Valentine's Day since has even come close to measuring up. The day has always approached with such promise and then withered into such disappointment that I grew into that kind of adult who disguises the love holiday as yet another manipulative invention of the groveling-card cartel. And I began to

wonder exactly what might have happened had Lori Lee
not disappeared from my world at the conclusion of our
fourth-grade year.

In this day and age, any man who goes on a search for
a lost love from twenty years ago must immediately be
suspected of several potentially dangerous psychotic disorders. But the failed Valentine's Days were stacking up
like broken limbs behind me, and although I had not once
seen or heard anything of Lori Lee since moving thousands of miles away from her at age nine, the image of her
had never quite left my mind. It was sometime around
last Valentine's Day that the idea got stuck in my head. I
needed to find Lori Lee.

1972. A neighborhood in Southern California that looks
very much like the one where the Brady Bunch lived, only
without Sam the butcher. For two years I have been completely in love with Lori Lee, the angelic creature who
lives across the street. That Lori is the defining love of my
life has been clear to me for some time, but the situation is
complicated by a couple of factors. First, Lori's older
brother, Ted, also happens to be my best friend. Second, I
am a grotesquely bashful child in Lori's radiant presence.
In the company of friends and family I am a sparkling wit,
already a budding journalist and critic of the world. With
Lori, my primary form of communication consists chiefly
of grunts and rudimentary hand gestures.

Although she is always sweet to me, outwardly at least,
Lori's heart does not appear to be pounding to the same
desperate rhythm as my own when we walk home
together from the bus stop each day. These walks become
the highlight of my young life, but never once am I able to
summon the courage of my feelings after school and
invite Lori inside my house for a discreet game of Twister.

The whole thing comes to a head on Valentine's Day.
In class there is the usual ritual. A festive atmosphere

prevails as we kids pass out store-bought valentine cards following that school role from time immemorial: if you bring a valentine for one person, you bring one for everybody. So, we pass out our humdrum cards, and I get a generic "Be Mine" from Lori and the other twenty-six kids in class, and we all get sick eating candy hearts and get to go home early, and that's that. The same as it ever was. Or so I thought.

The walk home from the bus stop with Lori that day seems pretty much like all the ones that have preceded it for the past two years, but when we arrive at the spot where our paths split, Lori stops and says, "I have something for you." I go numb. She pulls an oversize red envelope from her Snoopy and Woodstock school bag, presses it into my hand, and takes off running into her house without a word.

I rush to my bedroom, carefully open the envelope, and find inside the most beautiful handmade card of red construction paper with a big white doily and shiny stars and all sorts of heart stuff attached. On the inside, Lori has spelled out "I love you" in Elmer's glue and then covered the perfect white cursive lettering with glitter. (Even with glue and glitter, an A in penmanship! What a girl!)

Such drama! The perfect expression of sentiment! Can anyone blame me for feeling only disappointment at the feeble Valentine's Days that were to follow! Could any Valentine's Day be anything other than pallid by comparison? The sheer momentum was dizzying, and the pace might even have picked up from there—Lori and I might be married now for all I know—if not for one Godless extenuating factor: my older brother, Mike.

After reading it thirty or forty times I'd hidden the card under a pile of socks in my dresser drawer, but for some reason—which to this day remains unexplained—Mike happened to have his vile paws in my dresser that

evening and, or course, stumbled upon the big, red envelope. Now, my brother wasn't extraordinarily sadistic, but
he was an older brother and, as a sixth-grader, given to
the sport of adolescent cruelty that earns big brothers
such bad reputations. Mike was so amused by my valentine from Lori that he promptly marched the thing across
the street to show Ted, my best friend and Lori's older
brother, and then paraded it with thunderous enthusiasm
all over the neighborhood. Needless to say, a tremendous
commotion ensued, all of which mortified both Lori and
me and pretty much rushed any major developments in
this early love of our lives.

The will of love may be strong, but the taunting of children can be just as intense. Lori and I spent the remainder
of the school year exchanging restrained looks of longing—a few quick words in corners here and there—but it
all came crashing down when my father announced that
our family would soon be moving to, of all places, Alaska.
It seemed a rather severe place to be exiled from the sum-
mery smile of Lori Lee, but there was little I could do.
Scrambling for a way to be near the source of my heart's
flame, I suggested that I might be able to stay behind and
live in an orphanage, and my father didn't sound entirely
unintrigued by the idea. In the end, I was resigned to
leave town with the rest of the family.

On the last day of school, Miss Lockhart organized a
good-bye party for me. She was even thoughtful enough
to have prepared a short lesson on Alaska in my honor—
complete with an SRA reader, *The Last Frontier*—and after
class, all the kids lined up to say good-bye. The whole
time, though, all I could do was stare at Lori, who, for the
first time since Valentine's Day, stared back at me with
her great, liquid eyes.

The final sublime moment came on the school bus,
when, with very deliberate intent, Lori took the seat next

to mine, grasped my hand in hers, and held it the entire way home and then down the street. At my door, I searched furiously for words to describe the terrific bursting in my chest.

"Well," I finally managed, "bye."

"I'm really sorry you're leaving."

"Me, too."

That said, she kissed me on the cheek and once again darted into her house across the street.

Our family moved the next day, and I never saw Lori Lee again.

It had crossed my mind more than once that a search for a fourth-grade sweetheart is not something that indicates an entirely level mind. Times being what they are, men on such quests might be referred to by courts of law as "stalkers," or worse. But where there had once been romance, I had faith that some shred of feeling remained, and if I had wondered all these years what had become of Lori, she too, must have wondered at least a little what had become of me. I was determined to find Lori, travel to wherever it was the winds of fate had taken her, and then. . . . Well, who knows what then? Trust nature to do its work.

The search began promisingly with a tip from some old friends that the Lee family had possibly relocated to Hawaii. An expensive trip, to be sure, but if I was to go through with the promise to myself to see Lori, what better location? It looked good when I found, through a friend's computer phone directory and credit-reference database, no fewer than four Lori Lees in Hawaii who were approximately my age. Alas, upon calling, none turned out to be my Lori—although one sympathetic Lori offered to be—and it was back to the drawing board. Phone calls to the old school and past acquaintances turned up nothing. Even three weeks working with a private investigator drew only blanks.

With hope dwindling, a lawyer named Lee in Sacramento—himself the result of a dead-end lead—suggested a Tempe, Arizona-based company called Finders, Ltd., which specializes in locating hard-to-find individuals. Almost miraculously, operating only on the sparse information I could provide, Finders was able to track Lori within an hour of my call, and, quite unexpectedly, I suddenly found myself in my living room holding a scrap of paper with Lori Lee's San Francisco-area address and phone number written on it. Moments before, twenty years had stood between Lori and me, now only eleven digits on a telephone separated us, and I was faced with an emotion I hadn't anticipated: panic.

It occurred to me that until this instant Lori had been at least half based on whimsical fantasy, but the phone number and address were frighteningly real pieces of information. Did I really want to do this? Had I really ever known this person in the first place? Was it worth risking the desecration of one of my most sacrosanct childhood memories for what might turn into a very strange and disappointing experience?

"No sense in going all the way to the ocean and not jumping in," an uncle once said to me, even though his ocean was the North Atlantic and it was freezing cold and I didn't really want to go in, even if it had taken us five hours in the car to get there. But I did get into the water every time we went, and that is what I remembered from one childhood memory as I stood on the precipice of another. It would be stupid to finally get this close to Lori and then stand on the beach gazing out at the blank horizon, forever wondering. Even so, I chickened out on the phone call, deciding it might be less of a shock for Lori to receive a letter. Also, it was easier for me.

"Dear Lori," the letter began. "I hope you haven't forgotten me . . ." An entire afternoon was spent on that letter, writing about what had happened in my life and how for a long time I'd regretted moving away in fourth grade and how, even though I realized we were both grown up now and had lives of our own, it might be fun to get together. "If this whole thing doesn't sound too bizarre to you," I finished up, "I hope you will call or write and let me know what you think."

I expressed the letter overnight. The phone rang the next evening.

"Of course I remember," the voice began as soon as I answered.

"Lori?"

"You had a dog named Walter."

"Yeah."

"You wore an Oakland Raiders jacket to school every day, even when it was too warm for a jacket."

"Yeah."

"You slugged a kid at the bus stop for making fun of me when I had the chicken pox."

"Lori."

"Hey, stranger."

For the next hour we talked. A little tension, but nothing too weird. A few uncomfortable silences and the voice was a little different, but Lori Lee was as charming as ever. She told me about her brother, Ted, and I told her about my brother Mike, and we laughed about what a couple of jerks they were to us. Somewhere in the conversation she got around to her job and her husband and her two sons, the oldest starting school this year. My life seems to have followed more of an undefined random circle than your productive linear path, I told her; but I reviewed the high parts and she seemed genuinely interested. With only a hint of skepticism, she agreed to meet me at my favorite Italian restaurant in San Francisco the following week.

For two hours after hanging up the phone, I was

stricken with paralysis and only able to stare blankly out
the window.

"You are Mr. Thompson?" This is the waiter asking me
as soon as I arrive at the restaurant. I nod. "A message
from Lori. With regret she will be one hour late." I buck up
and take the news pretty well, all things considered. In
fact, Lori's tardiness comes as something of a reprieve. My
stomach has been knotted all day, and it might be a good
idea to have a few moments to collect myself. I order ver-
mouth, rocks, twist of lemon, thinking this will calm me.
Instead it makes me wonder if an hour alone in a crowded
restaurant is probably more time than one needs to collect
himself. Two drinks later I'm convinced that an hour here
will surely do me more harm than good. Every damn eye
in the place has already identified me as some wounded
piece of meat who is obviously being stood up. I don't like
this at all. Would they be good enough to hold the table
while I go out for some air? Certainly, sir. (God, I love this
restaurant. Viva, it's called, and for the romantic reader,
worth checking into.)

Out on the street, I walk a few laps around the block
with still half an hour to kill and my mind inventing a
hundred possible explanations for Lori's delay: City traffic
is murder. She had to work late. Cold feet. Couldn't find a
sitter for the kids. A huge row with her husband, some
insane rage-a-holic with a purple vein that bulges from his
forehead when he's angry, who has vowed to crush my
spleen while she wails at him with high-pitched ululations
of protest and the neighbors call the cops. Though my
romantic experiences have not always been pleasant, they
have usually been educational and I have come to accept
the fact that it is a woman's prerogative to be as late as she
pleases in situations such as these.

But this isn't the way it was supposed to work out
with Lori. At once I am overtaken with a great epiphany; I

cannot go through with this. I don't need to satisfy my curiosity about what she looks like now, what she acts like now, or what might have been. Suddenly my mind is clear. I've known all along what I needed to know about Lori Lee.

The trouble is, you see, that while one can always maintain realistic expectations of the world, the fact remains that nobody really wants to be faced with living proof that their grade-school love has somehow gotten away, grown up, gotten married and had twin kids. Nobody wants to find that twenty years have muddled whatever connections there once might have been, not made it more heroic. That the phone calls can be tainted by those dreaded moments of naked silence. Those may be the things that life is all about, but they are not what fourth-grade love affairs are about. And they are surely not what Valentine's Day is about.

Not far from the restaurant I find a stationery store still open for business late in the day and buy about $15 worth of paper, pens, envelopes, glue and glitter. Sitting on a stoop outside, I write a brief note to Lori apologizing for not keeping our date, and at the end I finally write something that satisfies the thing in me that has wanted to speak for all these years.

> *Lori,*
>
> *I'm sure we would have had a wonderful time tonight, but all I really wanted to do this whole time was just finally say thanks for the valentine card you gave me a long time ago. It may now feel like a small gesture to you, but those are the types of gifts that seem to sum up everything that is good in the world, and I will never forget you for it.*
>
> *Yours, Chuck*

After carefully folding the letter, I spell out Lori's name in Elmer's glue across the front of the big, red envelope, sprinkle gold glitter over it, and wait for it to dry. Back at the restaurant, I seal the envelope with the most innocent look I can manage, place the card on our vacant table, and walk quietly out the door as a single girl with familiar-looking eyes walks in. I feel sad that the world is no longer the simple place it once was, but satisfied just the same that some things, even if remaining forever just beyond reach, never really change at all.

Chuck Thompson

CLOSE TO HOME JOHN McPHERSON

Vern was starting to sense that
Sheila's interest in him was fading.

Angel on the Beach

If you want to know how much I love and care for you, count the waves.

Kenneth Koh

"Thank you."

"I appreciate all you have done."

"It was kind of you to come."

The same words over and over again. None of them would bring Tom back, nor would any of the flowers, charitable gestures, cards or notes. He was dead—dead! My best friend, lover, husband would no longer come through the door, cook his specialties, leave his socks on the floor or hold me with a warmth I had never known before.

Tom suffered a terrible end. No dignity, just pain—endless pain. The cancer had ravaged his body so he was no longer the person I knew physically. However, his aura, his being never changed and his bravery amazed me every day. We had the life together people hear about but never really believe exists outside of the movies or books. "Twenty-six years and holding—and not letting go!" Tom would say and then hug me. "Not sure I'm going to keep her, I may want a younger version soon."

My reply was an automatic, "And what would you do with a younger version, my dear?" Our routine amused our friends and family but it also confirmed our commitment to each other. A commitment based on love, trust and true friendship.

Tom and I were confirmed "singles" prior to our meeting. He was forty and I was thirty-two when we met— neither one interested in a relationship. "Too old for that nonsense," we said. Friends decided we would be the perfect match for companionship since our interests were similar and included fine dining, classical music and the theater. We both had successful careers and no interest in a relationship. Absolutely no interest in a relationship.

Our first meeting was not at all what we expected or wanted. It was not love-at-first-sight but it was certainly something-at-first-sight. We were very attracted to each other, but since we were sophisticated New Yorkers, we tried to be "cool" about the attraction. It did not work. We talked only to each other and totally ignored everyone at the party. We left at the first possible moment and were married three months to the day we met.

Friends and family were sure we had both lost our minds and that the marriage would not last as long as the courtship. We knew better. Tom and I had found our missing parts. We complemented each other in every possible way. We enjoyed the same things, but each one brought something new to the relationship. We reveled in our sameness but respected our differences. We loved to be together but loved being alone. We were friends.

Our careers were demanding but fulfilling for both of us. However, our careers never took control of our lives and we always had time for each other. We traveled, kept an active social life, and surrounded ourselves with family and friends. We had not been blessed with children, but we accepted that fact easily, for our lives were full and happy.

The change came when we were preparing for one of our trips. "Tom, please pack your suitcases today or at least lay out your clothes and I'll pack for you," I shouted up the stairs. "Tom, Tom, do you hear me?" He quietly replied, "Hon, I don't feel well, please come up here." That was the beginning.

A feeling of great fatigue came over Tom, very unusual for a man who was never tired. We went to the doctor (doctors, really), had countless tests, and then the diagnosis. "They are wrong. Doctors make mistakes. We'll go to other medical centers, other doctors, anywhere, this is not correct!" But it was.

We were soon totally consumed by the disease. Every waking moment was turned over to doctor visits, hospitals, chemo, radiation and medication. It was all we talked about and all we read about. New and innovative treatments. Holistic approaches. Traditional medicine. Surgery. Everything was tried and nothing helped. Tom was leaving me. Every day he got weaker, unable to hold on, and then he was hospitalized for the last time.

As we entered the hospital room, a volunteer followed with magazines, books, toiletries and a gift. "The gift of hope," she said, "for no matter what happens, you must have hope." She placed a tiny angel pin on Tom's hospital gown and it stayed with him the entire five days he was in the hospital. On the fifth day, the doctors asked if he would like to go home "to rest more comfortably," but we both knew the end was near. We decided to go to our beach house since it was a place we both loved dearly.

We entered the beach house together and spent the next two weeks holding on to whatever we could. Friends and family visited for short periods to not tire him. I did not leave his side and, with the help of an aide, was able to care for his needs. I read to him, I talked to him, I loved him for as much time as we had left together. And then he was gone—one year from the diagnosis.

I took early retirement from my job and stayed at the beach house. It was where we loved to be and where he had spent his last days. I needed to keep his memory alive. I wanted nothing to do with anyone because they took my thoughts away from Tom, and I could not have that!

I kept his clothes near me because they smelled like him. I wore his favorite sweater because it felt like him. I read our favorite books and listened to our favorite music over and over. It was the only way to hold him close. Our favorite time to walk the beach was at dusk—just before the sunset. That became my ritual.

Time went on and the first anniversary of his death arrived. I truly believed I had no life without Tom. Absolutely no reason to go on without him. Friends intervened, family called, visited, nothing helped. I needed Tom to tell me what to do. I needed him to answer me when I spoke to him. I needed a sign.

With the help of friends, I agreed to clear out Tom's closet, bureau, desk and bookcases. However, after hours of sorting, I could not find the angel pin that Tom had close to him at the end. Where was it? Was it still in the house, or had it been thrown out in the confusion of his last hours? I wanted the angel pin because it had been a part of Tom's last hours, and it represented hope to me. Hope for the future, if I really had one.

With the cleaning out of Tom's belongings, I decided to return to our apartment in town and close the beach house until the summer. It was close to dusk and I decided to take a walk on the beach. My walk was brisk and invigorating, and I felt refreshed. As the sun set, it sent a glow over the ocean and a bright reflection on the sand. I bent over, picked up a shiny object and, in disbelief, cradled it in my hand. It was the angel pin that had been lost since Tom had died.

An omen? A message from beyond? The sign I had been asking for? I did not know. All I did know was that I felt a calm I had not felt for years and, suddenly, I knew everything would be all right.

Helen Xenakis

6

LESSONS IN LOVE

*The good, the bad, hardship, joy, tragedy,
love and happiness are all interwoven into
one indescribable whole that one calls life.
You cannot separate the good from the bad,
and perhaps there is no need to do so.*

Jacqueline Bouvier Kennedy Onassis

Visions of Art

I never knew how to worship until I knew how to love.

Henry Ward Beecher

One afternoon I toured an art museum while waiting for my husband to finish a business meeting. I was looking forward to a quiet view of the masterpieces.

A young couple viewing the paintings ahead of me chattered nonstop between themselves. I watched them a moment and decided she was doing all the talking. I admired his patience for putting up with her constant parade of words. Distracted by their noise, I moved on.

I encountered them several times as I moved through the various rooms of art. Each time I heard her constant gush of words, I moved away quickly.

I was standing at the counter of the museum gift shop making a purchase when the couple approached the exit. Before they left, the man reached into his pocket and pulled out a white object. He extended it into a long cane and then tapped his way into the coatroom to get his wife's jacket.

"He's a brave man," the clerk at the counter said. "Most of us would give up if we were blinded at such a young age. During his recovery, he made a vow his life wouldn't change. So, as before, he and his wife come in whenever there's a new art show."

"But what does he get out of the art?" I asked. "He can't see."

"Can't see! You're wrong. He sees a lot. More than you or I do, the clerk said. "His wife describes each painting so he can see it in his head."

I learned something about patience, courage and love that day. I saw the patience of a young wife describing paintings to a person without sight and the courage of a husband who would not allow blindness to alter his life. And I saw the love shared by two people as I watched this couple walk away with their arms intertwined.

Jeanne Knape

A Different Kind of "Trashy Secret"

Let your love be stronger than your hate or anger. Learn the wisdom of compromise, for it is better to bend a little than to break.

H. G. Wells

It was one of those stupid fights a couple has after five years of mostly blissful marriage. I had just come home from another long day at work. Of course, as we were a modern married couple, my wife had only arrived home a couple of minutes before me, after HER long day at work.

"Hey, babe," I said cheerily, dropping my keys and wallet off on the wicker table in the foyer.

"Don't you 'hey, babe' me," she grunted over a load of laundry she'd just started.

Puzzled, I looked at her for a minute, just before the fireworks started, it turns out. She was still in her fashionable work outfit, tailored slacks, silk blouse, crested blazer. Her hair was pulled back and stray wisps from the long day spilled over her beautiful face. Even after five years, catching her in moments like this one still took my breath away. If she only knew how—

"Don't you stand there in front of me with that 'innocent dreamer' look of yours, either," she said, advancing on me with a handful of colorful plastic. "Would you mind explaining . . . these?" she finished with a flourish, opening her clenched fist to reveal several candy bar wrappers, no doubt left behind in the load of my khaki work pants she was slipping into the washing machine.

I smiled for a minute, hoping my still-boyish charm might soften her concern.

"That's it?" she asked instead, slamming the candy wrappers down next to my wallet and keys. "You're just going to stand there and smile while your arteries clog by the minute?"

The upscale publishing company I worked for had recently offered blood tests to all of its employees. When my results came in, my wife and I were both surprised to see my cholesterol levels so high. Since then, she'd been urging me to eat better.

Snickers and Baby Ruths were definitely not on her list.

"Fine," she spat, deserting her load of laundry and grabbing her purse and keys off the wicker table instead. "If you don't want to be around to enjoy our twilight years together, then I don't know why you ever married me in the first place."

Embarrassment at getting caught, frustration from a long day at work and the "mother hen" tones of her afternoon "scolding" suddenly combined to raise the hackles on my neck.

"Me either," I spat pettily, just before she slammed the door in my face.

Minutes later, of course, I felt the first twinge of post-flare-up guilt and quickly finished her load of laundry and began tidying up the house to make myself feel better.

Noticing a bulging trash bag in the middle of the kitchen floor, I caught my wife's not-so-subtle hint and headed out the front door for the quick trek to the apartment complex Dumpster.

On the way past the deserted tennis courts, a faulty seam in the dollar-store trash bag stretched to its limit and split right in two. Cursing myself for making such a cheap purchase, I began stuffing the scattered coffee grounds and banana peels back into the remaining half of the bag.

I stopped when I noticed the glaring labels of products we'd never bought before and that looked completely unfamiliar. Fat-free cheese slice wrappers hastily rewrapped around regular, oily slices of cheese. Low-fat sour cream containers still mostly full. Healthy Choice cereal boxes full of regular raisin bran and Apple Jacks. A coffee can claiming it contained "Half the caffeine of regular brands" still full of rich-smelling, regular coffee. "Lite" lunchmeat and dessert wrappers. Low-fat potato chip bags in which the chips had been replaced by regular, greasy Ruffles!

No wonder things had been tasting differently lately! She'd been switching healthy products out with my usual, fattening ones! But when did she find the time? In between our hectic schedules and long workdays, I could only imagine her getting up half an hour early each morning and stealthily replacing my usual chocolate chip cookies with dietetic ones by moonlight. The socks on her always-cold feet padding around the darkened kitchen floor while I slept two rooms away snoring peacefully, none the wiser.

Maybe she really did want me around for the rest of her life, after all.

Gathering up the devious garbage, I made two trips and dumped all of her "evidence." Then I washed my hands, grabbed my wallet and keys, and drove to the one place I knew I'd find her: the deserted movie theater near our apartment complex.

Once a week she called from her office and asked if I wanted to see a twilight movie with her after work. And once a week I declined, claiming some fictional last-minute meeting or looming deadline. The fact was I liked my movies at night, where crowds swelled, laughter roared, popcorn flowed and everyone had a good time.

Twilight shows were for little kids and old folks. Not to mention one lonely wife who was quietly begging her husband for a little weekday romance . . .

I parked next to her car in the empty parking lot and bought a ticket to the first chick-flick I saw. Out of habit, I headed straight for the concession stand.

Balancing a diet soda, licorice and a huge bag of popcorn, I found her in the third theater I tried, watching exactly the kind of blaring action-adventure movie she never let me rent in the video store!

Creeping up behind her, I sat down with a flourish. She looked startled to see me, but not just because I'd snuck up on her.

"What are you doing here?" she smiled, our fight quickly forgotten. "You never come to the movies with me after work."

"I missed you," I said honestly, not telling her about the garbage bag discovery. "I'm sorry I blew up at you. . . . I'm just—"

"We're both tired," she finished for me, reading my mind. "And you shouldn't be such a sneak and . . . I shouldn't be such a nag."

I held her face in my hands in that darkened theater and told her, "No . . . you should."

She smiled warmly until she saw the bag of popcorn resting gently on my armrest. "Honey," I explained, "I didn't get any butter on it. And look, it says these Twizzlers are 'low fat.'"

She looked surprised, if not exactly happy. "Well," she

grunted, holding my hand as yet another car chase played out across the giant screen in front of us, "that's a start, I guess."

Not really, I said to myself, still amazed at how much effort she'd made to keep me healthy and how much she loved me. It was more like a new beginning.

Rusty Fischer

Love or Infatuation?

Infatuation is instant desire. It is one set of glands calling to another. Love is friendship that has caught fire. It takes root and grows—one day at a time.

Infatuation is marked by a feeling of insecurity.

You are excited and eager but not genuinely happy. There are nagging doubts, unanswered questions, little bits and pieces about your beloved that you would just as soon not examine too closely. It might spoil the dream.

Love is quiet understanding and the mature acceptance of imperfection. It is real. It gives you strength and grows beyond you—to bolster your beloved. You are warmed by his presence, even when he is away. Miles do not separate you. You want him nearer. But near or far, you know he is yours and you can wait.

Infatuation says, "We must get married right away. I can't risk losing him."

Love says, "Be patient. Don't panic. Plan your future with confidence."

Infatuation has an element of sexual excitement. If you are honest, you will admit it is difficult to be in one another's company unless you are sure it will end in intimacy. Love is the maturation of friendship. You must be friends before you can be lovers.

Infatuation lacks confidence. When he's away, you wonder if he's cheating. Sometimes you check.

Love means trust. You are calm, secure and unthreatened. He feels that trust, and it makes him even more trustworthy.

Infatuation might lead you to do things you'll regret later, but love never will.

Love is an upper. It makes you look up. It makes you think up. It makes you a better person than you were before.

Ann Landers

Overlook It

Sheila and I just celebrated our thirtieth wedding anniversary. Somebody asked her, what was our secret? She answered, "On my wedding day, I decided to make a list of ten of Tim's faults which, for the sake of our marriage, I would always overlook. I figured I could live with at least ten!"

When she was asked which faults she had listed, Sheila replied, "I never did get around to listing them. Instead, every time he does something that makes me mad, I simply say to myself, 'Lucky for him, it's one of the ten!'"

Tim Hudson

"Okay, I'm ready for our bridge game, Blanche."

The One Who Got Away

*The greatest happiness of life is the conviction
that we are loved—loved for ourselves, or rather,
loved in spite of ourselves.*

Victor Hugo

I think every woman has one—that ex-beau who
niggles his way back to consciousness after a family fight,
a bout of stretching the weekly paycheck or even after the
oaf you really married leaves his dirty socks smack in the
middle of the living room floor.

You know the guy I'm talking about. And who cares if
you can list fifteen reasons that you're glad you didn't
marry him?

So what if he talked too much—or was too shy, too arro-
gant, too possessive? So what if he gambled and his relatives borrowed money? This man would never do a strip
tease on the rug and he'd have too much couth to yell if
you forgot his mother's birthday or spent ten bucks over
budget on bedroom drapes. Best of all, he would understand and cherish your finer emotions.

Even knowing you really wouldn't want him doesn't

make the man less desirable in times of marital stress. Believe me. Like the fish that got away, the guy I almost married has had moments of near perfection.

The only problem with my romantic past is that, after twenty years, I was fated to meet "him" again at a wedding.

I knew he'd be coming, and let me tell you, there's nothing like knowing you'll meet an old boyfriend to make you feel young again. Or regress to adolescence.

After buying two dresses, both of which looked ugly, I had a row with my husband over the expense. I got a perm—row number two—at which point, my hair frizzed and looked terrible. I hadn't been vain enough to wear a girdle for fifteen years, and the one I found in the attic was two sizes too small. Talk about depression!

More than anything, I was positive I would (a) break out in zits, (b) catch a red-nosed cold or (c) come down with the plague the morning of the big event.

Unfortunately, no disaster occurred and, tightly girdled, I tottered off on heels I usually have sense enough not to wear. I also wore enough makeup to have supplied Detroit.

The makeup might have caused row number three had I been listening to my husband on the way to the church. I was too busy worrying about the wrinkles that even creams couldn't hide. What if my dream man didn't recognize, after all, what really were laugh lines in disguise?

The amount of time I'd "hogged the bathroom" (that much of my husband's complaints got through) made us late and the church was packed. Craning my neck and missing half the ceremony, I couldn't spot my old flame. Tension grew until finally, at the reception, there he was!

He was blue-veined, pudgy, short. So short that he never met my eyes when we talked. He was too busy trying to hide the thin spots of hair—not quite as robustly auburn as I recalled—by tilting his head back and staring at some illusive spot six inches above me.

The man—my ideal!—was prudish, opinionated, a bigot. The sort of yo-yo who'd not only shed socks in the living room, but wear two pairs a day so he could shed them in the kitchen, too. How could I have imagined he would understand me?

I walked away from that reception deeply thankful to be married to a fine, tall man who had hair and lacked racial opinions. By the time my husband and I arrived home, I'd forgotten all about my dream man. And as I shed the girdle and sluiced the makeup from my face, I vowed to tell my real man much more often how much I appreciated him, flaws and all!

Margaret Shauers

"Giving" . . . The Unforgettable Gift

*F*or *a crowd is not company; and faces are but
a gallery of pictures; and talk but a tinkling
cymbal, where there is no love.*

Francis Bacon

We were college students when my husband and I first
noticed each other in church in San Jose, California. I sang
in the choir, and Bob played his trumpet in the orchestra.
Mine was not the most outstanding voice in the choir,
contrary to the sounds that came from his most cherished
horn, which I later learned he had been playing since the
fifth grade.

Our college Sunday-school class retreat was held in
Yosemite National Park that year. This is where we
shared our first moments together amidst the casual
atmosphere and comfortable laughter of close friends.
The exchange of a few glances along with some light ban-
tering ignited an eternal flame of devotion.

This occurred almost thirty-five years ago. Bob was a
young lieutenant in the midst of a transition from the
California National Guard into the regular army. That

meant he would be forced into temporarily relinquishing the pursuit of his college degree in order to attend helicopter flight training as a medical evacuation pilot. Concurrently, his job—building saunas for a California-based manufacturer in San Jose—was phased out while he awaited orders that would provide the path toward our future.

During this overlapping of obligations, we were engaged to be married in March 1969. Despite the forthcoming orders and lack of a job, Bob surprised me with a sparkling, one-carat diamond engagement ring, which I assumed took most if not all of his life savings. At Christmastime, I was also shocked to receive a beautiful suede coat with a genuine mink collar. Needless to say, these lavish gifts were wonderful, but I was more enraptured by the thoughtful personality of this officer and gentleman who had stolen my heart.

Soon after our marriage, Bob served a year in Vietnam. Then we were off to his next assignment in West Germany where our only child was born.

Life couldn't be sweeter, and I have such a wonderful husband, I thought as I counted my blessings on the way home from church one Sunday evening near Landstuhl. Quietly reminiscing in the car over earlier days, I in the choir and Bob in orchestra, it suddenly occurred to me that during all of our moving I had not seen Bob's trumpet among our household goods.

"Bob, where is your trumpet?" I asked. There was silence. "Bob, your trumpet. Where is it?" If it hadn't been in our household goods when they were unpacked in Germany, where could it be?

Sheepishly he answered me with a question, "Do you remember that suede coat I gave you the Christmas before I left for flight school?"

"Yes."

"Well, I hocked my trumpet to get you that coat."

I couldn't believe it. Tears coursed down my cheeks as we continued our drive home. I was humbled by this revelation. My thoughts resumed the counting of my blessings. One of the greatest I had received was Bob's giving of a gift from the heart. The coat had disappeared into never-never land; however, I will *never* forget the unspoken love that was given through this precious, selfless and silent "giving" of this unforgettable gift.

Phyllis A. Robeson

A Romantic Hammer

During the story that follows, you will gain insight into an especially romantic evening amidst a very difficult financial time in my life. My husband, our two children and I lived on a very tight, shoestring budget for a number of years. We were in the ministry and our little church could barely afford to pay us as their pastor and family. But out of lack come great things from the heart, things that make memories, things that mold character, things that make strong marriages, things that will never be forgotten. And from this, I tell my story. . . .

As I walked into the room that had earlier been off limits to me, I could see that careful preparation had taken place to assure that our wedding anniversary celebration would be a wonderful surprise. Most of the day had been spent carefully following my husband's instructions to spend the afternoon outdoors, which in itself made me suspicious. For several months, I had become totally absorbed with juggling our financial situation—so much so that the word "surprise" wasn't even in my vocabulary. I certainly was not prepared for what I was about to receive. My husband knew that we didn't have the extra finances for an evening out, so instead he and our two children worked together to create the most romantic anniversary evening right in our very own home.

Standing directly in front of our dining room entrance was my husband who said with a smile, "The evening awaits you, my lady." My face blushed like a new bride anticipating what was to happen next. My eyes were immediately drawn to the table, which was beautifully covered with a fine linen cloth and my best china dishes. Napkins were neatly folded by each plate, but above one of the plates were several packages wrapped in brown paper. A single source of light came from the center of the table, where a rather large candle was burning. Balloons of varied shapes and sizes danced along the ceiling as if in accompaniment to the beat of the soft music playing in the background. My daughter emerged from the kitchen proudly carrying the cake she had just baked for the celebration while my son stood tall with a strong posture as he wore a white linen towel draped carefully over his arm, as to take on the position of maître d' for the evening. My husband was dutifully orchestrating all the last-minute details before he pulled out the chair for me as guest of honor at the head of the table. It was obvious that each member knew their assigned duties and had rehearsed them several times for this occasion.

Only a queen could feel this regal, I thought. Glancing at my husband throughout the evening, I could sense romantic overtones to his smile and the way in which he addressed me to the children. This was life at its finest, and I was savoring every moment of it when my son said, "Come on, Mom, it's time to open your presents!" I could see in their eyes that this was the moment, the unveiling if you will, the frosting on the evening. So I proceeded to unwrap the first gift. It was from my daughter. She had given me a book of coupons on which were written different chores that she would do for me as I had need of them. The second gift was from my son. It was his treasured silver dollar.

Then there was the last gift. It was from my husband. Anticipation loomed across their faces like you would see seconds before a touchdown. At this point, I felt like part of the winning team, and that this box contained a special something just for me. And as I removed the last piece of wrapping paper and opened the tightly closed box, there was a still silence, and then, there it was!

"A hammer?" As they were cheering, I was gasping as I tried to hide my bewildered expression. Was this a joke? Had I missed something? Not knowing what else to do, I gave my husband a quick kiss, hoping this diversion would eliminate any detection of ungratefulness on my part. Gathering my composure, I said to my husband, "How did you know that I wanted my own hammer?" All the time, my son was saying, "Gee, Mom, this is great!"

Sometimes, we cover our disappointments with gratitude, especially when our spouse has that special sparkle in his eyes that speaks loudly of the pride he feels after having purchased the perfect gift. How could I be anything but happy for all they had done for me? But the romance was fading fast! How could I be ungrateful when in all reality we had very little money for anything extra? Yet I had secretly hoped for a bottle of perfume or a renewal on my favorite magazine subscription. Had I forgotten to convey that to my husband over the course of the week before our anniversary? A hammer? What was he thinking? Next it'll be a tool belt or staple gun. Doesn't he know that a woman savors the romantic things, especially on her wedding anniversary? And here I was at forty, already feeling my esteem fading with the discovery of new facial wrinkles, graying hair and a thicker waist. I tried to keep in mind that it was the thought that counts, but every time I envisioned that hammer, my heart sank even deeper. How could our thinking be so far apart? My resolve would be to simply misplace the hammer, perhaps in a box under my bed, and never let on of my disappointment.

But there is a moral to the story. . . . My husband was much more discerning than I ever gave him credit for being. I have always been a decorating bug, always changing and rearranging the furnishings in our home. Since then, I have realized that his hammer was a gift that spoke volumes to me of the confidence my husband had placed in me and my abilities to transform the interior of our simple little home into a place of beauty. The hammer was like receiving his stamp of approval. Today I can see the purpose in the gift in a far greater way than I did the day I received it. And I am impressed with the fact that my husband knew me better than I knew myself.

As I look back on that situation, I can laugh and even tell you the story. I've also learned an important lesson about prejudging a gift. What I would have chosen for myself at the time would not have benefited me half as much as this gift has. And you know what else? Every time I have used this handy tool throughout the years, I have thought of my husband and the romantic anniversary evening he so lovingly planned for me. It generates a continuous romantic feeling each and every time. So it really was a romantic hammer after all.

Catherine Walker

CLOSE TO HOME

"Children or non-children?"

Three Kisses

During our marriage, my wife and I have always exchanged not just one kiss, but three kisses when we departed company. It has brought snickers and chuckles from others, usually our daughters. What is the significance of the three kisses?

The three kisses are not to say good-bye, but are a reminder of the completeness and meaning of our marriage union.

The first kiss is Heart, an expression of how our hearts are joined in mutual love and understanding.

The second is Mind. Our minds are of one accord in thought, and we have, through many trials and tribulations, brought those thoughts together into an expression of our love. We do not agree at times on some issues, but when it comes to the meaningful and important ones, we are of one mind and decision.

The third is Soul, an expression of how our souls are in a harmony that will be everlasting. We have gained this harmony over the years through working hard on our relationship.

I can endure the snickering and the chuckles, because I know and feel the true meaning of our three kisses.

Knowing my wife feels the same way gives me peace and makes me love her even more.

Thomas Webber
Submitted by Sandra Webber

My Dad's Story

My father and I were sitting next to the fire, drinking hot cocoa on a late night in December. I said, "Dad, tell me a story."

Even though I'm forty years old with a family of my own, I become a six-year-old asking his dad for a bedtime story when we are alone. He says, "Well, let me think a moment." My dad had the look of someone trying to recall the past, with his index finger pointing to his chin.

Finally, he started. "A long time ago, when I was in high school, there was a girl named Jennifer in my graduating class. She was one of three Asians in the entire school. She was tall, lean and had a smile that had a lasting impression. You know the feeling at the exact moment when your heart skips a beat?"

At that moment, I thought of when I met my wife for the first time. She smiled and my heart melted to the floor. And I knew that was the smile I wanted to see for the rest of my life when I asked her to marry me. So I gave my father a small nod with a smile.

He continued, "I had four classes with her my senior year. I fell in love with her smile but also with all of her being. The scent of her perfume, the way her hair moved when the wind blew and her heart of kindness. One day, Jennifer confessed her love for me in a letter. I was in shock and happy all at once. Unfortunately, my happiness did not last long. My friends got ahold of the letter. They said we could never be, for we were complete opposites. I felt that they had my best interest at heart so I covered my feelings for her. I got my schedule changed, and I made a new route to all of my classes. I didn't give her an explanation, but I disappeared from her life.

"From graduation to my junior year in college, I thought of Jennifer—the scent of her perfume and the way her hair moved in the wind. I bumped into some of her friends at a local café. I think their names were Emily and Stephanie. Anyway, they told me how I had broken Jennifer's heart without an explanation. She decided to go to college in Washington because of me. That's when I realized how much of a jerk I was. I thought of my friends and how I hadn't seen them since graduation. I knew what I had to do."

My mom was leaning on the doorway when my dad finished the story. The beautiful Asian girl my dad had fallen in love with had changed with time, but she came into the living room, kissed my dad on the cheek and smiled her beautiful smile.

Chin Pak

Goodnight, Sweetheart

Some people believe in love at first sight. I can't say that I do. However, I can say that I believe a single moment can teach you more about it than you could ever imagine. I was lucky enough to experience one of those moments on the night of November 23, 2001.

On that night, my husband and I had only been married seventeen months. During our brief courtship and the year and a half following our marriage, I had gradually worked toward developing a sense of history and understanding of his family. His father, whom I refer to as Mr. Ralph, was hard to know. This was mostly due to his failing health. He had suffered numerous heart problems and strokes that affected his speech and memory.

Every now and then, Mr. Ralph would feel good and begin telling me stories of when he was young. He loved to tell me about when he drove fruit trucks from Durham, North Carolina, all the way to Baltimore, Maryland. I believe he thought it was ironic that he had probably passed by my father who had worked at Bethlehem Steel during those years. Other stories he liked to tell revolved around the pride he had for his family, the significance of being born on the Averasboro Battleground, and the fine privilege of growing up in Falcon, North Carolina, where God and country were at the center of life. Everything else I knew of him, I learned from his wife and children.

My husband's mother, Mrs. Janice, also took some time to know. She was an excellent listener and was always very supportive and encouraging, but she didn't talk much about herself. Most of her time was spent caring for Mr. Ralph when he was sick and trying to help him relish the good times when he was feeling better. I knew all the heart attacks and strokes had significantly affected his personality. He had been a very vibrant, intelligent, opinionated man, and still could be from time to time. But, usually he was more like a child. That never seemed to matter to my mother-in-law. She still took him most everywhere she went, whether to church, the beauty parlor or their daily trip to Bojangles. When they were home, she sat beside him on the couch, held his hand and filled in all the missing words he couldn't find.

In November, Mr. Ralph's health began to deteriorate very quickly. He had congestive heart failure and was in the hospital for a week. During all that time, my mother-in-law got very little sleep. She never left his side for more than a few minutes at a time. Her presence brought him comfort and freedom from anxiety, and she was not willing to deprive him of that, regardless of how tired or uncomfortable she became.

When he came back home, the doctor said his heart was functioning at about 30 percent. We all knew that we could lose him at any time. The only thing we knew to do was to just keep living each day and try to get the best from it that we could.

On Thanksgiving Day, she decided to keep him home. She felt he needed to be away from all of the noise and excitement the grandchildren would bring. Halfway into the afternoon, he perked up and said, "Where are my people? I want to be with the people that love me." So, she bundled him up and drove him to my brother-in-law's house to be with his family for a short visit.

The next afternoon we received a phone call from the hospice nurse. She said she believed Mr. Ralph would soon pass away and urged us to come to the house. We quickly jumped in the car and sped the quarter mile from our house to theirs. We found him in his bed with Mrs. Janice to his right and his "baby girl" at his feet. His "tomboy" was sitting behind him with her arms around him to hold him up because he did not want to lie down. He stubbornly fought death back for several hours even though all of his children told him it was okay and my mother-in-law kept saying she would help him. Eventually, he seemed to regain some strength. His breathing became more relaxed and he conceded to lie down and let himself be made more comfortable in the bed.

At bedtime, Mrs. Janice quickly brushed her teeth and changed into her pajamas while we all stayed in the bedroom to watch over him. Then, the moment happened. She came back in, finished her nighttime routine and crossed the room to her side of the bed. She pulled back the covers and gently slid into place beside him. We watched as she turned to look at him through tears, and suddenly, we all knew in our hearts that it was the last time she would do this. It was her last chance to say "Goodnight, sweetheart." It was the last time she would cup his cheek and brush his thin hair off his forehead. It was the last time she would lay beside him and help wash away the hardships of a day with the warmth of her love. This was it. The end was coming.

In that moment, I began to understand why the scriptures say, "Love is as strong as death ... unyielding as the grave. It burns like a blazing fire ... many waters cannot quench it; rivers cannot wash it away." Love had grown stronger with each passing day just as death had. There is no escape from death. Likewise, there is no escape from true love. It grows stronger until death separates you from it, and even then, it does not die.

Love's strength was made evident in the way my mother-in-law graciously let my father-in-law go. She was able to find comfort and joy in knowing he would be at peace and they would only be separated for a while. She may have let him go, but she will not let him be forgotten. I will not soon forget what love looks like in its finest hours.

Karen Lucas

The Lovers

His wife was away visiting family, so he took time to explore some unfamiliar hiking trails. His choice that late summer day was the Morris Creek grove of old-growth western red cedars in northern Idaho.

The short walk from the road to the massive trees was through a field abloom. Showy scarlet Indian paintbrush mingled and yet contrasted with white daisy-like flowers. There were a dozen or more varieties of wildflowers blooming in various hues. It was a picture you would see on a postcard, but there it was in real life. He made a mental note to buy a wildflower field guide so he could identify them.

The old, tall trees were not far up the gently sloping hillside. Not far into the eighty-acre grove, an odd tree twenty feet off the path caught his eye. He moved slightly up the path to view the tree from a different angle. It was then he realized that there were actually two trees. The larger of the two cedars was as big around as a large refrigerator and taller than two bus lengths. Immediately beside it was a smaller tree, perhaps two-thirds the girth of the larger. The trees had distinctly different root systems, but rose vertically from the forest floor side by side. For the first eight or ten feet of their height there was no space between them and then an inch or two for twenty feet, and again none for another twenty feet, where again they stood apart ever so slightly.

About twenty feet above eye level the larger cedar had a bough that looped out from its trunk and then divided into two smaller limbs. The first division of the branch was a substantial tendril that followed the curve of the smaller tree's trunk in a wooden embrace. The second fork of the branch subdivided several more times until it mingled with twigs from a branch of the smaller tree, becoming visually indistinct, like fingers laced together when two lovers hold hands.

"The Lovers" he mentally labeled the trees. These lovers started their embrace before Sacagawea led Lewis and Clark in their nearby westward trek. These lovers stood side by side in their adolescence, during a time before the United States was a nation.

His mind shifted to his wife on the other side of that nation. Her return had been delayed, and she would be away yet another week. Her return was now delayed until the day after their anniversary. It was amazing how much he missed her, and he wished she was with him at that moment, looking at "The Lovers."

He contemplated their relationship. In spite of his temporary loneliness and in fact in conspiracy with that feeling, he still felt he was the luckiest man alive. He had been fortunate enough to be formed, to stand side by side, to embrace and hold hands with his wife, his lover, his friend for thirty years. They will not make three centuries, as the old lovers in the forest have, but each day with her in his life was a blessing. He knew this.

He also knew he would return to this spot one day soon, wife by his side, and he would stop in front of "The Lovers." He would put one arm around her, hold her hand with the other, and show her the two old trees and say, "This is you and I, my love."

Daniel James

Change of Heart

A psychiatrist asks a lot of expensive questions your wife asks for nothing.

Joey Adams

A woman seeking counsel from Dr. George W. Crane, the psychologist, confided that she hated her husband and intended to divorce him. "I want to hurt him all I can," she declared firmly.

"Well, in that case," said Dr. Crane, "I advise you to start showering him with compliments. When you have become indispensable to him, when he thinks you love him devotedly, then start the divorce action. That is the way to hurt him."

Some months later the wife returned to report that all was going well. She had followed the suggested course.

"Good," said Dr. Crane. "Now's the time to file for divorce."

"Divorce!" the woman said indignantly. "Never. I love my husband dearly!"

The Best of Bits & Pieces

Learning to Love

Recently, I asked my husband Philip if he still loved me even though I had aged since he fell in love with me. That afternoon I had seen beautiful, slim, young women look at him with interest and had suddenly felt the need for confirmation. He looked into my eyes, smiled and wrapped his arm around me. "Of course, dear." He snuggled up close and started to tell me a story about his granddad and him.

"I guess that I was about thirteen or fourteen years old when it happened. My mother dropped me off at Granddad's house. She and her sister were going to London for a few days. I have to admit that I did not mind having to stay with my granddad since we got along splendidly and had a special bond. I was really looking forward to the next few days.

"When I entered the room, I saw a black-and-white photo of a beautiful woman I had never seen before on the cupboard. I took it and showed it to my granddad. 'Who is that in this photo?' I asked spontaneously.

"'Do you see her eyes?' Granddad asked with a smile.

"'Yes, they look very intriguing, just like the rest of her face. She is so beautiful,' I agreed.

"At that age," my husband explained to me, "I was

already looking at the fairer part of the opposite sex with interest and the woman on the photo sure could compete with the best. Therefore, I wanted to find out why Granddad suddenly had put this photo on the cupboard.

"'Is this your sweetheart?' I asked jokingly. Granddad started to smile but still did not take his eyes off the photo. His smile suddenly faded and with a serious face he looked into my eyes. 'Yes, Philip, this is my sweetheart. She has always been and always will be.' Stunned by his answer, I could not respond immediately. Granddad walked away and returned with the family photo album. 'Look, here I stand next to your grandmother when we were vacationing on the beach in Scheveningen.'

"'What has that got to do with this good-looking lady on the picture?' I asked impatiently.

"'It's the same woman,' Granddad said to me softly. 'Just look at her eyes, they are the same, even though she is much older in this photo.'

"Only then I realized, because of the clothing the woman in the picture wore, that it was indeed an old photo of my grandmother. I had only seen her fascinating face. Full of disbelief, I compared both pictures. 'But. But . . . ,' I stammered, 'if such a foxy lady turns into a crone, or does not age very well, it surely becomes difficult to wake up next to someone like that. There were probably enough other good-looking women around with less wrinkles and slimmer figures.'

"When I look back on it," Phillip confessed to me, "I am embarrassed, but I was after all just reacting like a typical teenager. Granddad must really have loved me in order to respond patiently to my impolite, cruel remarks.

"'You did not get to know your grandmother because she died before you were born,' Granddad continued. 'But even though she got old, she remained the same woman, the woman I loved with all of my heart. To put it into your terms: If you really love someone, you do not care much about . . . the package anymore.'

"I had to think about that, but told him that I still wondered how he had felt when he saw a younger and more beautiful woman pass by when he was in the company of his aged wife. 'Of course, I saw them, but then I looked into your grandmother's eyes, and I saw the fifteen-year-old girl I had fallen in love with, the girl in the picture. Her eyes never changed, even though she got older, her eyes always stayed the same—just like my love for her.'

"I had to admit that Granddad's words had touched me and deep inside made me wish that I also would find a woman I could love that much. I compared both pictures and said, 'Granddad, I can see it, on both pictures her eyes are still the same.' But I didn't get a reaction for a short while. When I looked aside, I saw Granddad staring lovingly at both pictures. I remember him mumbling, 'Even for an old woman, she was still beautiful, but you are still too young to see that.'

Phillip turned to me. "Granddad was right. I was too young to understand then. But now I know what he meant. I've learned that it's not a person's appearance you fall in love with but their soul. When I look into your eyes, darling, I still see the same young and beautiful girl I fell in love with. I still love you and my love for you is not based on your appearance but on who you really are. Like the old proverb says, 'The eyes are the mirror of the soul.'

As Philip held me close, I breathed a deep sigh of contentment, and I silently thanked his granddad for teaching his grandson, so many years ago, the true meaning of love.

Carin Klabbers

7

FOR BETTER OR FOR WORSE

*The marvelous richness of human experience
would lose something of rewarding joy if
there were no limitations to overcome.
The hilltop hour would not be half so
wonderful if there were no dark valleys to
traverse.*

Helen Keller

Sage Advice from the
Stepfather of the Bride

Christy and Carl are getting married.

Christy's my stepdaughter, a beautiful, intelligent and seemingly normal young woman who started channeling Martha Stewart about six months ago and has now color coordinated everything within six square blocks of our house, including Sam, our mauve-and-blush-colored cat.

Carl's the lucky young man and soon-to-be former surfer.

It'll be an "intimate affair." In wedding terms that means taking approximately the same number of people who usually attend a professional sporting event and doubling it, the theory being that some family members, especially those still incarcerated, won't show up.

Truthfully, though, I haven't had to worry too much about the intricacies of "the event." Oh, occasionally, I'm asked whether I think yellow roses create a more spiritual aura than white, but I just smile and tell Christy how beautiful she is and how beautiful the wedding will be and how even the cat has finally started coming out of the hall closet again. This usually earns me a peck on the cheek and the opportunity to slip away before the "Greatest

Weddings of the Twenty-First Century" video starts up again.

My only wedding responsibilities will be to keep the DJ sober and to impart a few words of wisdom to the young couple during a tearfully tender toast.

I've never made a toast before. I did have to stand up once at a company Christmas party and apologize for giving Leslie, the new guy who took over the mailroom, a scented bath loofah, but other than that my public speaking career has been limited.

However, I have learned six important rules of survival that I hope will be of some help during the tricky transition part of marriage known as the post-honeymoon, or "what-the-heck-was-I-thinking," phase.

1. Be careful choosing pet names for each other. Remember . . . some wild and crazy night at the state fair you could end up thinking, "Hey! matching tattoos would be cool!", only to wake up the next morning with "snoogly-woogly little pookey bear" etched onto your butts.

2. You should both learn some standard marriage-saving responses as soon as possible, like: "Wow, you make dinner really fun, dear. I've never had meat loaf that bounces." Or: "Thank you, honey, for sharing the excruciatingly minute details of the groin pull injury that kept you out of the all-star game. I'll never forget it."

3. Try to master the subtle differences in personal hygiene. Facial foundation and bath oil beads are just as important as athlete's foot ointment and nose hair clippers, though I'm not really sure why. Also, Kleenex and toilet paper are two different products and, yes, they should match the bathroom decor, which will, unfortunately, be determined by the discriminating tastes of the people you invited to the wedding.

4. Speaking of decor . . . one partner's couch may be another partner's excuse to rent a Dumpster. That's why

they invented beige. Nobody likes it, but at least it's not plaid. Wall hangings must also be a compromise. Japanese art prints aren't really all that bad, especially if you light them with a red neon Budweiser sign.

5. Learn to share your space. Your first apartment may be rather small, in that people are always mistaking it for a phone booth. Learn to give a little. Be willing to part with at least one pair of shoes for every concert-logo T-shirt and funny-slogan hat relegated to Goodwill.

6. Finally, there will be occasional bumps on the road to marital bliss. But it's better never to go to sleep angry with each other, especially if you have a waterbed and just received three sets of Ginzu knives at the reception. Instead, analyze both points of view, apologize, kiss and make up. After all, the only alternative is to go running home and guess what . . . your rooms have already been converted into entertainment centers.

So good luck, God bless and have a wonderful life. Now, if you'll excuse me, the DJ's lying under the keg again. . . .

Ernie Witham

The Missing Candelabra

A little girl at a wedding afterwards asked her mother why the bride changed her mind. "What do you mean?" responded her mother. "Well, she went down the aisle with one man, and came back with another."

Author Unknown

It was one of the largest weddings ever held at Wilshire. Fifteen minutes before the service was scheduled to begin, the church parking lots were overflowing with cars, and scores of people were crowding into the foyer, waiting to be properly seated. It was the kind of occasion that warms the heart of a pastor.

But that was fifteen minutes before the service.

At exactly seven o'clock the mothers were seated, and the organist sounded the triumphant notes of the processional. That was my cue to enter the sanctuary through the side door at the front and begin presiding over the happy occasion. As I reached for the door a voice called from down the hall, "Not yet, Pastor. Don't open the door. I've got a message for you."

I turned and through the subdued lighting I saw the assistant florist hurrying as fast as she could toward me. Her speed didn't set any records, because she was about eight months pregnant and waddled down the hall with obvious difficulty. She was nearly out of breath when she reached me. "Pastor," she panted, "we can't find the candelabra that you are supposed to use at the close of the ceremony. We've looked everywhere, and it just can't be found. What on earth can we do?"

I sensed immediately that we had a big problem on our hands. The couple to be married had specifically requested that the unity candle be a part of the wedding service. We had gone over it carefully at the rehearsal—step by step. The candelabra, designed to hold three candles, was to be placed near the altar. The mothers of the bride and groom would be ushered down the aisle, each carrying a lighted candle. Upon reaching the front of the sanctuary, they were to move to the candelabra and place their candles in the appropriate receptacles. Throughout the ceremony the mothers' candles were to burn slowly while the larger middle one remained unlighted. After the vows had been spoken, the bride and groom would light the center candle. This was designed to symbolize family unity as well as the light of God's love in the new relationship.

I felt good about all this at the rehearsal. I had a special verse of scripture that I planned to read as the couple lighted the middle candle. We had it down to perfection.

We thought.

The notes from the organ pealed louder and louder as I was stalled in the hallway. I knew that the organist by now was glancing over her left shoulder wondering where in the world the minister was.

"Okay," I said to the perplexed florist, "We'll just have to wing it. I'll cut that part out of the ceremony and improvise at the close."

With those words I opened the door and entered the sanctuary, muttering behind my frozen smile, *What on earth are we going to do?*

The groom and his attendants followed me in. The bride and her attendants came down the left aisle of the sanctuary. When the first bridesmaid arrived at the front, she whispered something in my direction.

The puzzled look on my face was a signal to her that I did not understand.

She whispered the message again, opening her mouth wider and emphasizing every syllable. By straining to hear above the organ and through lip-reading, I made out what she was saying: "Go ahead with the unity candle part of the ceremony."

"But . . . how?" I whispered through my teeth with a plastic smile.

"Just go ahead," she signaled back.

We made it through the first part of the ceremony without any difficulty.

Everyone was beaming in delight because of the happy occasion—everyone except the first bridesmaid who had brought me the message. When I looked in her direction for some additional word about the candelabra, she had a stoic look on her face and her mouth was tightly clamped shut. Obviously, she was out of messages for me.

We continued with the ceremony. I read a passage from Corinthians 1:13 and emphasized the importance of love and patience in building a marriage relationship. I asked the bride and groom to join hands, and I began to talk about the vows they would make. There wasn't a hitch. I was beginning to feel better, but I still had to figure out some way to conclude the service. Just now, however, we needed to get through the vows and rings.

"John, in taking the woman whom you hold by your hand to be your wife, do you promise to love her?"

"That's the funniest thing I've ever seen," the bride interrupted with a loud whisper. I turned from the bewildered groom to look at her and noticed that she was staring toward her right, to the organ side of the front of the sanctuary. Not only was she looking in that direction, so were all the attendants, and so was the audience! One thousand eyes focused on a moving target to my left. I knew it was moving, for heads and eyes followed it, turning ever so slightly in slow-motion style.

The moving target was none other than the assistant florist. She had slipped through the door by the organ and was moving on hands and knees behind the choir rail toward the center of the platform where I stood. The dear lady, "great with child," thought she was out of sight, beneath the rail. But in fact, her posterior bobbled in plain view six inches above the choir rail. As she crawled along she carried in each hand a burning candle. To make matters worse, she didn't realize that she was silhouetted—a large, moving, "pregnant" shadow—on the wall behind the choir loft.

The wedding party experienced the agony of smothered, stifled laughter. Their only release was the flow of hysterical tears while they fought to keep their composure. Two or three of the bride's attendants shook so hard that petals of the flowers in their bouquets fell to the floor.

It was a welcomed moment for me when the vows were completed and I could say with what little piety remained, "Now, let us bow our heads and close our eyes for a special prayer." This was a signal for the soloist to sing "The Lord's Prayer." It also gave me a chance to peep during the singing and figure out what in the world was happening.

"Pssst. Pssst!"

I did a half turn, looked down and saw a lighted candle being pushed through the greenery behind me.

"Take this candle," the persistent florist said.

The soloist continued to sing, "Give us this day our daily bread. . . ."

"Pssst. Now take this one," the voice behind me said as a second candle was poked through the greenery.

". . . as we forgive those who trespass against us . . ."

I was beginning to catch on. So I was to be the human candelabra. Here I stood, with a candle in each hand and my Bible and notes tucked under my arm.

"Where's the third candle?" I whispered above the sounds of ". . . but deliver us from evil . . ."

"Between my knees," the florist answered. "Just a minute and I'll pass it through to you."

That's when the bride lost it. So did several of the attendants. The last notes of "The Lord's Prayer" were drowned out by the snickers all around me.

I couldn't afford such luxury. Somebody had to carry this thing on to conclusion and try to rescue something from it, candelabra or no candelabra. I determined to do just that as I now tried to juggle three candles, a Bible and wedding notes. My problem was complicated by the fact that two of the candles were burning, and the third one soon would be.

The dilemma was challenging, a situation that called for creative action—in a hurry. Nothing in the *Pastors' Manual* addressed this predicament. Nor had it ever been mentioned in a seminary class on pastoral responsibilities. I was on my own.

I handed one candle to the nearly hysterical bride, who was laughing so hard that tears were trickling down her cheeks. I handed the other to the groom, who was beginning to question all the reassurances I had passed out freely at the rehearsal. My statements about "no problems," and "we'll breeze through the service without a hitch," and "just relax and trust me," were beginning to sound hollow.

I held the last candle in my hands. They were to light it together from the ones they were each holding. Miraculously, we made it through that part in spite of jerking hands and tears of smothered laughter. Now we had three burning candles.

In a very soft, reassuring voice, I whispered, "That's fine. Now each of you blow out your candle."

Golly, I said to myself, *we're going to get through this thing yet.*

That thought skipped through my mind just before the bride, still out of control, pulled her candle toward her mouth to blow it out, forgetting that she was wearing a nylon veil over her face.

Poooff!

The veil went up in smoke and disintegrated.

Fortunately, except for singed eyebrows, the bride was not injured.

Through the hole in the charred remains of her veil she gave me a bewildered look. I had no more reassurances for her, the groom or anybody. Enough was enough.

Disregarding my notes concerning the conclusion of the ceremony, I took all the candles and blew them out myself. Then, peering through the smoke of three extinguished candles, I signaled the organist to begin the recessional . . . now! Just get us out of here! Quickly!

Everything else is a blur.

But I still turn pale when prospective brides tell me about "this wonderful idea of using a unity candle" in the ceremony.

Bruce McIver

CLOSE TO HOME

Knowing that wedding receiving lines are notorious for being dull, Pete and Gloria did their best to liven theirs up.

A Wife's Greatest Gift

Nate suffered a devastating blow when he lost his job. His boss had spoken curtly, "Your services are no longer needed." Nate left the building a broken man filled with despair. By the time he reached home, he was in a deep depression. When he entered his house, he blurted out to his wife Sophia, "I lost my job. I am a complete, utter failure." A tense silence followed. Then a smile crept across Sophia's face. "What great news!" she responded. "Now you can write the book you have always wanted to write."

"But I have no job and no prospect of a job," he objected, completely without hope. "If I struggle to be an author, then what will we live on? Where will the money come from?"

Sophia took her husband by the hand and led him to the kitchen. Opening a drawer, she took out a box that was full of cash. "Where on earth did you get this?" Nate gasped. "To whom does it belong?"

"It's ours!" Sophia replied. "I always knew that one day you would become a great writer if only you were given the chance. From the money you gave me for housekeeping every week, I have saved as much as I could so you would have your chance. Now there is enough to last us one whole year."

What a surprise! What encouragement! What a wife! Nathaniel Hawthorne *did* write that year, and the novel he wrote became a literary masterpiece. The book is *The Scarlet Letter.*

Marilynn Carlson Webber

Mourning the Loss, Mending the Heart

Love cures people, both the ones who give it and the ones who receive it.

Dr. Karl Menninger

When I was first diagnosed with rheumatoid arthritis in my fingers, wrists, elbows, shoulders, hips, knees, ankles and feet three years ago, my first reaction was shock and denial. I had always been so active—hyperactive actually—and involved in everything! I kept wondering if the doctor might not be wrong about the diagnosis. I also hid my symptoms, even from my family. I guess I thought that if I didn't acknowledge to anyone how much pain I was experiencing, it wouldn't be as bad. I'm sure it was also difficult for me to admit to others that I had a debilitating disease. After all, everyone would see me differently, wouldn't they? I felt I would be less of a person than I had been before if everyone knew.

I went through months of being the "little trouper" with my husband Chuck, coworkers and two sons, Kevin and

Keith. Every time I was asked how I was, my answer was always "fine" or "okay." I didn't realize that my masking of pain and sickness was only preventing me from receiving the support I so desperately needed. Everyone assumed I was really "fine" or "okay," because I said so.

Eventually, my husband began to realize what I was doing. He came to me one evening as I was sitting in the TV room and asked if he could talk to me. I agreed and turned off the television. He knelt down on his knees in front of me. I immediately wondered what on earth he was doing! Several times throughout our marriage he has pretended to have some serious news for me, saying, "I just don't know how to tell you this," and once he knew he had me worried he would say, "Just wanted you to know I love you." One of my famous punches to his chest would always follow! This time, he remained serious. "I understand that you have been going through a tremendous amount of pain and have been having problems coping with all the changes that are happening because of the new physical limitations you have," he said. "Please don't shut me out any longer. I want to go through this experience with you because you are my wife, I love you and I don't want you to feel like you have to handle this alone."

Then the sweetest, most precious moment came, one that I will treasure all of my life. He asked me whether it would be all right if he mourned my loss. At this point, I was still feeling a little unsure of what he was up to, but I agreed it would be okay.

He began to cry and held my swollen, tender hands in his as he expressed to me how sorry he felt that I could no longer hold a telephone very long at work and now had to use a headset, and I had to use a cane to walk sometimes, and the Methotrexate shot I received every Friday made me so sick to my stomach that I was ill every weekend. I had to resign as the worship leader and choir director at our church because I was so fatigued and it was painful to sing. As he sincerely mourned all those losses, and others, his teardrops began to fall on my hands. Suddenly, a flood of tears burst forth from the inner depths of my soul and we held each other as we both sobbed.

Later, I began to open up to him about everything that I had been keeping to myself for so long. I felt so light and happy, and I no longer felt so isolated. He told me that he never wanted to hear "fine" or "okay" again, unless it was really true. We decided to use the pain scale that I use with my rheumatologist, zero to ten, ten being the worst pain, to communicate how I'm doing.

In the past year, I've been using some of the new RA drugs and am doing *much* better. I can walk farther, rarely need the cane and the pain is much more manageable. There are even days when I have no pain at all! But through the past three years, my husband has greatly surpassed the level of support, understanding and frequent nursing that I could have imagined! When I flare up so badly that I have to stay in bed for a week, he prepares my meals (many from his hip pocket), gives me lots of hugs, brings me the heating pad, water to drink, medicines, magazines or books to read, takes time away from his business to drive me to the doctor thirty miles away to get cortisone shots, whatever I need.

We've purchased a wheelchair to use for activities that require quite a bit of walking, such as shopping or touring Yellowstone Park. He has never once made me feel like I am a burden or that he resents the extra household duties he has had to take on.

Because of his support and encouragement (and the great working relationship I have with my rheumatologist), I am still working full time as a legal administrator for a local law firm. Chuck had arthroscopic surgery on his left knee last summer and I was able to do things for him for a change, and that felt great!

Our marriage has bonded even more deeply because this is *our* problem—not just mine. I thank God for giving me this wonderful man.

Sandy Wallace

Slaying My Dragon

*Love takes off masks that we fear we cannot live
without and know we cannot live within.*

James Baldwin

"I want to lighten your load," he said as he dug out all
the loose change and assorted foul and unidentifiable junk
from the bottom of my pocketbook. His eyes lit up, scan-
ning the oodles of quarters and nickels that had taken up
residence in the black hole of my bag. "We can use this at
the casino," he said.

I let the words echo in my brain. *The casino*. Other people
would think of it as a nice day trip. But me? This was the
sign that dreams come true, that miracles happen, that
love can cure anything.

Even agoraphobia.

I hadn't left my house in two and a half years. I had an
overwhelming panic disorder that made me feel mostly
like I was falling out of a plane in the middle of a hurricane
with no parachute whenever I walked out my front door.

My world shrunk until I couldn't even have friends
over, or eat in front of anyone, or . . . any of the social

activities that most people take for granted.

Prior to that, I was a very social person. I went to college, I was a professional actress, I threw great parties. There was no hint anywhere in my life that I would ever become afraid of the world. But, lo and behold, it happened.

Over the course of a few months, I started having panic attacks whenever I was in a crowd. Bars, restaurants, parties, stores—I avoided all of them because whenever I tried, I failed. I would walk into a place, and everything would turn into a bad movie. Sounds would be amplified, people would be out of focus, the ground would move beneath me, my heart would beat so loudly that I was sure it was audible to everyone around me, and I'd feel drugged—like I'd just overdosed on cold medicine.

I thought, surely, there had to be a medical reason for this. Maybe it was low blood sugar, or a heart malfunction, or brain seizures. Anything other than what it really was—a mental illness.

I had to move back in with my parents, and along with relinquishing my independence, I also gave up my self-esteem and all of my dreams for a successful life of career and marriage and adventure. If you told me then that I would find my recovery in the form of a blind date, I'd have said you were crazier than I was.

But here I am today to tell you that's exactly what happened.

Through the years of panic, I gave up on relationships. How could I ever meet anyone if I was trapped in my house? But, as the old cliché goes, you always find what you need when you stop looking.

I had worked for a wedding band, and my ex-boss wanted me to meet the band's new saxophone player, Anthony. I told him to forget it. I wasn't ready to have my heart broken when I found out that no man would be able to deal with dating a woman who couldn't leave her parents' home. He was persistent, though, and gave Anthony my e-mail address.

My screen name was "Violetfairy," since I love all things fairy-related.

His e-mails intrigued me. He sent me poems and song lyrics and riddles, knowing all along about my agoraphobia. I wrote back, even though I'd only seen a photo of the back of his head.

I finally gave him my phone number and, after several marathon phone calls, had the bizarre inclination to invite him over one night at midnight. Even though he had to wake up to teach in the morning, he came.

Somewhere in the course of that night, we both fell in love.

The next day, he brought a beautiful book of fairy prints with descriptions of how to "lure" them. He watched nervously as I read the page marked "Augustine, The Violetfairy," which said she could be lured with lilacs.

That's when I noticed he'd pressed a fresh lilac into the page.

Just a month later, I found myself in his car, headed out of state for a day trip to a casino. A casino, of all places! Hundreds of people, the sounds of clanking and ringing machines, excitement, tension . . . and I stood right in the midst of it all, enjoying every second.

How in the world did this happen? It was a feat that three medications and four psychologists couldn't accomplish. This man had helped me find my life again.

My panic didn't disappear when he showed up. In fact, I still have panic attacks now. But when we're out in a crowd now and he notices that I'm getting anxious, he'll sing me ridiculous German lullabies, or pull me in close for a slow dance in the middle of the grocery store, or piggyback me outside and sit with me in the car until we're both ready to give it another try.

He helped me learn that my panic didn't make me worthless, and it didn't make me unattractive, meek, boring, crazy or any of the other things I had convinced myself I was. Suddenly, I was me again. I was a funny, exciting, smart, sexy woman—who happened to have a panic disorder.

I'm very proud to say that, despite the fact that we lost a whole lot of money in the casino that day, we walked out feeling like millionaires. And for one day, I forgot to panic.

That lilac sure did work. He lured me back into the world, where I've learned everywhere feels like home when you're with a man who leaves construction paper hearts under your pillow and stomps "I love you, Violetfairy" in snowy lawns at sunrise while you're fast asleep.

Jenna Glatzer

Women and Fiction

A fellow walked into a bookstore and asked the woman behind the counter, "Have you got a book called, *Man, the Master of Women?*"

"Try the fiction section," said the woman.

The Best of Bits & Pieces

Reprinted by permission of Randy Glasbergen.

A Mistake I Will Not Repeat

The first duty of love is to listen.
Paul Tillich

Ah! Valentine's Day . . . a day for lovers, romance and flowers. A day for hearts, candy and jewelry, but apparently not a day for appliances.

I give up. I will never be able to figure out the unspoken language between men and women. And to think I got married two months ago secure in the knowledge that I had finally figured out how to play the game. I was wrong.

You see, I proudly presented to my new wife, on our very first Valentine's Day as young newlyweds, a food processor for her St. Valentine's Day gift. She gazed upon this appliance—one she had mentioned week after week that she desperately needed—and said, "Oh. A food processor."

I have always heard that when someone says what the gift is upon receiving it, it's not a good gift (i.e., "Oh. A Chia pet"). Did I mention that my wife has repeatedly said how much she wanted a food processor?

See, I am of the school of thought that says when I ask, "What's wrong?" and my wife answers, "Nothing," I assume nothing is wrong. And when my wife tells me she wants something, I want to get it for her. She wanted a food processor. She got it. So why did I have to sleep on the couch Wednesday night?

My coworkers laughed at me when I pleaded my case to them. I guess they all attended Gift-Giving 101. I must have missed that class. My boss asked me, and I quote, "Are you an idiot?" I suppose I am.

To make matters worse, my wife's coworkers scoffed at my gift, wondering why she would even consider marrying a heathen like me. How dare I? A food processor, indeed!

I'm not a complete idiot. It's not like I gave her a lawn mower or a subscription to *Sports Illustrated*. I didn't even get her that certificate for a free oil change I was tempted to buy. I gave her what she wanted. And she didn't want it.

I was informed by a female friend of mine that the proper action to take was to buy my wife the food processor on Arbor Day or Flag Day or some random Monday. Never on Valentine's Day.

Another friend said gifts like mine conjure images of housework and stuff that has absolutely nothing to do with romance. What happened to "It's the thought that counts"?

I had no idea there were guidelines for which days to give what. The food processor, I am told, was not personal enough for Valentine's Day. How personal do I need to get? I'm not buying underwear, or anything else she would have to wear, for that matter. If you knew anything of my fashion acumen, you'd agree with me.

I was probably the only person in the world who knew she wanted a food processor. Everyone else got flowers and candy. She got a major appliance. That's pretty personalized, don't you think?

I think my gift blunder has less to do with outright stupidity on my part and more to do with a general communication breakdown between the sexes. I have recently discovered that "Watch whatever you want" does not include *SportsCenter*. I just learned that "Whatever you want to do" does not mean that I can play golf with my friends on Saturday afternoons. I used to think that females found the stereotypical male behaviors cute, even charming. You know, hanging my ties on the doorknob, never making my bed, cold pizza for breakfast, memorizing *Caddyshack*, cleaning out my refrigerator maybe once every time Neptune orbits the sun.

It's all so guy-ish and adorable.

I was wrong on all counts. And I obviously didn't know that "I really wish I had a food processor" meant "Don't you dare give me anything with a cord and a plug for Valentine's Day!" I know now. And I promise to spread the word to all males who are considering shopping at Sears or Home Depot for Valentine's gifts.

For now, I guess I'd better start thinking of a way to make this up to my wife. I should probably start by returning the sewing machine I was going to give her for her birthday next week.

Michael Seale

"Today's our anniversary—can you gift-wrap it?"

A Message from the Angels

*. . . and if I have faith that can move mountains,
but have not love, I am nothing.*
The Apostle Paul (1 Corinthians 13:2)

Angels and people, different entities, or are they?
Angels. Just the word brings soothing comfort to those
who have experienced the pleasure of meeting them face-
to-face. Though I have read many stories of people and
their experiences with angels, that was what I thought
they were, stories. But my skepticism was turned around
by my experience with angels.

At some point and time in each of our lives, some of us
will be placed in a situation where we have to make a life-
and-death decision regarding a loved one. I never thought
in my wildest dreams that I would be placed in such a
position. But life is a challenge for both the living and the
dying. My mother always told me that God gave us only
that which we could handle. I never truly understood that
until I was faced with the biggest decision of my life.

Death. We tremble when we hear that word spoken. It's
a violent word. It's a violent action. It's a word whispered

rather than spoken aloud. But it comes to each and every one of us, eventually.

In May 1995, death came to my husband. It was not a quick death, though in reality it was, for late one evening my husband's heart stopped functioning. A call was placed to 911 and the paramedics arrived at our home. Since my husband was not breathing due to the stopping of his heart, he was without oxygen for a dangerous amount of time. The paramedics worked on his body until they eventually had his heart functioning again. A considerable amount of time had elapsed, and though his heart was pumping with assistance, his mind and body were gone. He was placed in intensive care, and put on life support equipment. I knew what was coming, the decision.

My husband and I were very close. He had polio, and throughout our many years of marriage, I took care of him. He always told me that he never wanted to be hooked up to life support, and to please let him die with dignity. I knew this, but I loved him very much. The final decision, the right decision, was up to me. I always tried to protect him in life and was so afraid to let him go. I did not know what would happen to his soul, and that concerned me. I fought and fought within myself to do the right thing, to do what he wished, to do what he wanted. I was selfish, afraid for him, afraid for myself.

I was at his bedside every day, except to go home to sleep. My daughter was my strength, and she was at my side every minute of every day. On the third night, daughter and I came home from the hospital exhausted and went directly to bed.

While I was sleeping I had a dream, and in that dream my daughter and I were met by two angels who came down from the heavens and spoke with us. I told the angels that I could not let my husband leave this earth because I did not know where he would go. The next thing I knew we were upon their wings, and we flew through the air, and as we were flying we began to see a bright light and the higher we seemed to go the brighter the light. It was so intensely bright that we could no longer look at the light. Though no words were spoken to us, our minds were filled with their words. We were engulfed by this bright light and as the angels released us, the light was no more. What we saw was so beautiful. The angels were shimmering light, and as we gazed upon them we could see that each one was engulfed in a bright light, but this light did not hurt our eyes. One angel came up to us and she spoke, not in words, but through our thoughts. She told me that it was time to let my husband go, that he was needed there, and that his work on earth was complete.

The words that were communicated from her were very comforting, with a gentle soft voice she spoke again and asked if we would like to see the place they had made there for my husband. Yes, we so wanted to see, and with a flash we were standing in a garden with beautiful flowers, and then she pulled back what seemed like a sheer curtain, and she said, "We are building this brook for your husband," and we could see the angels working on the brook, laying rock, and making bridges. I told her that my husband cannot walk, and she said that in heaven everyone walks, and everyone is free of all pain, and that each angel has a specific job to do, and that my husband's job was waiting for him there in heaven. I asked what was the job, but of this she would not say. We were able to see clouds all around us and when we looked down at our feet they were floating; we were not standing on anything solid. I held my daughter's hand tight and we both started to cry, not because of sadness, but because we were so happy that at last my husband was going home, no more pain, no more crutches, no more machines.

When I woke up the next morning, I ran into my daughter's room and woke her up to tell her about my dream. What she said to me made my blood run cold. She said, "Mom, it wasn't a dream, I was right there with you." We just hugged each other and started to cry.

At last I was able to let my husband go, because I knew what a wonderful place he was going to. You might think this was the end of my story, but in fact it was the beginning of a whole new meaning to my life. The love that my husband had for me on this earth was so strong that it carried over after his death. Yes, I believe in angels, and yes, I believe that our souls continue to watch over our loved ones after our death. To say that heaven and earth are not joined by a link is greatly understated—for what happened to me after my husband's passing greatly enforced my belief that love never dies.

Mary Ann Stafford

8

THE FLAME
STILL BURNS

*R*eal love stories never have endings.

Grandfather's Favorite

May you live as long as you wish and love as long as you live.

Robert A. Heinlein, *Time Enough for Love*

He sat in his easy chair, looking every minute of his ninety years. A long-sleeved, white cotton shirt hung from his bony shoulders, once broad and strong, and from his arms now shower-rod thin. His worn khaki pants were belted high above his waist, held in place by gray and red suspenders. The "flood" length trousers, as teens refer to them, revealed his swollen ankles and feet hosed with white stockings and squeezed into house slippers, evidence that Grandfather had no intention of going outside the house. Maneuvering with a walker had simply become too taxing and was reserved for only the most essential errands. His wispy hair had been neatly combed, and I could smell Old Spice aftershave lotion.

Grandmother groomed him daily, shaving him with an electric razor, combing his hair and brushing his teeth. The rest of his toilet required assistance from someone else having more strength than Grandmother, even though she was in relatively good health. Grandfather was a tall, big man—now weighing much less than he did when he was younger, when he labored as a beekeeper, farmer and cattle rancher. The hard work that seemed to delay Grandfather's aging had finally, and suddenly, overpowered his mortal body, and perhaps his mind because, though he returned my hug and kiss and greeted me warmly, I was not sure he recognized me. It was hard to say. His smile was sweet and genuine, but then he always had been a gentleman.

I turned, and hugged and kissed Grandmother, who was looking beautiful as ever. Her caftan with oriental motif flowed to the floor, settling in an exotic, colorful cloud around her feet. Beaded and sequined slippers peeked from under her gown and I knew she would be wearing knee-high hose. Properly dressed women are never without hosiery or jewelry. Today, her jewelry included her wedding ring, matching broach and clip earrings, and multi-colored rhinestones set in a dark metal. Her thick hair was swept up into barrel curls, which framed her ears and the colorful earrings. Rouge blushed her cheeks as she smiled, showing her teeth clean but aged, gold dental work apparent on several teeth. I smiled back at her, shaking my head a little, amazed that at their age, nearly a century, they still had their own teeth, were still in their own home and still had each other. Pretty fortunate, really.

I sat down on the couch across from their little, symmetrical nest. Matching walkers stood poised next to matching easy chairs angled in such a way that Grandmother's left knee and Grandfather's right knee nearly touched. Between the chairs sat a single lamp table with lamp atop a doily surrounded by all manner of necessities and comforts: eyeglasses, a flashlight, magnifying glass, pen and paper, glasses of water, the news-paper, Kleenex, a book of crossword puzzles, playing

cards and the TV remote. Each item kept there reduced
the need for an excursion on the walker.

Grandfather was hunched back in his chair. His eyes,
though open behind his wire-rimmed glasses, were dim
and distracted. Grandmother sat regally with back
rigid and head upright, each arm lying lightly on an arm
of the chair. She graciously asked about my husband and
our children and grandchildren, her great- and great-
great-grandchildren. Our family was growing so fast, she
found it somewhat difficult to keep the names of the
great-great-grandchildren associated correctly with their
parents. Still I was impressed at what she did remember.
I often found myself struggling to keep the little ones'
names with the right person.

"So what have you been up to?" I asked. A silly question, obviously, because what they could do was very
limited given their health and physical condition. Grandmother recited a few of their ailments and what they were
doing about them. Then she shrugged her shoulders
slightly and twisted her head away from me, fluttering
her eyelids and pursing her lips, mannerisms she displayed when she was embarrassed or self-conscious.
Tentatively picking up an old work-boot box from the
floor between her chair and the lamp table, she stroked
the lid and paused as if deciding whether to lift it or not.
With a slight shrug of her shoulders, she smiled at me,
opened the box and showed me her latest project.

Inside the box was a strawberry-shaped pincushion
with its green felt calyx holding on by one petal, pins and
needles sprouting from the berry. At one end of the box
was a rainbow of spools of thread, mostly pastel but one
each of white, bright red and black. Scraps of material
were neatly stacked at the other end. On top lay several
sizes of Kewpie dolls, orphaned and rescued from thrift
stores and garage sales, each in various stages of dress.

One man's waste is another man's treasure, they say. Each doll had been scrubbed clean, its face repainted and body clothed in a unique little garb. One had a tiny blue floral skirt gathered around her waist with tinier lace straps over her shoulders. Others were outfitted in a kimono, pajamas, or a diaper and baby blanket.

The dolls and their outfits were delightful, and I was glad Grandmother had something to occupy her time. Too bad Grandfather didn't have something as engaging for him. I glanced at Grandfather; he was still withdrawn. Trying to bring him into the conversation I asked, "Which doll is your favorite, Grandfather?" He thought quietly, then his eyes gradually focused on me. Puzzled, he cocked his head and scrunched his brow. Pointing at the Kewpie dolls, I smiled and repeated very loudly and slowly, "Which . . . one . . . is . . . your . . . favorite?"

He looked at Grandmother with the Kewpie dolls scattered on her lap. As he turned back toward me, a smile lit his face and his eyes twinkled. Leaning slightly toward me, he winked one eye and balled his fist, extending his thumb. In slow motion he gestured his thumb and nodded his head toward Grandmother. With a big grin he said, "She's my favorite."

Grandmother blushed and smiled, again exhibiting her singular mannerisms of embarrassment. This time she shrugged her shoulders and ducked her head away more deliberately, chin almost resting on the shoulder opposite Grandfather, even as she coyly leaned her body toward him. I could well imagine them seventy-plus years younger sitting on a porch swing, flirting, her parents waiting up in the parlor just inside the front door discussing in whispers whether or not they should turn up the gas lantern.

"Oh, Walter," she murmured as she straightened up and sat back in her chair, arranging the caftan at her knees so, again, only the tips of her slippers showed. The dolls tumbled around on her lap. As she started rearranging them in the box, she looked up at Grandfather and smiled coquettishly. For another brief moment his face remained luminous as he smiled back at her. Then he shrunk back into his chair, countenance fading, eyes dimming, once again far away.

Betty Tucker

The Three Men I Married

To fall in love is easy, even to remain in it is not difficult; our human loneliness is cause enough. But it is a hard quest worth making to find a comrade through whose steady presence one becomes steadily the person one desires to be.

Anna Louise Strong

I have been married to three kinds of Rodneys over the past two decades. The Rodney I met right after college asked my father for my hand in marriage, but he never proposed to me. He claimed bragging rights among his fraternity brothers. He didn't have to bend a knee to a woman. It never occurred to him that his boast offended me. When I brought it to his attention after the newlywed sweetness dampened, he said, "You married me, didn't you?" As a young attorney, he made an unarguable point. I looked at the traditional solitaire diamond ring and remembered June 10, 1978, the day of our wedding. Though he hadn't officially asked me to marry him, he'd given me his solemn vows that day—vows we both intended to keep.

The week before our tenth anniversary, June 10, 1988, Rodney and I fought long-distance. I was 150 miles away at a work-related conference. Each phone conversation left me in frustrated tears. I arrived home five days later in a foul mood with a sour disposition. I knew it was the end of a difficult relationship, and as much as I didn't want to leave the marriage, I convinced myself that he wanted out.

When I arrived home, I only wanted to see our three children. Rodney was the last person I wanted to spend time with, but he was the only person waiting for me. He suggested a walk downtown in the heat. The vapors rose from the sidewalk on that June day and steam seemed to be pent up inside me as I tried to feel happy to be home. As we walked he tried to engage me in small talk. He took my hand. Sweat mingled in our palms, and I thought of all the sweat and toil that had gone into keeping both of us sane through so much fighting over the years. Our marriage felt like the dry leaves clinging to the trees under which we walked.

He said, "Sit down," and indicated the courthouse steps. I knew what was coming, and though I didn't want it to happen, I felt unprepared to stop it. I held my breath, shut my eyes and waited for the word "divorce."

"Would you marry me again?"

My eyes popped open as I said, "What?"

Rodney held a ring box gingerly before me. He laughed a gentle laugh and dropped down on one knee. "I said, would you marry me again?" As he opened the box, a deep blue sapphire and diamond ring caught the sunlight and winked at me. I let my held breath out with a rush and said, "Yes!" I'd never been more startled.

"I didn't like you being gone this week," he offered as an explanation for his incessant fights.

"That's what all that was about?"

He looked sheepish, but he nodded and grinned. "Surprised you, didn't I? You said you'd do it again, and now you can't take it back."

I smiled at him and thought to myself—*and so I will do it again.*

As we walked home hand-in-hand, the leaves didn't seem as dull; I'd finally gotten my down-on-one-knee proposal. This time though, I entered the "engagement" with less hope than I'd entered the marriage. Proposal or not, things had to change. We talked about that too.

We changed all right, and when the third Rodney came to propose, he did it with a flourish and a gentled heart.

The morning of our twentieth anniversary, he called me from work. "Let's go to the Versailles exhibit in Jackson, Mississippi, today," he said, as if it were normal to take three-hundred-mile day trips. I've learned to say "okay" over the years to my impetuous husband, so I willingly agreed. The trip was pleasant. We talked and laughed and shared our dreams. Before we crossed the Mississippi River, he suggested we change drivers. We stopped at a small convenience store, and while I was inside, he snuck out the back door to retrieve a small box from the glove compartment. When he slipped back inside, I was buying Junior Mints to celebrate. I never knew he'd been gone.

Back on the road again, we soon approached the Mississippi River Bridge. Right in the middle of crossing, he popped a ring box open and held it at the height of the steering wheel. "Will you marry me?" he asked with a grin plastered on his gorgeous face. The sun glinted off the diamond and emerald ring. I gazed at the green ring against the backdrop of the verdant bridge high above the water below; it's a wonder I didn't crash the car. Rodney had planned the perfect proposal for me, his incurably romantic wife. We exited on the other side and talked a security guard at the Mississippi hospitality center into capturing the moment on film. All my questions of when and how were answered with a hug and a smile. He'd been listening to my heart and taking notes for twenty years; he knew me well.

It's like I always tell young brides, "You don't often get the sensitive caring husband you long for on the day you marry him. That process takes years. You grow there together."

Pamela F. Dowd

"She's into serious recycling.
This is the third time she's married him."

Metamorphosis

Accept the things to which fate binds you, and love the people with whom fate brings you together, but do so with all your heart.

Marcus Aurelius

She gazed into her mirror
And beheld an aging face . . .
The woman looking back at her
Seemed strangely out of place.

Time, wily thief, had stolen gold
And left her only gray . . .
She touched with rueful fingers
Lines that would not smooth away.

Lost in wistful contemplation
She was really unaware
As the door behind her opened
With her husband standing there.

Are you ready yet, my darlin'?
Lady, aren't you a sight . . .

I can see why blue's your color!
Girl, you'll knock 'em dead tonight!

With startled gaze she met his eyes
Reflected in the glass . . .
And as he smiled the strangest thing
Of all had come to pass.

It may have been a change of light
But gray returned to gold . . .
And the woman in the mirror now looked
Young instead of old!

Helen V. Christensen

Forever in Their Eyes

Early one morning, I witnessed romance at one of the least-expected places in the world—a long-term care facility. At the time, my father shared a room with three other gentlemen. While it wasn't an ideal situation, it was the best the administrator could do at the time.

A few days before this particular visit, an elderly couple was admitted to the facility. Since there wasn't a double room available, they were forced to separate the couple. The gentleman, Mr. West (name has been changed) was placed in the bed beside Daddy. His wife, Mrs. West, shared a room with several other ladies down the hall.

When I went to see Daddy that morning, I met Mr. West. Three employees were working with him. He hadn't eaten a bite of food since he was admitted several days earlier. I could tell by the expression on the nurses' faces that they were worried about him. While one nurse was trying to get him to open his mouth with spoonfuls of gelatin, another nurse was trying to coax him to drink a health shake from a straw. The third nurse was standing nearby with a cup of water. Mr. West refused to open his mouth for any of them.

"Let's try this," one of the nurses said. She pulled out a lollipop, tore off the paper and offered it to Mr. West. His lips were clamped together tightly. He refused to listen to reason. Finally, he uttered something about his sweetheart, who was resting down the hall.

"Go get Mrs. West," the nurse instructed her helper, while handing her the lollipop. "Maybe Mr. West will eat for her."

In a few minutes a kind-looking lady was wheeled into the room. She held the lollipop in her hand. Her smile was contagious and Mr. West smiled brightly. I felt as though I was intruding on a private moment, but I couldn't take my eyes off the couple. The love between them was obvious, as Mrs. West patted Mr. West's hand and then caressed his forehead.

With a soft voice, Mrs. West convinced Mr. West to eat. To everyone's surprise Mr. West opened his mouth and began to enjoy the lollipop and his wife's company. While the nurses fed him, he stared at his sweetheart with a smile on his face. Mrs. West began humming a tune to him. The expression on his once solemn face became even brighter.

Tears filled my eyes. The nurse then pulled the curtain around the couple to give them some quality time alone to visit. I discovered that romance doesn't only exist when we're young and in love. Romance lasts a lifetime and grows stronger with age. Before long I heard snores of contentment coming from the bed beside me.

Today, Mr. and Mrs. West reside together in a place where there are no limitations, nursing homes or wheelchairs. There are no tears in their eyes or rooms dividing them. I am convinced that the West marriage went well beyond "till death us do part" and will last throughout eternity. Not only did I witness a memorable romance that day, I saw a glimpse of forever in a loving couple's tired and worn-out eyes.

Nancy B. Gibbs

A Joy Forever

Every season brings its own joy.

Spanish Proverb

John Keats wrote, "A thing of beauty is a joy forever." Perennial, enduring love is a thing of beauty, rather like a rose can be.

Every time I catch the scent of a rose, I think of enduring love. Being a freelance journalist, years ago I had the pleasure of interviewing an elderly man. James Charlet had an interesting story, beginning two decades earlier when he lost his beloved wife, who been a great lover of roses.

So deep was his grief when she died, so enduring was his love, that he asked his church if he could plant roses by the church walkway in his wife's memory. Of course, the priest there said yes.

James started with a few rose bushes. He planted lovely pinks, deep yellows and fragrant reds with names like "Yesterday" and "Golden Chersonese" and "Chrysler Imperial." The roses grew and flourished under his never-ending care, for he also had retired and had a great deal of time on his hands.

He told me that those few roses didn't seem to be enough; they were insufficient to fully express his love for his wife. He asked the priest if he could plant some more roses; again, the priest said yes.

James planted some different kinds of roses this time: rare burgundies and hard-to-find violet roses, silver roses and hybrid roses created in the memory of others. Roses with names like "The Doctor" and "Alba Celeste" and "Honorable Lady Lindsay."

Still he was dissatisfied with what he called a paltry outward show of his inner feelings. He again approached the priest, asking if he could use part of the vacant lot next to the church that the church owned. Again, he was told yes.

James planted more roses and then went on to plant roses by the sidewalks up and down and around the entire city block, surrounding the church and grounds. Roses with names like "Red Meidiland" and "Trumpeter" and "Pikes Peak."

Now, rose bushes numbering in the hundreds are everywhere; the scent of them fills the air, the pied blooms catch the eye and blossoms float on the breeze along with the laughter of the children playing in the church playground. Couples strolling along downtown walk past the roses and instinctively take each other's hand. The altar-guild ladies cut great, fragrant bouquets of roses to decorate the church and altar, filling the interior with the color and perfume of love.

Decades after he began his project to honor his wife's memory, and years after I interviewed him about what he had done, James and I visited that rose garden one afternoon. The roses are tended now by someone hired by the church, as James is no longer able to care for them himself. So old and feeble is he now that his nurse and I half-carried him to the garden, helping him settle in his wheelchair in the midst of the blossoms. We sat under an arbor, one of his favorite places to sit in the hot summers when he'd been more vigorous.

I sat with him there in companionable silence, among the scent of a myriad of rose blossoms. What was it that kept his love going inside him? What did the two of them have, even after one of them had died, that so many of us spend our lives desperately seeking?

It occurred to me then that some people are like prisms: Anyone with a light in them can be near that person and have their light refracted into many different colors, like the colors of the roses around us. Prisms by themselves cannot make light, and light by itself cannot divide into the lovely colors of the rainbow. James Charlet's wife must have been like a prism, being there to magnify and refract her husband's light. He made her complete because she completed him. I thought at that moment how she must be smiling upon him, seeing all these gifts he had planted for her.

As I took his thin, old hand and saw him smile at me— a bit sadly, in spite of the lovely midsummer day—I found myself hoping that the love I have found is less ethereal than the scent of a rose, that it can endure as James's love has.

To nurture this love so it can endure throughout all our lives, even through the infirmities old age may bring, to care for one another and love one another even beyond the boundary that separates this existence from the next is my hope. Perhaps our love can remain as strong and as sweet as the roses that have endured and bloomed all these years, and be a thing of beauty, a joy forever.

T. Jensen Lacey

Tattooed Dreams

There are only two ways to live your life. One is as though nothing is a miracle. The other is as though everything is a miracle.

Albert Einstein

I didn't like going to the beach, but I had no choice. My boys were at that age where it was best to keep an eye on them. It wasn't that I didn't like to sit in the sun and feel ocean breezes tease through my hair, but at forty-five, I felt fat and out of shape. Middle age was not a good time.

Sounds of the old beach stirred up emotions. I sat in the sand chair wrapped like a mummy in a long beach cover-up. Ageless aromas breezed from concession stands carrying memories of my teenage years, especially the good times with Jimmy. We had spent summers on the beach jumping through waves, kissing under bubbling foam, holding hands as we walked under starry summer skies.

Mother never liked Jimmy. Her comments were always laced with negative remarks. "He's irresponsible. He'll never amount to anything."

For me, it was love at first sight. Jimmy was cool. He drove a souped-up Plymouth sedan. He wore chino pants and white tee shirts. His dark, shiny hair dipped across his forehead in an enviable wave. It didn't take long to learn his tough veneer covered a sensitive, loving person. He treated me like the best thing that had ever happened to him.

Sitting on the old beach, listening to the rhythmic sounds of rolling waves, the toasty sun lulled me back to the past. Sleepily, I eased from my beach chair to stretch out on the striped towel, and then discreetly slipped off my cover-up.

Daydreams wandered off to the time when Jimmy and the guys had gotten tattoos. A flowery heart surrounded my initials, CLG. At first, I was annoyed. I didn't like my middle name and never used the initial, but when Jimmy rolled up his sleeve, I was proud of the statement his tattoo made: I was his girl.

We made plans to marry right after high school. Then Jimmy broke my heart. He and a couple of friends quit school. "We joined the army." Mother was thrilled over his enlistment. It was as if her prayers were answered.

He shipped out to the Far East. I spent my senior year alone. During the following summer, Mother found me a promising husband. She promoted my relationship with Chet, an engineer with an engaging personality. At Mother's urging, our marriage took place, quickly. Chet and I moved across the country to California and began our new life.

Through the years, I had no contact with Jimmy. Every once in a while, thoughts about him slipped through daydreams. When I asked Mother if she'd heard how he was, she'd always cut the conversation short. "Heard Jimmy married one of those overseas girls," or "Heard Jimmy was MIA."

I tried to be an attentive wife, but I felt empty inside. Every once in a while, I escaped the confusion of marriage with thoughts of my first love. When I did, it seemed as if Chet could read my mind. He'd become nasty and lectured blatantly about the responsibilities of marriage. He didn't seem to care how I felt or that past times needed closure. I quietly submitted to his demands and covered up my feelings.

Chet's controlling directives forced me into a Stepford wife existence to promote his advancements at work. Unexpectedly, my life took a dramatic turn. While away on business, Chet had a heart attack. He died in the Chicago airport.

For the first time, I took control of my life. Somehow, I managed to keep all the balls in the air, except for money issues. Moving back East with Mother had helped financially, but had stirred up the past.

Lately I had been thinking, *If I could drop a few pounds and tone up this mess, I could settle down, again. But this time, do it right.*

"Ma! Ma!" A panicked call broke beach daydreams. My son screamed as he struggled through the waves trying to rescue his brother, who'd been caught in a riptide. I bolted to the water's edge. The lifeguard's chair was empty.

Suddenly, a man dashed past and dove into the water. He swam, hard and strong, out to my son, who wrapped his arms around the man's neck and almost drowned them both. The man managed to make headway when the lifeguards showed up and pulled them to safety.

My son was fine. The middle-aged man gasped breathlessly. "How can I ever thank you?" I said.

"Don't worry," he replied. "Saving your son is thanks enough. I only wish the same had been done for me." His eyes teared.

"Why?" I hesitated, and then asked, "What happened?"

"Several years ago, we capsized off the 'Nam coast. Soldiers pulled me in, my wife and son drowned." He brushed tears away. The kids and I were devastated. I didn't know what to say. My boys gathered around and sat quietly with our heroic stranger. His friendly manner eased us into conversation. As I looked into his eyes an old, comfortable feeling washed through my thoughts. I forgot about my middle-aged appearance. I forgot I wasn't hiding under my cover-up.

As we talked, one of my sons asked, "What's that picture on your arm?" My son's directness embarrassed me.

Our rescuer chuckled, "It's a tattoo."

"Like Popeye?"

"That's right. And it had my girlfriend's initials right there," he said pointing to the flowery heart. "Under that blue line. I covered them up because I married someone else."

"That's kinda like my first boyfriend, Jimmy," I blurted. "He had my initials tattooed on his arm." My boys' eyes widened. "Wonder what he did?"

The kids gasped, then giggled. Our new friend chuckled. For the first time, I took a hard look at our rescuer. His bald head was fringed with gray, and his belly overlapped his bathing trunks. I wondered, *Could he be . . . ?* I glanced at his eyes.

He grinned. Then his upbeat voice distracted me. "Guess he did what I did," he laughed.

Something seemed familiar about his tone. I don't know why I said, "You're kinda like him." Our hero filled my nagging emptiness. Maybe daydreams tricked me. I liked not having to cover up my feelings or my middle age. Then, I remembered, through all our conversation, we hadn't introduced ourselves. I smiled and extended my hand. "I'm sorry. I should have introduced myself. I'm Carol. . . ."

"Yes, I know," he interrupted gently. "You're Carol Lee Gebhardt. And yes, I'm Jimmy. And you haven't changed a bit."

As impossible as it seemed, it was true—we had found each other again. Our magical reunion turned into a marriage that has been solid for eighteen years. His wonderful, caring personality won the boys over, and they think of him as a father figure.

When people see the blanked-out area inside the tattooed heart on Jimmy's arm they think somebody else's initials are under there. I laugh and say, "I'm really under there!"

Carol MacAllister

Oh, to Be Loved Like That!

When you have loved as she has loved, you grow old beautifully.

W. Somerset Maugham

When I arrived at the beauty salon, the operator said, "I can start with you, but Mrs. Smith [now under the dryer] has a doctor's appointment, and I will have to comb her out as soon as she's dry." And that's just how it happened. Her time under the dryer was up, I was asked to wait, they brought her wheelchair to the dryer chair and transferred her to the operator's chair to be combed out.

When she was almost finished, her husband drove up, made out a check for her permanent, got her coat and waited for her to be brought to the front of the salon where he stood. It was very obvious to me by this time that the woman had a rather severe disability and that her husband was heavily burdened by her illness. As she was wheeled toward him, he looked at her and said, "I don't think we should go to the party this evening." Her face fell with disappointment, and she asked, "Why?" He replied lovingly, "As pretty as you look, I'm afraid someone will steal you from me."

Mary L. Ten Haken

"You have an inordinately long shelf life, for a cup-cake."

The Sun Had Come Out

To love and to be loved is to feel the sun from both sides.

David Viscott

Their love story began in high school when Martha Fleming began dating Glenn Stockton. On September 22, 1934, they were united in marriage.

They were never separated from that time until just after Christmas last year when Glenn became a resident of Wesbury United Methodist Retirement Community. Diagnosed with Alzheimer's disease, his family could no longer care for him. In January, Martha, who had been deaf since she was six, became ill with severe back pain.

Diane Dickson, the couple's daughter, recalled that only after tests were completed March 24 was it determined the incredible pain was coming from a huge mass, which turned out to be a tumor.

Diane and her brother, David Stockton, took turns staying with their mother from that point on, with assistance from family members and from the staffs of Visiting Nurse Association and Hospice of Crawford County.

Diane said, "Hospice care was very, very, very good . . . and much appreciated by the family for their support," including the pain management care so her mother could rest comfortably. Grandson Mike Dickson said, "The VNA and Hospice—they do wonders."

Martha's illness worsened very quickly and soon she was unable to eat, Diane recalled, adding her mother had to be fed through a syringe. They never told Mrs. Stockton her illness was lung cancer, not a heart condition.

In the meantime, her husband had frequent visits from family members and never failed to ask about his sweetheart.

Diane believes that somehow her father sensed how it was with his wife. When he asked, he was told she wasn't well. His physical health continued to deteriorate to the point Wesbury staffers informed the family they thought he wouldn't live long. The nurse asked if he wanted to go home and see his wife and he said yes.

Diane said she told her son, "Bring him home." They knew it wasn't just for a visit, but for the rest of his life. They didn't know how short a time that would be. The entire family was there for the homecoming Friday.

Glenn Stockton couldn't talk much and neither could his wife. But words weren't really necessary between these two who'd spent their entire lives together.

She was bedridden. He was wheeled to her bed in a wheelchair.

She opened her eyes, looked up, and there he was. The love of her life, once more holding hands, offering her comfort, assuring her of his love. The body was weak but the love was not.

Family members agree the moment was unforgettable, the emotions so real, the feeling so deep, the picture so complete.

After a while, she closed her eyes and he indicated he too was ready to lie down. But not before he said the last words they would hear him say.

He squeezed Diane's hands tightly as he said, "Thank you." Another family member had to bend down to decipher the words.

The thanks was for bringing him back home, to say I love you and good-bye to the woman he had loved for so long.

Diane said her father looked terrible, but while lying in a room in a hospital bed next to his wife, he looked "more comfortable, more peaceful" now that he was home.

Neither Glenn or Martha was well enough to be out of bed.

But they were in the same room preparing for another chapter of their lives. Diane recalled that several times her mother opened her eyes and looked around the room and her eyes opened wider each time she noticed her husband. And as their grandson said, "They let nature takes its course." They didn't hasten their deaths; they only lived until God had chosen for them to die.

Shortly before 1 A.M. Sunday, the family left the room, some to go to their separate homes for a night's sleep after a long vigil. No one was in her room with Mrs. Stockton except her husband, who was sleeping in the bed a few feet away.

When her son returned to the room after only a few moments, Martha Stockton had made her final journey.

Grandson David Dickson is convinced Grandma had the last word, including when she would peacefully pass from this world to the next.

"She just quit breathing," he said. "It's pretty amazing."

Knowing how frail his grandfather was, the family wondered how long Mr. Stockton would live after his wife died. When they removed her body from her bedroom early Sunday morning, her husband was asleep. But their daughter believed he sensed something.

The hospice nurse came at 8 A.M. and told the family that death was very near.

"It was like he knew she was gone and he wanted to go, too," Diane Dickson said.

She recalled the family sitting by his side and saying their last farewells. She remembered assuring him, "Mom's waiting for you; take good care of her."

Twelve hours and forty-five minutes after his wife died, Glenn Stockton, like his wife, "just stopped breathing."

Their grandson noticed that five minutes later, the rain which had made the day so dreary stopped, and the sun shone through.

He said it almost was as though his grandmother was at peace.

He said he could just hear the woman who always told him what to do getting through to her husband and saying, "Get your butt up here."

And somehow heaven became a brighter place because Glenn Stockton had followed his wife on their final journey.

The family believes she who was so strong had two last wishes: that her family be spared seeing her die and that she always be with her husband.

She got those two wishes the day she left this Earth.

And although they grieve the death of two at once, her family members are comforted by the belief that both are together again.

"It's like it is the way God wanted it," Mike Dickson said. Diane agreed.

"Even though it's hard," she said. "It's God's way of saying, 'I'm going to keep them together; everything is going to be fine.'"

The love they left behind, the love the family shared, especially during those last forty-eight hours, was far too incredible to forget, Diane Dickson said.

But especially the memory of seeing two longtime sweethearts share one last handclasp, one more smile, one more memory.

The family found the experience so incredible, so inspirational they will remember the time of dying as not just of sadness, but also of love.

For to them, the love shared by Martha and Glenn Stockton is a love story which really has no end.

Jean Shanley
Submitted by Mrs. Rebecca Lucas

Golf Course Romance

My husband, Roy, had always wanted to play golf. I had heard the horrid "golf widow" stories and never encouraged the game. After quite a few years of marriage and raising three children, we were informed by our twin sons, Brad and Chad (now young adults), that they were taking up the sport of golf. Needless to say, they wanted their daddy to play with them. They begged and pleaded, but he had lost interest several years earlier.

Our sons surprised Roy with a set of golf clubs one Father's Day. During our vacation that year, the three of them played a round of golf. Since he had so much fun, Roy wanted to share the experience with me.

"Let's go to the golf course," he begged one Saturday afternoon.

"Why on earth would I want to play golf?" I asked.

"You can drive the cart," he replied. "Please." I saw a pitiful look on his face—just like a little boy with no money in a candy store.

My first thought was, *Sure I can, but I could also drive my car to the mall. It would be cooler and a lot more fun.* I looked back at his sad face and finally agreed to go.

"Now how long will this take?" I asked with a twinge of resentment in my voice.

"We will only play nine holes," he said. He whistled as he got his equipment together. We headed for the green grass of the golf course.

I moaned as I got out of the car and sat down in the driver's seat of a little white golf cart. This was not my idea of a good time. Before I started up the engine, Roy started trying to teach me the rules of the road.

"What rules?" I shouted as I took off, driving full speed.

"Slow down," he begged. I laughed and kept driving. "You can only drive in designated spots," he sternly informed me.

"And who is going to stop me?" I joked. I was already feeling rebellious.

When we reached the tee box at hole number 1, he was shaking his head.

It was clear that he was relieved to get off of the speeding golf cart. He set up for his first swing while I watched, wondering why people think golf is so much fun. It looked mighty boring to me.

He hit the ball but had no idea where it went. For the next fifteen minutes we searched for it.

"Oh, this is fun," I chided him.

"We'll just get another ball," he placated me, as he opened the pouch on his golf bag and pulled one out.

Back we went to the tee box. *This could take all afternoon,* I grumbled to myself. When Roy hit the ball a second time, we found it down the fairway a little way. After quite a few strokes, the ball went into the hole. I can't remember the last time I saw my husband that happy.

What was the big deal? I wondered.

The driving game was on. We were off and speeding to the next hole. I was driving the cart, and he was walking. He said he needed the exercise, but I knew he was afraid of my driving. He spent a great deal of time hitting the ball and then looking for it, while I watched the squirrels and rabbits play.

Something entirely unexpected happened by the time we reached the fifth hole. We were laughing, harder than we had in many years. The financial stress associated with putting three kids through college was gone. The strain of "too much work and too little play" was replaced by happy hearts and smiling faces. To my utter amazement, a golf course romance was born.

By the time we got to hole number 6, I had fallen in love again. I felt like a young bride accompanying her Prince Charming. Suddenly, he looked so cute trying to keep up with that little white ball.

When we got to hole number 7, I sensed that he was watching me more than the ball. "Keep your eye on the ball," I reprimanded him.

"But I can't," he replied. "I like looking at you."

At that point, he decided that he would ride with me again. This time, he didn't get upset when I drove too fast. By the time we reached hole number 8, we were holding hands. I don't know if he was holding on for dear life or if he enjoyed holding my hand, but nevertheless, I liked it.

It had been a long while since we last held hands.

The last hole, number 9, was the best hole of all. Before he stepped off the cart, he leaned over and kissed me. "I'm glad you came," he said.

"I had so much fun. Can we come back next week?" I asked. A smile covered his face—and mine.

"Yes, and next time we'll play eighteen holes," he asserted. He smacked the ball and it soared off into the woods. We both giggled as we drove off to find yet another lost ball.

This time, it didn't matter to me. My husband was happy. I was enjoying his company. Golf was just a good excuse to be together. We were not only finding lost balls. We were finding each other again, too.

Nancy B. Gibbs

Lost and Found

"You should get home more often."

This is the phrase my conscience lovingly chided me with as I approached the driveway of my childhood home in rural Indiana. I hummed to myself as I parked my car and merrily waltzed over the sidewalk that had been the canvas for many a chalk drawing and hopscotch court in my youth.

It was a warm July evening. The screen door stuttered behind me as I entered the house. I dropped my bags and rushed through the house to where I knew my parents would be during any pleasant sunset . . . at the picnic table sharing tea and conversation. Being a part of this ritual is a little slice of wonder. How many times had I crawled under that table to eavesdrop on their familiar discussions? My life's truest lessons had been learned there. I settled in across from them and kicked off my shoes so my toes could drink in the green of the freshly mown grass.

We exchanged kisses and giggles and I complimented my dad on how beautiful the yard looked. He thanked me and then announced, "Your mother has a story to tell you." Even at twenty-six, I still loved to listen to my mother tell a story. She fills them with inspiration, humor, love and, above all, truth. I smiled at her and said, "I'm ready."

She took a sip of tea and began. "Well, this will certainly cause you to believe in miracles if you don't believe in them already." I rolled my eyes and laughed. I was hardly the skeptic in the family. That title of distinction belonged to my eldest brother. You can count on the oldest sibling for that sort of thing. I grinned. "Okay, Mom, I'll keep an open mind."

"A couple of days ago I was putting away some shirts in your father's closet and my ring got snagged on a shirt-sleeve. I managed to get untangled from it and then I noticed the diamond was missing from my ring! I quickly began to rummage through the closet to try to find it. I pulled shoes out and turned them upside down, I shook his clothes and crawled all over the floor.

"It didn't seem to be in the closet, so I began to retrace my entire day. I had potted some plants outside, so I went through my gardening gloves and the potting soil. I even yanked my philodendrons out of their new homes and shook the poor things until their roots were clean. Every step I had taken that day, I took again. I went through containers I had washed and then disheveled an innocent loaf of bread thinking I might have lost it in the bag. I stirred the pot of soup I was cooking for dinner, retossed the salad and wiped down the counter hoping I would hear it 'clink' or that I might see a sparkle. I returned to your dad's closet for one last look when your father came home from work."

She paused and I looked down at her left hand. It was gone. The ring that she had never taken off, the ring that had stayed on during the birth of four children, the ring that was deemed fit for kneading bread dough as well as dinner parties . . . was gone. Tomorrow would be their fortieth wedding anniversary, and I couldn't help but feel my heart fall a little as she continued.

"I wasn't going to tell him until after dinner, but as soon as I looked up at him I started to cry. I was sobbing and could barely get the words out. He just kept saying, 'It's all right, it's only a thing, it's all right.' I wiped away the tears and decided we had better eat dinner. I even teased your father and said, 'Careful of the salad, there may be half a carat in there.'

"We pondered over how such a thing could happen so close to our anniversary, and we began to talk about how amazing the past forty years had been. We revisited fond memories as if they were good friends and we marveled at how much we had grown—especially in the times when it seemed we had so little. A bit of diamond starts to seem pretty insignificant when you consider how a blind date became a great love story. As we finished our dinner my tears had turned to happiness, and I gave your father a kiss as I picked up our plates to take them to the kitchen.

"I stepped into the kitchen and nearly dropped the plates onto the floor. There in the middle of a clean counter, right where I had run my hands at least one hundred times in my search—was my diamond! I just stood there and called to your father to make sure I wasn't seeing things. He walked in and just looked at me and mirrored my expression of disbelief."

She looked at me with a grin and said, "Now, what do you make of that?"

I laughed and with tears in my eyes gave them a heartfelt round of applause. Then I asked, "Where is the ring now?"

My mom smiled lovingly at my dad and he began to blush. He put his arm around her and said, "I decided to wait and give it back to her tomorrow, when I ask her to marry me again."

Ami McKay

The Ageless Dance of Love

*A*ge *does not protect you from love, but love to some extent protects you from age.*

Jeanne Moreau

The hot line rang loudly, awakening me from a sound sleep. I picked up the old-style black phone and heard the voice of an alert dispatcher: "We have an elderly male who is not breathing at Angler Courts, Cabin Four. It's the second cabin on the left from the Fulton Road entrance." I hung up the phone, jumped into my paramedic uniform, and stopped in the bathroom to check my eyes for mascara rings and finger through my big Texas hair. A possible cardiac arrest; the adrenaline streaked through my veins. Our south Texas resort area had mainly trauma in summer and cardiac in winter because of the northern retirees who spent the colder months here.

As I pulled onto the highway in the early dawn, I hit the switch that causes eye-popping lights of red, blue and white to bounce reflections from surrounding buildings. That tends to wake me up. I held off on the siren, since no real need existed at that hour.

I pulled into the given address and parked near a sher-
iff deputy's car. Volunteer EMTs were already on the
scene. As I walked up the steps to the little clapboard
cabin, a deputy spoke quietly to me. "It looks like he's
been down awhile, Wendy."

I saw a small woman standing by the bed, clutching the
front of her blue quilted robe. Her short white hair fluffed
into curls around her face and reminded me of a Tiny
Tears doll I had as a child. As I placed the jump kit on the
floor and the Life-Pak heart monitor on the bed, I asked
the burly EMTs what they had assessed to this point.

"We found him breathless and pulseless. We didn't start
anything, but if you want us to. . . ." I picked up the old
man's hand; they were right. Lying on his back, pillow
under his head, he looked peaceful. The thought passed
through my mind that he had no problem greeting death
tonight. I placed the paddles on his chest to monitor his
heart rhythm and found none. An absolute flatline. I
asked for his age. "He would have been eighty-six next
February," his wife said softly. I asked the deputy to
notify the funeral home in the next town. We all knew it
would take at least an hour. We would wait with her.

Another paramedic stood with me as I took the
miniature-looking hand of the new widow. "Ma'am, I am
sorry, but your husband's heart has stopped, and it has
been too long for us to attempt any sort of resuscitation.
It appears that he may have died quietly sometime in the
night." She acknowledged by gently nodding her head.

"When did you notice that he wasn't breathing?"

"Well, sweetie," she said, "we went to bed around midnight. We just lay there and talked, like we do every
night. We aren't like most folks our age; we stay up late
and sleep late. Our friends just hate that about us.
Anyway, we talked until about 1 A.M., then we began to
make love."

There was a sharp intake of breath from the paramedic next to me and he suddenly began to fidget with the gear on his belt.

"I'm sorry, ma'am, you did what at about 1 A.M. . . . ?"

"We were having sex, making love." She graciously deadpanned her delivery. "We finished about an hour later, and I got up to go to the bathroom. When I came back, he was lying just like that, like you see him now. I told him goodnight, but now that I think about it, I'm not sure he answered."

Every person in the room had discovered some obscure duty that demanded their immediate attention. No one would look in our direction. Backs were shaking slightly from held-in laughter. Law enforcement officers suddenly needed to go outside, medics were packing up equipment, and no one, absolutely no one, would make any eye contact. This precious little woman never shied away from her description of the evening, had no embarrassment of it, and seemed to believe their behavior standard—for octogenarians to engage in sex for one hour.

"When I woke up to visit the bathroom at 6 A.M.," she said, "I couldn't arouse him." Poor choice of words with this audience. We were instantly alone in the room. The guys nearly knocked down the door getting out. I envisioned the chuckle-stifling crew hidden on the other side of the ambulance.

"I just cannot imagine it, though. We have sex most every night and it never killed him before." But instead of laughter, I felt immediate respect and admiration for this couple who had remained close emotionally and physically until their ultimate separation.

"You must have had such a grand love for one another." I moved her to a chair and had her sit down. "May I make some coffee while we wait for the funeral home folks? Do you want to talk for a while?"

"That would be nice. You've all been nice and so prompt. Yes, coffee . . . I suppose. I have a lot of things to do now. I should call my daughter in Illinois. I should. . . ." She looked at her husband as her eyes welled up with tears. "I will miss him, I already do. . . . You know, I remember the day we met."

"Please tell me about it. We can make the calls later, after they have come for him. How did you meet?"

I sipped hot coffee and held the hand of a lovely farm girl from Kansas. As she spoke, I saw in her eyes a twenty-year-old seeing her first love, her only love, her constant love. Through the hardships of farming, raising children, losing two children and growing old, they had remained true to each other.

A habit had formed early. Each night they talked in bed for about an hour and then made love to one another. Emotional and physical communication had kept their relationship fresh for sixty years. They never viewed each other as old, never saw wrinkles, never noticed the changes that naturally happen to a body with age. At night, they were ageless—connecting, moving and swaying to a dance of their own creation. No "if onlys" will exist in her mind, only dear sweet memories of a man and a marriage made in heaven.

Wendy J. Natkong

Fifty Years of Love

The last time we had a family reunion was at my parents' golden wedding anniversary four years ago. We had piled into the house, shouting and hugging, suitcases spilling over, phone ringing, friends and relatives dropping in.

My two brothers, their wives, my husband George and I had planned the event—the invitations, the ceremony, the food, musicians and the hall. We reveled in the excitement, happy to be able to present this celebration as our gift to them.

Fifty years. Taken all together in a lump, they boggled my mind, and yet they had accumulated like thick snowflakes covering the landscape, piling into drifts, soft mountains of love and caring.

Looking at their marriage, I saw my own thirty married years flipping past like pages in a book—some chapters better than others, some sparkling, some full of anguish, some exciting or plodding or confused. Had it been the same for them? What did all of those years together mean?

Years of commonplace things, of routine, of excitement over the events and crises of life: the miles of scrubbed floors and tons of ironing; the endless days my father left for work and came home in snow or searing heat; the countless fall picnics and Sunday dinners; the time David broke his arm riding his bike and fourteen-year-old Jerry came home from delivering newspapers drunk on cheap wine; the discipline, their encouragement to study and to be fair and honest in our relationships; the times they stood aside in the pain of letting go, and the treasured moments of closeness.

The solemnity of the occasion struck me most at the reception. As the hall quieted, we three children stood in front of the huge gathering while I read a short tribute to our parents.

"We, your children, thank you for the gift of life, the guidance towards responsibility, and the model your life has been for caring for each other. We, your family and friends, salute you for this past half century of life together and join you in joyous celebration and anticipation of the years to come."

I thanked them now for what I had once rebelled against—their way of life, which had seemed so solid and dependable that it was stultifyingly, so uneventful it was boring. And yet, it was just that enduring solidarity they represented that had influenced me the most that made me see the many faces of love and commitment. It was just that dependability, that capacity for sticking it out, that had carried me through many problems and crises.

I tried to picture them when they were first married, standing at the altar of that small church on the top of the mountain near their Pennsylvania farmhouse. They, too, had been starry-eyed young lovers—my father with pitch-black hair and a trim moustache, my mother slender and beautiful with auburn braids.

Earlier that morning when they had restated their vows, the church was quiet and unadorned. The ceremony was as practical and unpretentious as their lives had been. They stood there holding hands at the altar—my mother a little stout now, less sure of her step, her auburn hair short and wispy. My father's shoulders were still squared, but his hair was thinning and gray. They were very much alone up there, and their family and friends looked on with rapt faces as they repeated the vows with the same earnestness and the same belief in the tradition they had vowed to uphold fifty years earlier. But they were not alone. All those years they had shared were grouped around them, surrounding them in much more intimate company than any crowd of well-wishers could ever put them.

As I finished my speech at the reception, I looked at my parents, Dad spruced up with a big bow tie, my mother in a soft green dress. I wanted to rush over and hug them, pin a big medal with a long streamer of pride on them. How does one encompass all of those years with a few words of admiration and gratitude?

I realized our privilege in sharing this celebration with them—how rare it is becoming. We had such fun preparing for it, enjoying the occasion to be together, but it was much more. I had the distinct feeling of being a long-distance runner in a relay: We, the three married children, were now taking up the long tradition and carrying it on. Knowing how fragile marriage is, I wondered where we would be years from now. But I only wondered for a moment, for there they were—a testimonial to enduring solidarity and love. I accepted being a runner, being part of the relay, carrying on the tradition.

My parents are older now and show the fast changes that four years can bring to those over seventy. I notice that Mother listens to the radio and rarely turns on the television. I notice that Dad is doing all of the work in the house, the cooking and the shopping. He takes me aside and tells me not to mention it if I find egg on a spoon. "Your mother can't see that well now." He's rearranged the house, moving their bedroom into the dining room so she won't have to climb the stairs.

My husband and I had planned to invite them to Europe with us this year, and to take them where my father has always wanted to go, to Rome. I wanted him to fly across the Atlantic and see the world he has always been so curious about. Now I know he won't go. Mother can't go, and he wants to be by her side. That is his responsibility and no dream could ever be stronger than the bond he has with her. He gives his devotion not out of duty, but out of love. They have cared for and taken care of each other throughout their married lives, their love has been compounded of alternating disappointment and joy, and now it is no different.

Such a bond and, especially, such mutual dependence are regarded negatively today. It is felt that something must be wrong with marriage if it fosters such reliance on another person. What about freedom? What about the individual? What about me? The individual is truly precious. We are no longer expected to sacrifice our total beings to marriage when it threatens our dignity as people. Yet I believe that although we have given up many of the traditional structures and expectations of marriage, we need not give up marriage itself. The concept of marriage is flexible; it can stretch to accommodate the new "you" and the new "me" because it is being made by, and for, "us."

I understand now the full meaning of marital commitment, of being the most important person to someone and having someone as your most important person. My parents give me a warm reassurance that two people can care for each other forever, that the virtues and values we have held as human ones are still alive and well, and that we can go on coping somehow, helping one another, achieving together dimensions we never thought possible.

Nena O'Neill

Who Is Jack Canfield?

Jack Canfield is one of America's leading experts in the development of human potential and personal effectiveness. He is both a dynamic, entertaining keynote speaker and a highly sought-after trainer. Jack has a wonderful ability to inform and inspire audiences toward increased levels of self-esteem and peak performance.

He is the author and narrator of several bestselling audio- and videocassette programs, including *Self-Esteem and Peak Performance, How to Build High Self-Esteem, Self-Esteem in the Classroom* and *Chicken Soup for the Soul—Live.* He is regularly seen on television shows such as *Good Morning America, 20/20* and *NBC Nightly News.* Jack has co-authored over fifty books, including the *Chicken Soup for the Soul* series, *Dare to Win, The Aladdin Factor, 100 Ways to Build Self-Concept in the Classroom, Heart at Work* and *The Power of Focus: How to Hit Your Business, Personal and Financial Targets with Absolute Certainty.*

Jack is a regularly featured inspirational and motivational speaker for professional associations, school districts, government agencies, churches, hospitals, nonprofit organizations, sales organizations and corporations. His clients have included the American Heart Association, the Children's Miracle Network, the Boys Club of America, Reading Fun, the American Dental Association, the American Management Association, AT&T, Campbell's Soup, Clairol, Domino's Pizza, GE, ITT, Hartford Insurance, Johnson & Johnson, the Million Dollar Round Table, NCR, New England Telephone, Re/Max, Scott Paper, TRW and Virgin Records.

Jack conducts an annual eight-day life-changing workshop to build self-esteem and enhance peak performance. It attracts educators, counselors, parents, corporate trainers, professional speakers, ministers and anyone else interested in transforming their lives and teaching those skills to others.

For further information about Jack's books, tapes and training programs, or to schedule him for a presentation, please contact:

Self-Esteem Seminars
P.O. Box 30880
Santa Barbara, CA 93130
phone: 805-563-2935 • fax: 805-563-2945
Web site: *www.jackcanfield.com*

Who Is Mark Victor Hansen?

Mark Victor Hansen is a professional speaker who, in the last twenty years, has made over four thousand presentations to more than two million people in thirty-two countries. His presentations cover sales excellence and strategies; personal empowerment and development; and how to triple your income and double your time off.

Mark has spent a lifetime dedicated to his mission of making a profound and positive difference in people's lives. Throughout his career, he has inspired hundreds of thousands of people to create a more powerful and purposeful future for themselves while stimulating the sale of billions of dollars' worth of goods and services.

Mark is a prolific writer and has authored *Future Diary, How to Achieve Total Prosperity* and *The Miracle of Tithing.* He is coauthor of the *Chicken Soup for the Soul* series, *Dare to Win, The Aladdin Factor* and *The Power of Focus* (all with Jack Canfield) and *The Master Motivator* (with Joe Batten).

Mark has also produced a complete library of personal empowerment audio- and videocassette programs that have enabled his listeners to recognize and use their innate abilities in their business and personal lives. His message has made him a popular television and radio personality, with appearances on ABC, NBC, CBS, HBO, PBS and CNN. He has also appeared on the cover of numerous magazines, including *Success, Entrepreneur* and *Changes.*

Mark is a big man with a heart and spirit to match—an inspiration to all who seek to better themselves.

For further information about Mark write:

MVH & Associates
P.O. Box 7665
Newport Beach, CA 92658
phone: 714-759-9304 or 800-433-2314
fax: 714-722-6912
Web site: *www.chickensoup.com*

Who Are Mark and Chrissy Donnelly?

Mark and Chrissy Donnelly are a dynamic married couple working closely together as coauthors, marketers and speakers. They began their marriage with a decision to spend as much time together as possible—both in work and in spare time. During their honeymoon in 1995, they planned dozens of ways to leave their separate jobs and begin to work together on meaningful projects. Compiling a book of stories about love and romance was just one of the ideas.

Mark and Chrissy are the coauthors of the #1 *New York Times* bestsellers *Chicken Soup for the Couple's Soul, Chicken Soup for the Golfer's Soul, Chicken Soup for the Sports Fan's Soul, Chicken Soup for the Father's Soul, Chicken Soup for the Baseball Fan's Soul* and *Chicken Soup for the Golfer's Soul: The 2nd Round.* They are also at work on several other upcoming books, among them *Chicken Soup for the Friend's Soul, Chicken Soup for the Working Woman's Soul* and *Chicken Soup for the Married Soul.*

As cofounders of the Donnelly Marketing Group, they develop and implement innovative marketing and promotional strategies that help elevate and expand the *Chicken Soup for the Soul* message to millions of people around the world.

Mark grew up in Portland, Oregon, and unbeknownst to him, attended the same high school as Chrissy. He went on to graduate from the University of Arizona, where he was president of his fraternity, Alpha Tau Omega. He served as vice president of marketing for his family's business, Contact Lumber, and after eleven years resigned from day-to-day responsibilities to focus on his current endeavors.

Chrissy, COO of the Donnelly Marketing Group, also grew up in Portland, Oregon, and graduated from Portland State University. As a CPA, she embarked on a six-year career with Price Waterhouse.

Mark and Chrissy enjoy many hobbies together, including golf, hiking, skiing, traveling, hip-hop aerobics and spending time with friends. Mark and Chrissy live in Paradise Valley, Arizona, and can be reached at:

Donnelly Marketing Group, LLC
2425 E. Camelback Rd., Suite 515, Phoenix, AZ 85016
Phone: 602-508-8956 Fax: 602-508-8912
E-mail: *chickensoup@cox.net*

Who Is Barbara De Angelis, Ph.D.?

Barbara De Angelis, Ph.D., is one of America's leading experts on relationships and a highly respected leader in the field of personal growth. As a bestselling author, television personality and motivational speaker, she has reached millions of people with her positive messages about love, happiness and the search for meaning in our lives.

Barbara is the author of eleven bestselling books, which have sold over five million copies and been published in twenty languages. Her first book, *How to Make Love All the Time,* was a national bestseller. Her next two books, *Secrets About Men Every Woman Should Know* and *Are You the One for Me?* were number one on the *New York Times* bestseller list for months. Her fourth book, *Real Moments,* also became an overnight *New York Times* bestseller, and was followed by *Real Moments for Lovers.* Her most recent books are *Confidence, Ask Barbara, The Real Rules, Passion, Secrets About Life Every Woman Should Know, What Women Want Men to Know* and the #1 *New York Times* bestseller *Chicken Soup for the Couple's Soul.* She also writes regularly for magazines including *Cosmopolitan, Ladies' Home Journal, McCall's, Reader's Digest, Redbook* and *Family Circle.*

Barbara's first television infomercial, "Making Love Work," which she wrote and produced, won numerous awards. Barbara appeared weekly for two years on CNN as their *Newsnight* relationship expert, dispensing advice via satellite all over the world. She has hosted her own daily television show for CBS-TV, and her own radio talk show in Los Angeles. She has been a frequent guest on *Oprah, Leeza, Geraldo,* and *Politically Incorrect,* and a regular contributor to *Entertainment Tonight,* and *Eyewitness News* in Los Angeles. In 2001, Barbara wrote and produced her own special, "Love Secrets," on PBS-TV.

For twelve years, Barbara was the founder and executive director of the Los Angeles Personal Growth Center. She is presently president of Shakti Communications, Inc., which provides production and consulting services. Her clients have included YPO, Sharp Health Care, AT&T and Pritikin. She lives in Santa Barbara, California.

For further information about Barbara's books and tapes, or to schedule her for a presentation, please contact:

Alison Betts
Shakti Communications, Inc.
12021 Wilshire Blvd. #607
Los Angeles, CA 90025
310-535-0988, e-mail: *askbarbarad@aol.com*

Contributors

Christina M. Abt is a newspaper columnist, magazine profiler and radio commentator. Her work has been featured in *Chicken Soup for the Soul of America* and on the *Heartwarmers.com* Web site as well as in Heartwarmer's books and Petwarmer's CD. She is the wife of one awesome husband, Michael, the mother of two terrific kids and will always be her mother's daughter. She may be contacted at *christinaabt@hotmail.com* or 9411 Sand Rock Rd., Eden, NY 14057.

Dave Barry is a humor columnist for the *Miami Herald*. His column appears in more than five hundred newspapers in the United States and abroad. In 1988 he won the Pulitzer Prize for commentary. Many people are still trying to figure out how this happened. Dave lives in Miami, Florida, with his wife, Michelle, a sportswriter. He has a son, Rob, and a daughter, Sophie, neither of whom thinks he's funny.

Barbara Bartlett finds being a wife and mother a rewarding life. She enjoys music, reading and the outdoors immensely. She is intensely private person who is keenly interested in others, other cultures and current events, and armchair travel. Her motto is to seek simplicity in life.

Marion Benasutti was born in Philadelphia, Pennsylvania. She has written countless stories and articles for magazines and newspapers throughout the country including *Reader's Digest, McCall's, Mademoiselle, Redbook, Seventeen,* the *Literary Review, American Home, The Inquirer Magazine* and *The Philadelphia Inquirer*. Her 1966 novel, *No Steady Job for Papa,* was published in the United States, Germany and Italy.

Katherine Grace Bond is the bestselling author of *Legend of the Valentine, Sleepytime Dance* and poetry collections *The Sudden Drown of Knowing* and *Yielding to Calliope*. Her work has appeared in *Focus on the Family Magazine, Virtue, Today's Christian Woman* and *Dark Moon Lilith*. "Head to Toe" also appears in *Stories for the Family's Heart*. Katherine lives in Washington State with her darling husband, four children, two dogs and two cats. Her house is never clean.

Cindy Braun was born and raised in Flint, Michigan, where she met and married her husband, Dennis. They have been happily married since their "Honeymoon Flight" for twenty-three years. They currently live in Georgia, with their teenage daughter, Ciara, who fills their life with joy, learning and adventure. Cindy is grateful to her parents, Harry and Norma Chestler, and her extended family for always showing her love and support.

Michele Wallace Campanelli is a five-time national bestselling author. She lives in Palm Bay, Florida, with her husband, Louis V. Campanelli III. She is the author of *Hero of Her Heart, Margarita, Keeper of the Shroud* and more novels published by Americana Books. Her short stories have been included in dozens of anthologies. Her personal editor is Fontaine M. Wallace, instructor of humanities at Florida Institute of Technology. To contact Michele, go to *www.michelecampanelli.com*.

Valerie Cann returned to school at age forty after raising her son. She is studying computer information systems and technical communications at Austin Community College, Texas, and works as a paralegal in a family law practice. Upon graduation in May 2003, she hopes to live and work in Ireland for a time. She can be reached by e-mail at *ivalerie@austin.rr.com* or *panda826@yahoo.com.*

Helen V. Christensen has been writing poetry all her life. Her verse has appeared in various papers and magazines, and she has published two books of poetry with her husband. In her early years she was a reporter and once had an exclusive interview with Eleanor Roosevelt. She is also a musician, having served as church organist and singer for many years. In 1997 she was named Poet Laureate for Life of Harlingen, Texas, by then Mayor Card. Until her husband's death in 2000 she had been married to him for almost fifty-eight years. She may be contacted at 5626 Ben Hogan Cir., Harlingen, TX 78552.

Suzanne C. Cole, former college English professor, has published books, essays, poetry, plays and fiction in many commercial and literary magazines, newspapers and anthologies including *Newsweek, Houston Chronicle, USA Today, Troika, Personal Journaling* and *Writing Your Life Story.* She also wrote *To Our Heart's Content: Meditations for Women Turning 50.* A new grandmother, she does not anticipate future "one-sweet-potato Thanksgivings" but will accept them if they come for their different blessings. She may be reached at 4226 University Blvd., Houston, TX 77005.

Mary J. Davis has been married to Larry since 1967. The have three children and six grandchildren. Since Mary's 2001 bout with cancer, Mary and Larry have been closer than ever. Mary has published over five hundred articles, thirty-four Christian education books and five children's journals. In addition, she has sold numerous greeting cards, calendars and other items. She can be reached at *ninepine@interl.net.*

Michele Davis is a sixteen-year-old student from Ontario, Canada. She loves dancing and has always found the time to just sit down and write. She is grateful for her mom, dad and Joel, and wants to thank Lauren for always telling her to just do what makes her happy. She lives by the saying "There is never any traffic along the extra mile!"

Pamela Dowd is the author of "Cookie Jar Greetings," a line of inspirational cards published by Warner Press. She also writes for DaySpring and Leanin' Tree. Pamela was featured in a July 2001 *Writer's Digest Special Issue* article entitled, "In Their Words—Seven Successful Writers Share the Joys and Challenges of Working in Today's Inspirational Writing World." Pamela has written for several magazines and anthologies such as: *Christian Parenting, Pray!, Evangelizing Today's Child, Catholic Parent, On-Mission, The Christian Communicator, Byline, Why Fret That God Stuff?, An Expressive Heart, Season's of a Woman's Heart* and *Heart-Stirring Stories of Romance.* She and her husband, Rodney, have three daughters. Contact Pamela at *grammargurl@hotmail.com.*

April Felts is a graduate of Northeastern State University in Tahlequah,

Oklahoma, and a retired kindergarten teacher. She spends her time writing stories for her grandchildren and recording tales of her family's genealogy for the next generation. She may be contacted at 109 Grandview Blvd., Muskogee, OK 74403, or via e-mail *afelts@mynewroads.com*.

Rusty Fischer is a professional freelance writer who works at home with his beautiful wife of nine years, Martha, who is also the main character in most of his stories. Together they enjoy walking, going to the movies and enjoying theme parks in sunny Orlando, Florida. He may be contacted via e-mail at *Freelancer86@aol.com*.

Katherine Gallagher is a wife, mother of three and an avid reader. Her love for family and for writing has led her to share some experiences through short stories and essays. She is a member of a local writer's club, participates in writing workshops at the local community college, and writes poetry and letters to the friends and family willing to read them. She may be reached at 1 Vineyard Way, Mt. Sinai, NY 11766, e-mail *kathycg@optonline.net*.

Nancy B. Gibbs is an author of two books, a weekly religion columnist and freelance writer. She has been published in numerous anthologies, such as *Guideposts* books, *Honor* books, *Chicken Soup for the Nurse's Soul* and *Chicken Soup for the Grandparent's Soul*. She has also had articles appear in magazines such as *Angels on Earth, Family Circle, Decision* and *Woman's World*. She is a pastor's wife, mother of three grown children and the grandmother of a precious little girl. She can be contacted at P.O. Box 53, Cordele, GA 31010, e-mail *Daiseydood@aol.com*.

Jenna Glatzer is the editor-in-chief of *Absolute Write (www.absolutewrite.com)*, a free online magazine for writers. She is the author/editor of several books, including *Conquering Panic and Anxiety Disorders* (Hunter House, fall 2002), an anthology of success stories from people who have overcome anxiety disorders. She and Anthony live in New York with Kira, the greatest cat in the world. She may be contacted at *jenna@absolutewrite.com*.

Diane Goldberg is a member of the IAFW&T writers association as well as the Horror Writers Association. She lives in Charlotte with her tolerant husband and demanding garden. You can find out about her fiction writing or contact her at *www.dgkgoldberg.com*.

Lisa Bade Goodwin, forty-two, was born, raised and currently lives in the northern suburbs of Chicago with Pat, her husband of twenty-four years. They have two adult daughters, Kelly and Jenny. At the age of thirty-nine, after many years as a stay-at-home mom, Lisa decided to pursue her love of writing and landed a job as columnist for the *Gurnee Sun*. She is currently a columnist for a daily newspaper, the *News Sun* in Waukegan, Illinois. Her columns are about day-to-day life: sometimes funny, sometimes sad, sometimes curious, but always true to life. She may be contacted at 329 W. Maple Ave., Libertyville, IL 60048, by phone at 847-549-8572, or via e-mail *Lisabgood1@aol.com*.

Norma Grove lives in Tucson, Arizona (where she was born in 1922), with her "new" husband, Bob, and Shih-Tzu, Bonnie. She has four living children (out of eight) and nine grandchildren ranging in age from thirty-five to seven years, none of whom live in the Tucson area. As coeditor of the newsletter for the Tucson Chapter of The Compassionate Friends (an international organization that provides support for the persons who have lost a child or children, grandchild or sibling), she has had the opportunity to be of support to other grieving parents. Her hobby is photography, and she is a member of the Society of Southwestern Authors, currently writing memoirs. She also studies Spanish. She can be reached at 520-885-5860, or e-mail *Ngrove22@comcast.net.*

Bruce Hanna is a father who lost his wife to melanoma. He writes and leads groups on feelings and observations of value in everyday experience. His current focus is helping people deal with impending death and terminal disease. He has worked in marketing, communications, software technology and education. He may be contacted at 1211 Plaza del Monte, Santa Barbara, CA 93101, or via e-mail at *b@piweb.com.*

Joe A. Harding is an enthusiastic motivator of pastors and laity. He is known across the United Methodist Church as the author of *GROWTH PLUS: The Vision* and coauthor with Ralph Mohney of *VISION 2000: Planning for Ministry in the Next Century.* As past director of VISION 2000, he is calling the United Methodist Church to move away from negative images of decline and to lean forward into positive biblical images of new vision and hope. VISION 2000 has been adopted by thirty-six annual conferences representing 46.8 percent of the total United Methodist membership. Born in Missouri, Joe is an honors graduate of Emory University. He attended Candler School of Theology and is a cum laude graduate of Boston University School of Theology. He received his doctor of ministry degree from San Francisco Theological Seminary. Joe was organizing pastor of a new congregation in Salem, Oregon, which grew to eight hundred members in eight years. He has served as Seattle district superintendent and was senior pastor of one of the largest and most rapidly growing congregations in the Western Jurisdiction.

As a newspaperman (*Louisville Courier-Journal* and *New York Times*) **Philip Harsham** made African affairs a primary interest, but his magazine-article subjects have been limitless. Now retired and living in Florida, he and his wife Diane travel—often adventurously, most recently to Antarctica and Zimbabwe.

Timothy Hudson wears a lot of hats. At the University of Georgia he is the director of both Christian Campus Fellowship and the Institute for the Aberrant Group Studies. He is also a nationally ranked former powerlifter and current powerlifting referee. He has been married to Sheila S. Hudson, a freelance writer, for almost thirty-four years and they have two married daughters and three grandsons. Tim writes an e-mailed daily devotional called "Survival Guide," which currently has over fifty-one hundred subscribers. Tim invites you to receive a sample "Survival Guide" by sending a blank e-mail to *subscribe@ugaccf.com.* He may be reached at 161 Woodstone Drive, Athens, GA

30605, or via e-mail at *thudson@negia.net.*

Sherry Huxtable, at sixty years of age, has learned many lessons. Therefore, her priorities are now: her husband and children, her eleven grandchildren, her friends, and her job. Of course, her God always comes first in her life. She enjoys painting and writing. She has not always been successful in her writing, but continues to do it because it pleases her. She has been published several times. She enjoys Indy Car racing and attends as many races as possible around the country.

Daniel James lives with his wife in the northwestern United States. He is an observer of nature and human nature and is cursed or blessed with a dictate to wrestle with the wily word, which one day he hopes to do well. His writing appears frequently in *heartwarmers.com* and *hearttouchers.com.* He can be contacted at *danieljames@lycos.com.*

Barbara Johnson didn't write a word until she was fifty years old and now has sixteen books in print (over 6 million copies) in twenty-four languages and large print. Most of her books are Erma Bombeck sort of stuff for women . . . about frustrations with kids and husbands. Her newest book, *Plant a Geranium in Your Cranium,* is about her bout with a brain cancer tumor and handling cancer. She also has diabetes, and dealing with that and a cancerous brain tumor has been a challenge, but she hopes her books will encourage others. She may be reached at 2230 Lake Forest Cir., La Habra, CA 90631, or phone 562-691-7369.

LaVonne Anderson Kincaid is a real estate broker and her husband Tom is an architect, semi-famous for his designs and "one-liners." The great love of their lives, aside from their four children, is the Ile St. Louis in Paris where they go on wine-and-dining binges as often as time and income permit. She can be reached by phone at: 262-249-8909 or by mail at N1545 Linn Road, Lake Geneva, WI 53147.

Carin Klabbers's short stories until now have been published in the *Chicken Soup for the Soul* series. Besides her household duties and volunteer work as a PR person, she is currently working on her own inspirational book. Contact her at: C. Klabbers, Koninginneweg 75, 2982 AH Ridderkerk, The Netherlands, or via e-mail *pmklabbers@hetnet.nl.* Home page *www.home.hetnet.nl/~klabbers123.*

Jeanne Knape has published over three hundred inspirational, nostalgic, craft and children's stories and articles in a wide variety of national publications. She is active in both fine arts and crafts, working in many mediums, including watercolors, acrylic paints, collage, handmade paper and pressed flowers. Jeanne has been happily married to her husband, Ralph, for over twenty-five years. She earned her bachelor of fine arts degree and works as a part-time art teacher at an alternative high school. She volunteers over three hundred hours each year at a local library and a botanical center. Her hobbies include gardening, collecting antiques and traveling.

T. Jensen Lacey is a freelance journalist, teacher and author. Her books include two Native American histories, *The Blackfeet* and *The Pawnee* (Chelsea House),

Amazing Tennessee and *Amazing North Carolina* (Rutledge Hill Press), and a young adult novel, *Growing Season* (1st Books Library—order at *www.1stbooks.com*). She enjoys speaking to groups and giving writer's workshops. Lacey's Web site is *www.tjensenlacey.com*.

Mary Dixon Lebeau is a newspaper columnist and freelance writer living in South Jersey. She and her husband, Scott, share their Saturday nights—and the rest of the week—with their four children. She can be reached at *mlebeau@snip.net*.

Karen H. Lucas is a social worker at Falcon Children's Home and also serves as music director of her church. She graduated from Emmanuel College with a B.A. in psychology and is currently pursuing a career as a writer of children's literature. Mrs. Lucas shares her home with her husband, Chip, dog, Mike, and parakeet, Ellie. She enjoys living in the small, close-knit community of Falcon, North Carolina, where friends and family are close at hand. Her hobbies include singing, reading, writing songs and stories, playing musical instruments and making crafts. She also enjoys submitting articles about Falcon happenings to the local newspapers. You may write her at P.O. Box 111, Falcon, NC 28342, or send her an e-mail at *karenhlucas@aol.com*.

Carol MacAllister writes freelance historic-based and commentary pieces for local newspapers. She has received awards for her fiction writing and poetry from the NJ Wordsmiths, Florida State competition and numerous others. Her short stories are included in several trade paperbacks in the dark fantasy/horror genre. Her poem, "Martha's Jumprope," has been included in *The Year's Best Horror and Dark Fantasy for 2001*. However, she admits that writing children's stories for her grandchildren under the penname "Blue Grandma" delights her the most.

Meghan Mazour began writing when she was eight, filling tattered notebooks with her "novels." Currently, she is an AmeriCorps volunteer in New Mexico. During the day, she works at a middle school teaching peace and conflict resolution skills. At night, she fills tattered notebooks with her novels. Her stories and articles have been published in national magazines and literary journals. She may be contacted via e-mail at *meghanmazour@hotmail.com*.

Bruce McIver is a native of North Carolina. He was a graduate of Mars Hill College; Baylor University, which honored him with the Doctor of Laws degree and the George W. Truett Distinguished Service Award; and Southwestern Baptist Theological Seminary, which gave him its Distinguished Alumni Award. In 1997, Texas Baptists honored him with the Elder Statesman Award. McIver pastored the Wilshire Baptist Church in Dallas, Texas, for thirty years, and upon his retirement was named Pastor Emeritus. He authored four books, *Grinsights* (Harty Press), *Stories I Couldn't Tell While I Was a Pastor*, and *Just as Long as I'm Riding Up Front* (Word, Inc.). These last two were combined and published in a hardback edition by Guideposts. His fourth and final book, *Riding the Wind of God*, was published in March 2002 (Smyth & Helwys), three months following his death. He was a favorite speaker far and wide, telling stories from his books . . . and life. His favorite audience was his five grandchildren, who lovingly called him "Goose."

Ami McKay lives in Nova Scotia, Canada, with her husband and two sons. She is a poet, freelance writer and musician. She is a regular contributor to CBC Radio. Her most recent work includes a radio documentary, "Kitchen Ghosts," and an accompanying Webumentary, "The Midwife House." She may be contacted via e-mail at *amimckay@yahoo.ca*. Please visit her Web site at *www.hopes.com/midwife*.

Mary Mikkelsen grew up on a cattle farm in the Southwest Missouri Ozark region. In 1943 she received a B.S. degree in mathematics from Drury University. She was employed as a statistician by Eastman Kodak and Phillips Petroleum Company during World War II. As a stay-at-home mom she became an accomplished porcelain artist and a member of the Mid-Atlantic Porcelain Art Teachers Association. She has been an active volunteer in a number of community programs. Now in her eighties and living with her husband, Louis, in West Chester, Pennsylvania, she enjoys reading, searching the Internet and e-mailing her five granddaughters. She may be contacted via e-mail at *lavina@ccil.org*.

Susan M. Miller lives in Ocoee, Florida, and has been married to her husband, Jeff, since 1991. They have two children, Amanda and Matthew. She has been a paralegal since December 1987 and is currently employed with the law firm of Terry and Frazier, LLP, in Orlando, Florida.

Margo Molthan and her husband Mike reside just outside of the small East Texas town of Palestine, along with their two black Labs, two cats and various wild ducks. After years of being a furniture sales representative in the Dallas area, Margo now enjoys volunteer work and being with her precious grandchildren. She loves to write poems, and wrote her story about Mike and his transplant one afternoon while reflecting over her life and wanted to get it down on paper. Never did she think it would end up in one of her favorite books! She may be contacted via e-mail at *Margomolthan@aol.com*.

Wendy Natkong worked for thirty years in emergency medicine as a paramedic and instructor in Texas and Alaska. In 1999 she was diagnosed with progressive multiple sclerosis and now resides in her home state of North Carolina with her husband Don. She may be reached at 21549 NC Hwy. 210 East, Ivanhoe, NC 28447, or via e-mail at *natkong@intrstar.net*.

Nena O'Neill is an anthropologist and writer always fascinated with relationships, especially contemporary relationships and how they face change. With her late husband she wrote two award-winning bestsellers. She writes articles, essays, poetry, columns and is currently working on a memoir and a novel about the O'Neill clan.

Chin Pak writes as a hobby and enjoys reading as well. She may be reached at 2307 Big Sky Street, Caldwell, ID 83605, or via e-mail at *snow778@hotmail.com*.

Edmund Phillips served as a psychologist in various capacities throughout his professional career. He recently retired from his position as chief psychologist at the Veteran's Administration hospitals in Seattle and Tacoma, Washington. This is his first nonprofessional publication. The story is true. When people would ask how he and his wife met, his reply was, "I asked her to marry me before we met, and she said yes." The tale of their correspondence followed. He was encouraged to write the story by many who heard it. He enjoyed writing it as it demonstrates that romance and humor can go hand in hand. He may be reached at 10011 77th Street SW, Lakewood, WA 98498, by e-mail at *ritaed@mindspring.com* or by phone at (253) 582-5431.

Dennis Rach is a husband, father, writer and ministry professional living in Orlando, Florida. He authored the book *Dear Daddy* (Concordia Publishing House). Along with raising their two precious children, he and his wife Nikki (*Dear Mommy*, Concordia) serve as speakers and trainers for congregations in the areas of staff/volunteer development and ministry program formation. He may be reached at 3230 TCU Blvd., Orlando, FL 32817, or via e-mail at *wdr32063@aol.com*.

Margaret E. Reed is a home-schooling mom of three teenagers. She has been married nineteen years to her high school sweetheart, Chris. God willing they will have at least another nineteen years together. She enjoys writing and reading, as well as sewing, gardening and singing. She may be reached at 3560 High Bluff Drive, Dallas, TX 75234, or via e-mail at *mejreed@sbcglobal.net*.

Mary Roach's essays and features have appeared in *Outside, Salon, Health, The New York Times Magazine, Wired* and *GQ*, among others. She writes a monthly humor column called "My Planet" for *Reader's Digest* and is a contributing editor at the science magazine *Discover*. Her first book, *Stiff: The Curious Lives of Human Cadavers*, will be published by W.W. Norton in spring 2003. She lives in San Francisco with her husband Ed.

Phyllis A. Robeson, born and raised in San Jose, California, earned a bachelor of fine arts degree (majoring in art history and watercolor) at the University of Nebraska, in Lincoln, where she presently resides. She married a career U.S. Army office/aviator (retired) and has one daughter. Phyllis writes because of the encouragement of family and friends, and in the process she has published a number of articles in national publications. She loves working with color in decorating, painting, in the garden and also as a member of a floral arrangers guild.

Lori Robidoux is a chartered accountant and part-time writer who lives with her husband and two daughters near Winnipeg, Manitoba, Canada. She began writing for her children several years ago, and has written a number of midgrade and young adult novels. The story "Six Red Roses" was written after her children begged her to "tell us the story about you and Daddy again." She can be contacted at Grp 108, Box 18, RR1, Vermette, Manitoba, Canada, R0G 2W0, or by e-mail at *Lorirobidoux@aol.com*.

Victoria Robinson lives in a small Texas town with her husband, Asa. She is a homemaker and has written poetry and short stories all of her life to get the events of her life on paper. She has two children and four grandchildren. Now that her children are grown, she has settled down to do what she loves: writing. Having her work published is a dream come true. You may contact Victoria at 235 Port Road, Angleton, TX 77515, by e-mail at *victoria@computron.net,* or by phone at 409-848-3530.

Gwen Romero is a mother, wife, sister and friend who manages to teach English and creative writing in rural Utah high schools. She has had several articles published in local papers. Her real passions are literature and her family. She may be reached via e-mail at *gromero@morgan.k12.ut.us.*

Tina Runge lives with her leading man, Ray, and their three sons among cow pies and Amish buggies in a small town in northern Indiana. A published romance author, her debut novel, *Treasures of the Heart,* was released at the end of 1999 by Berley Jove and was a finalist in the Ohio Valley Notable New Author Contest. She enjoys sharing her publishing experiences and is a frequent speaker at writer's conferences, club meetings and schools. This romantic at heart loves to travel and swim and can be found most often sitting on bleachers rah-rahing her own young heroes in all of their sporting events. She's also a true hands-on researcher who likes to visit the places she writes about. Her most current trip was to Astoria, Oregon, the setting for her upcoming romantic suspense novel. Reading, writing and her husband are her passions. And not necessarily in that order! Tina can be reached at: P.O. Box 1468, Middlebury, IN 46540, or via e-mail at *tina@tinarunge.com* or at her Web site *www.tinarunge.com.*

Arthur Sánchez has degrees in theater and political science. He is presently residing in Peekskill, New York, with his wife Catherine and is finishing up work on a novel. "I hope Frances remembers me as fondly as I remember her." He may be reached via e-mail at *ASAN4950@yahoo.com.*

Susan Sarver is a senior editor for a university, a freelance writer and a former newspaper columnist. Her essays have appeared in *Reader's Digest, The Christian Science Monitor, Country Living* and *Grit.* Family is frequently a subject of her writings. Her two daughters, who often serve as editors and gentle critics, continue to inspire her work.

Chris Schroder graduated from the University of Virginia and worked for six Southeastern daily newspapers before starting his own three community newspapers in his hometown of Atlanta in 1994. He currently serves as general manager at Weltner Communications. He's a writer, a speaker and father to Sally and Thomas. E-mail: *schroder@mindspring.com;* Web site: *www.chrisschroder.com.*

Michael Seale is a columnist and a reporter for the *Daily Home* newspaper based in Talladega, Alabama. He writes local sports and news stories, and his column appears every Saturday. In addition to his vast number of writing assignments for the newspaper, he also writes short fiction and has done some freelance sports writing. He is an avid sports fan and has been active in his community's youth baseball league as an umpire for the last twelve years. He and his wife, Dee, live in Birmingham, Alabama. Michael can be reached at *MPSeale@hotmail.com.*

Jean Shanley has been a writer at *The Meadville Tribune* for forty years. She enjoys writing about people and how God uses their stories to affect the lives of others. She enjoys church, the historical society and helping bereaved parents. Her greatest joys have been her two children and her granddaughter.

Margaret Shauers has been a freelance writer for thirty-five years. She is a contributing editor to *Children's Book Insider*, field editor for *Taste of Home* and an online columnist of *write4kids.com.* She may be reached at *mshauers@cox.net.*

Kevin H. Siepel is an environmental scientist who teaches Spanish on the side. He has had essays, poems, and historical and pop-science pieces published in various journals, among them the *Christian Science Monitor, Reader's Digest, Virginia Cavalcade, Civil War, Wild West,* and *Notre Dame University Magazine.* He is the author of *Rebel: The Life and Times of John Singleton Mosby* (St. Martins Press, 1983; DaCapo Press, 1997), the first complete biography of one of the Confederacy's best-known military leaders. He may be reached at *ksiep@att-global.net.*

Susan Siersma recently left a career in special education to help with the care of a family member. In her spare time, she enjoys sharing the out-of-doors with her husband, Rodger. In June, she and her husband will celebrate their thirtieth wedding anniversary. One of her stories, *Gone Readin',* appeared in the March/April 2002 issue of *Inside Line* fishing magazine. She can be reached at *Ssiersma@msn.com.*

Andy Skidmore enjoys writing, photography and baking. She is a member of the Central Church of Christ in Cleveland, Tennessee. She has been published in *Woman's World, Christian Woman's* magazine, *Poetry Guild's* newest anthology, *Chicken Soup for the Woman's Soul* and *Chicken Soup for the Parent's Soul.* She won first prize in the North American Open Amateur Photography Contest. This story was written as her anniversary card to her husband on their thirtieth wedding anniversary. She may be reached at 4710 North Cree Lane, Cleveland, TN 37312, or via e-mail at *AndySkid@aol.com.*

Mary Ann Stafford is a mother of two and grandmother of two. She enjoys working with stained glass. The majority of her stained glass pieces are angels, which adorn many windows of her home and the homes of her family and friends. She also collects angels, which are placed throughout her home. Her other hobbies are reading, writing and giving psychic readings. She has performed many readings for family and friends over the years and finds this extremely enjoyable. She may be contacted at 2384 S. Nolting, Springfield, MO 65807.

When **Joyce Stark** was very small, her granddad used to offer to read her bedtime stories. She used to lie in bed and tell him her own made-up stories, and he would listen and then fall asleep, leaving her wide-awake, making up more stories! Not much has changed except that she finds people and real life so much more interesting than anything she could make up. She works full time in an office, but writes every spare minute she has.

Ed Stivender has been called "the Robin Williams of storytellers" by the *Miami Herald*. A Philadelphia native, Ed Stivender was the only son of an Irish Catholic mother and a Protestant father. His mother frequently prayed for him to become a priest but his father warned, "Son, never get a job where you have to wear a dress to work." He earned a master's degree in theology and taught religion in a parochial high school in Hartford, Connecticut, for several years. Since leaving his "day job" as a teacher in 1977, he has fabulated his way around the world, performing in schools, churches, theaters and storytelling festivals. Stivender is also a Shakespearean actor, banjo player, teacher, theologian, Mummer, dreamer, juggler and raconteur. He is a featured performer at the National Storytelling Festival in Jonesboro, Tennessee, where he has been a perennial favorite since 1980. He has toured North America, Ireland, Indonesia and New Zealand with his one-man shows. In addition to his storytelling, he has written two books of coming-of-age stories as well as several articles that have been featured in *Reader's Digest, Catholic Digest* and *Hartford Business Journal*.

Ken Swarner writes the syndicated humor column "Family Man" for newspapers in the United States and Canada. His first book appears on the Perigee label in spring 2003. He can be seen at *www.kenswarner.bigstep.com* or e-mailed at *noifs@aol.com*.

Mary L. TenHaken has been a lifelong resident of Sheyboygan County, Wisconsin. She grew up on a farm and loves the simplicity that goes with country living. She works as an executive assistant nearing retirement age, and she plans to work as long as she can to meet expenses for herself and her husband, who had a severe stroke at an early age. He now lives in an assisted living facility near her workplace, and so her personal boundaries have "moved in" a bit. She has recently begun writing short paragraphs purely for personal pleasure and to become part of a journal she will leave to her two sons. She may be reached at N2357 CTH KW, Oostburg, WI 53070.

Lisa Ferris Terzich lives in Arizona with her husband and soul mate, Ralph, and darling daughter, Alexis. In addition to writing, she enjoys all things crea -
tive. Her claim to fame with friends and family is being "an idiot savant of useless information." Lisa can be reached at *Habebe19@aol.com*.

Chuck Thompson was raised in Palm Springs, California, and Juneau, Alaska. He's the author of *The 25 Best World War II Travel Sites: Pacific Theater* (Greenline, 2002) and the former executive editor of *Travelocity* magazine. His writing and photography have appeared in *Atlantic Monthly, Maxim, National Geographic Adventure, Playboy, Islands, Reader's Digest, Publisher's Weekly*, MTV and many other outlets. This story originally appeared in the Valentine's Day issue of *American Way* magazine, February 1, 1995. He graduated from the University of Oregon with degrees in history and journalism.

Betty Tucker (Bee Tee to her friends and family) is a professor and departmental chairwoman of information systems and technologies at the Goddard School of Business and Economics at Weber State University in Ogden, Utah. She delights in the exchange of teaching and learning in education. Betty and her husband, Kent, believe in helping others help themselves, especially her grandchildren: Ashlee, Kyler, Koleby, Cailey, Jayden, Rylie, Trey, Parker and Camden. She can be reached at *btucker@weber.edu*.

Trish Vradenburg has written for *Designing Women, Family Ties,* and *Kate and Allie.* Her novel, *Liberated Lady,* was a Literary Guild and Doubleday Book Club selection. She has written humor pieces for *The New York Daily News, The Boston Globe, Ladies Home Journal* and *Woman's Day.* Her play, *Surviving Grace,* was produced at The Kennedy Center in Washington, D.C. and off-Broadway at Union Square Theater. Since her children refuse to be quoted, she is running out of family members to write about. She may be reached on e-mail at: *TGV3@aol.com*.

Catherine Walker with joy has counted it a privilege to share her story in *Chicken Soup for the Romantic Soul.* Some of her most memorable life experiences are wonderful stories of humor, lessons of living and reminiscent modeling of days gone by. She has had no formal literary training but rather writes from her heart and from the many experiences in life that have chiseled and molded her character the most. Her story is just one of those experiences. Encouraging young people, especially her children and grandchildren, to explore the love of writing and art has been a passion and a way of life for her. She may be reached at *CatherineLWalker@hotmail.com*.

Sandra Wallace and her husband, Charles, live in Newton, Kansas. They have two grown sons who live in nearby communities. This is Sandy's first short story. Her life centers on God, family and music, singing at local churches as a soloist or with family members. She enjoys cooking, making handmade crafts for gifts and, for ultimate relaxation, loves to curl up with a good book on the loveseat that sits in front of the home's sunny afternoon west window. She is a full-time staff member of a local law firm. She can be reached at *sandykay@cox.net*.

Evelyn "Wendy" Wander is a retired accountant. She and her husband Bob spend time between homes in Miami, Florida, with granddaughter Brianna, and Welch, West Virginia, where Evelyn is working on her first novel. She has had several short stories published. She can be reached at *wendy1dr@aol.com*.

Thomas Webber was a loving and caring husband to his wife Sandra for almost thirty-nine years before he passed away. He wrote "Three Kisses" for her birthday in 1998, three years before his passing. This story has brought her comfort even in these rough times of dealing with his death. She hopes reading "Three Kisses" will help people to appreciate what they have.

Ernie Witham writes a humor column called "Ernie's World" for the *Montecito*

Journal in Montecito, California. His humor has also been published in the *Los Angeles Times*, the *Santa Barbara News-Press*, and in six *Chicken Soup* anthologies. His first published collection, *Ernie's World* (the book), is available in bookstores and at *www.ernie@erniesworld.com*. He is also available to lead humor workshops for any age group and can be reached at *www.ernie@erniesworld.com*.

Helen Xenakis. *Chicken Soup* says tell me about yourself, dear. Keep it short, sweet and perfectly clear. Helen, who are you? Woman, educator, friend, wife, mother, grandma, writer with pen. All of the above and hopefully more. So proud to contribute with hope for lots more. Thanks for the chance, glad I am your pick for selection into *Chicken Soup for the Romantic Soul!*

Barbara Zukowski is a retired OB nurse, semiretired piano teacher, part-time musician and romance writer. Besides having published several romantic short stories, she has had writing-related articles appear in *Writer's Digest* and *Yellow Sticky Notes* magazines. When she's not busy creating at her Colorado home, Barbara loves to travel. And now that her son is college-bound, she hopes to find inspiration during her visits to as many exotic locations as possible! Therefore, the best way to contact her is by e-mail: *bz55@aol.com*.

Permissions

We would like to acknowledge the following publishers and individuals for permission to reprint the following material. (Note: The stories that were penned anonymously, that are public domain, or that were written by Jack Canfield, Mark Victor Hansen, Mark Donnelly, Chrissy Donnelly or Barbara De Angelis, Ph.D., are not included in this listing.)

The Right Approach. Reprinted by permission of Edmund Phillips. ©2000 Edmund Phillips.

Encounter on a Train. Reprinted by permission of Kevin H. Siepel. ©1988 Kevin H. Siepel. Previously appeared in the *Christian Science Monitor* on July 5, 1998.

"Falling" in Love. Reprinted by permission of Mary Mikkelsen. ©2002 Mary Mikkelsen.

Glads on Monday. Reprinted by permission of Chris Schroder. ©1994 Chris Schroder.

A Love Story. As cited in *Even More of. . . The Best of Bits & Pieces* by Rob Gilbert. ©2000 Lawrence Ragan Communications, Inc. Address: 316 N. Michigan Avenue, Chicago, IL 60601, USA. Phone: 800-878-5331 or 312-960-4100. Fax: 312-960-4106. E-mail: *cservice@ragan.com*. Web site: *www.ragan.com*. Please contact Lawrence Ragan Communications, Inc., directly to purchase this book or for subscription information on (or a free sample copy of) the monthly magazine version of *Bits & Pieces*.

Two Coins in a Fountain. Reprinted by permission of Joyce Stark. ©2002 Joyce Stark.

Six Red Roses. Reprinted by permission of Lori J. Robidoux. ©2000 Lori J. Robidoux.

Real-Life Fairy Tale. Reprinted by permission of Norma Grove. ©2001 Norma Grove.

To Infinity. Reprinted by permission of Lisa Ferris Terzich. ©2002 Lisa Ferris Terzich.

Just Call Me Cupid. Reprinted by permission of William Stanton. ©1971 William Stanton.

An Evening at the Waldorf. Reprinted by permission of Jean G. Ince and Eugene S. Ince. ©1978 Jean G. Ince and Eugene S. Ince. Originally appeared in *Gourmet Magazine* December 1978.

To Begin Again and *A Different Kind of "Trashy Secret."* Reprinted by permission of Rusty Fischer. ©2000 Rusty Fisher.

Love Notes. Reprinted by permission of Gwen Romero. ©2002 Gwen Romero.

I Love You Anyway. Reprinted by permission of Joe A. Harding. ©2000 Joe A. Harding.

A Fragment in Time. Reprinted by permission of Victoria Robinson. ©2001 Victoria Robinson.

Improving Your Life Every Day

Real people sharing real stories—for nineteen years. Now, Chicken Soup for the Soul has gone beyond the bookstore to become a world leader in life improvement. Through books, movies, DVDs, online resources and other partnerships, we bring hope, courage, inspiration and love to hundreds of millions of people around the world. Chicken Soup for the Soul's writers and readers belong to a one-of-a-kind global community, sharing advice, support, guidance, comfort, and knowledge.

Chicken Soup for the Soul stories have been translated into more than 40 languages and can be found in more than one hundred countries. Every day, millions of people experience a Chicken Soup for the Soul story in a book, magazine, newspaper or online. As we share our life experiences through these stories, we offer hope, comfort and inspiration to one another. The stories travel from person to person, and from country to country, helping to improve lives everywhere.

Share with Us

We all have had Chicken Soup for the Soul moments in our lives. If you would like to share your story or poem with millions of people around the world, go to chickensoup.com and click on "Submit Your Story." You may be able to help another reader, and become a published author at the same time. Some of our past contributors have launched writing and speaking careers from the publication of their stories in our books!

Our submission volume has been increasing steadily — the quality and quantity of your submissions has been fabulous. We only accept story submissions via our website. They are no longer accepted via mail or fax.

To contact us regarding other matters, please send us an e-mail through webmaster@chickensoupforthesoul.com, or fax or write us at:

Chicken Soup for the Soul
P.O. Box 700
Cos Cob, CT 06807-0700
Fax: 203-861-7194

One more note from your friends at Chicken Soup for the Soul: Occasionally, we receive an unsolicited book manuscript from one of our readers, and we would like to respectfully inform you that we do not accept unsolicited manuscripts and we must discard the ones that appear.